THE **HOME STYLE** SOURCEBOOK

THE HOME STYLE SOURCEBOOK

inspirational decorating schemes for every home

LESLIE GEDDES-BROWN, KATHERINE SORRELL

AND JUDITH WILSON

RYLAND
PETERS
& SMALL

LONDON NEW YORK

SENIOR DESIGNER Sally Powell

SENIOR EDITOR Clare Double

PICTURE RESEARCH Emily Westlake

PRODUCTION Patricia Harrington, Susannah Straughan

ART DIRECTOR Gabriella Le Grazie

PUBLISHING DIRECTOR Alison Starling

First published in the United Kingdom in 2004 by
Ryland Peters & Small
Kirkman House
12–14 Whitfield Street
London W1T 2RP
www.rylandpeters.com

10 9 8 7 6 5 4 3 2 1

Text by Leslie Geddes-Brown (Traditional
Country, Modern Country and Classic Period
style sections), Katherine Sorrell (Elegant
Modern, Scandinavian and Vintage & Retro
sections) and Judith Wilson (Finding your Style,
Sleek, Mellow Modern and Natural sections).

Text, design and photographs copyright
© Ryland Peters & Small 2004

ISBN 1 84172 676 1

A CIP record for this book is available from the
British Library.

Printed and bound in China.

The publishers cannot accept liability for any injury,
damage or loss to person or property, direct or
inconsequential, arising from suggestions made
in this book. The publishers recommend that any
structural, electrical or plumbing work is carried
out by a qualified professional.

CONTENTS

introduction

Choosing your decorative style is the fun part of creating a home, once the plumbing has been fixed and the crumbling plaster replaced – or when you've realized that your favourite place is looking a little tired and tatty. Now's your opportunity to give your home a makeover. Whether you want to revamp a single room or overhaul the decor of an entire house, *The Home Style Sourcebook* is a one-stop shop for the necessary inspiration.

Before you begin stripping off your old wallpaper and buying paint, have a look at Part One, Finding your Style. Thinking about how you use your home, whether you like to entertain, listen to music, pursue hobbies or spend hours in the bath, will help you determine your top decorating priorities. Look through the whole book and spot which photographs your eye is naturally drawn to, making a note of which looks they represent, as a start. Then turn to the Contemporary, Country and Period Style sections in Part One for an in-depth exploration of your chosen styles.

Once you have found a look you like, turn to Part Two. It works as a handbook of each style in each type of room (kitchen, bathroom and so on). A list of Key Features gives you a quick-reference digest of the main 'ingredients' of each look, and a Style Study shows how the ideas work in practice. Each Style Study includes a Why it Works list to identify the secrets of each room's success. Armed with these insights, you can create a home that looks great – and perfectly suits the way you live.

finding your style

gathering inspiration

We live in a design-conscious age; interiors have caught up with fashion in the race for ever-changing images. If it seems confusing to be bombarded with myriad decorating choices, the flip side is that there's never been so much design freedom. Finding inspiration is now one of the most enjoyable parts of divining your style.

ABOVE LEFT AND OPPOSITE BELOW LEFT: **A decorative accessory makes a great starting point, so re-evaluate all possessions with fresh eyes. The kooky aubergine and olive tones of this glassware might inspire a Vintage theme, whereas the curvy, romantic shapes of antique glass might prompt a Classic Period style.**

ABOVE CENTRE: **Furniture classics, especially the uncomplicated modern silhouettes of 20th-century pieces, may act as a springboard for an inspired new scheme. But weave such items into a Mellow Modern treatment, rather than slavishly copying a particular decade.**

ABOVE RIGHT: **Remain open-minded: the sharp silhouette of this lamp might inspire either a Sleek, or a Vintage, theme.**

Ask any designer how they garner ideas, and the answer will be revealing. Foreign travel or trips to galleries, street culture, fashion and the natural world are all key influences, not to mention seasonal fabric and furniture launches. And that's just the beginning. Design has undergone a mini revolution, with modern overtones in particular spilling over into every walk of life. Restaurants, boutique hotels, shop interiors and public spaces are all design-conscious now. So mimic the designers, and open your eyes to new visual influences. Filter out what works at home. You may not copy a trendy restaurant wholesale, but its mood lighting might be key.

In the early stages, it's vital to get a firm handle on interiors sources. Do your research, and go shopping – make it fun. Visit plenty of design stores, including specialist furniture outlets and antiques shops, and look at how pieces are styled and, even more importantly, how much it all costs. Buy or borrow a cross-section of decorating magazines and check out the Directory in this book for

ABOVE LEFT: **Textiles can be fabulously inspirational, be they an antique quilt, archive pattern or a modern-day print. Look at nuances of shade, texture or pattern as guides to a new look.**

ABOVE RIGHT: **Cast your net wide for ideas. The glamour of a hotel bedroom, visited fleetingly, may be a vital inspiration for an Elegant Modern look.**

new shops, websites or catalogues. Small or emergent companies are often great sources of inspirational products. Many high-street stores are spot on with inexpensive versions of designer looks.

Then repeat the research process for the 'ingredients' of your schemes: the paints, surfaces, fittings and fabrics. Only when you see what's on the market can you firm up appropriate colours or finishes, or what works at home. This needn't be exhaustive. It's often better to find two or three fabric companies whose products inspire, or a specialist paint range with a great complementary palette, than struggling with too many confusing choices. When it comes to major items like flooring or architectural fittings (from

fireplaces to door handles), don't forget that one-off pieces in salvage yards or junk shops can be as inspirational as modern ones.

Finally, hone down your favourite looks by gathering visual references. Either build up a mood board, as interior designers do, or buy a box file and amass cuttings. Tear out magazine pictures that attract you, take snaps of ideas in a hotel bar or friend's house (ask first!), request fabric cuttings or surface samples. You can be as specific or as vague as you like. In the excitement of gathering images, don't forget that the key influence should be your home. Scan the style of its windows and doors, its architectural detailing, and the views outside. Then add that information to the melting pot.

how you live

We all have hectic schedules, so it's crucial to choose a design style that works with, not against, your lifestyle. There's zero point devising a minimalist city pad if kids are part of the package, or creating a cluttered rustic look if streamlined living is your mantra. Examine how you live, then tailor your interior accordingly.

ABOVE FAR LEFT: **If you enjoy a relaxed lifestyle, then pick furniture to match. Nests of occasional tables, stacking chairs or modular furniture can be pressed into service for impromptu entertaining.**

ABOVE CENTRE: **Informal living calls for easy-care, shabby-chic furnishings. Loose covers in crumply linens, plump cushions, and casual throws tossed over a sofa are all key components. Unfitted furniture that's easy to move around, from sofas on castors to junk-shop storage, gives flexibility.**

Consider first who lives at home. If it's just you and a partner, then sleek and sophisticated can be the order of the day. But if there are children, a softer-edged, more practical style will be vital. The presence of lodgers, weekend guests or a home office may call for two looks: flexible and casual for the living quarters, chic and grown-up for your private zones. Consider your own personality. How do you like to run the home? Are you comfortable with a relaxed look, or are you a stickler for tidiness? Be honest.

Think about when you're at home, as the periods when you most use the space will affect your style choices. Peak times, of course, will vary according to lifestyle. A family home is most active during daylight hours, so practical yet crisp fabrics and a light, fresh colour scheme will be appropriate. A career couple need a space planned for after-dark entertaining, chill-out time and weekends. So elegant furnishings, lighting that looks good by night and cocoon-like textures are more appropriate. Think, too, about time (and money).

There's no point planning a high-maintenance Sleek look, for example, if you can't keep it pristine.

Evaluate, too, how you use the space. If friends are constantly in and out, tailor the decor to your entertaining style. Formal parties will call for 'wow'-factor finishes or grown-up furniture. Kitchen-table suppers, by contrast, will dictate a relaxed, yet chic look, capable of being dressed up at a moment's notice. If your home is a me-time retreat, then a soothing palette, or a streamlined interior and touchy-feely fabrics, may suit. Consider whether you are an indoor or outdoors person. If you live in the garden, then relaxed decorating is vital. If indoor pursuits are important, then mood lighting and deep, comfortable furniture should feature.

Where you live also has a bearing on style. There's no point investing in designer fittings if your flat is in a less than desirable area, as you may never recoup that initial investment. Match your look to the architectural shell. Unless very carefully managed, cutting-edge designer furniture can look inappropriate in a suburban-style home, just as chintz-patterned loose covers look at odds in a city flat. Look out of the window, and scrutinize the views. Is it unashamedly urban, or leafy and tranquil? Work the key textures or tones that you see outside into the planned style and decor. An all-white modern interior will calm down edgy, fast-moving city landscapes, whereas soft neutrals and gentle shapes will blend prettily with country scenes.

ABOVE LEFT: **In a city pad, aim for a look that is sharply tailored, yet deeply comfortable. With its leather bedhead, sculptural curtains and crisp bedding, this roomy penthouse bedroom looks sleek, yet for relaxed weekends is still supremely indulgent.**

ABOVE: **It's vital to pick a style that enhances the layout of a given space. In this flat, where wide linking corridors and open-plan rooms have been planned to cater for busy family life, the sleek, colourful style reinforces an already streamlined layout.**

RIGHT: **Here, traditional timber boards, alcove detailing and a cast-iron roll-top bath fuse with the bright, light palette of contemporary interiors to create the Modern Country look.**

BELOW LEFT: **Interpretation of a given style is key. For some, the Natural look will inspire the use of rough, traditional-looking timbers and stone surfaces. For the minimally minded, Natural can also mean sleek and clean design (see** OPPOSITE INSET**).**

FAR RIGHT AND BELOW RIGHT: **Look for recurring themes that link together two different styles. Both the Scandinavian-inspired room** (FAR RIGHT) **and the Retro room** (BELOW RIGHT) **use mid-toned wood veneers, low and lean furniture silhouettes and wood flooring as vital style components.**

mixing styles

Whatever styles we choose, it's impractical to adopt a look wholesale. The best interiors, like fashion, cherry-pick elements from a mix of influences, and in so doing create a new spin. Other looks, from Traditional Country to Scandinavian, are enduring classics.

OPPOSITE ABOVE LEFT: **The predominant overtones of this clear-cut, simple Natural dining room are the timber floorboards and the casually stacked alcove logs. Yet the modern purpose-built wood and metal table and benches, teamed with a vintage pendant lamp, give it a trendy new twist.**

OPPOSITE ABOVE RIGHT: **Mixing unexpected surfaces can create fresh new combinations. While this kitchen has a sleek contemporary stainless-steel cooker, and pristine white ceramic tiles, the deep wood tones of the doors add an Elegant Modern slant.**

OPPOSITE BELOW: **Furniture choices can take the architectural 'shell' of a room in one direction or another. Here, sleek stone detailing is softened with luxurious-looking upholstery and touchy-feely fabric wall textures, redefining the room as a Mellow Modern living space.**

It's not easy to pick a given design style, then stick to it. A few rare individuals have a strong look that is their unmistakable personal stamp. Homes designed by an architect or designer are permeated with one cohesive design thread, from the decoration to the furniture, surfaces to door handles. Yet, satisfying though it is, maintaining that single vision can be an uncompromising way to live.

Much more realistic, then, is to accept that our homes will be a mix of varied looks and influences. Just as we amass a wardrobe of clothes to satisfy different needs and tastes, it's fun to combine decorative styles. Contrast is the lifeblood of an interior: it's boring if every room looks the same. It is also a good way to control the visual pace at home: moving from a Sleek entrance hall, say, to an Elegant Modern drawing room, then back to a minimalist kitchen.

Added to that, we live in a culture that positively encourages mixing influences. These days, the choice is phenomenal. Suddenly it's OK to juxtapose a Fifties table with a Directoire armchair or contrast pink silk curtains with a limestone floor. The advantages are manifold. In an age where high-street style rules – and there's a tendency for everything to look the same – learning to mix guarantees individuality, and provides an enticing sense of surprise.

Yet the prospect of confidently mixing styles can fill many of us with trepidation. So do some visual research before putting ideas into practice. Leaf through a pile of interiors

magazines. Analyse the houses and decorating features, which will reflect a number of styles. What treatments work, and which don't? Home in on examples where varied looks have been deliberately contrasted for drama, or subtle combinations have been seamlessly blended together. Create a mixed style mood board. Choose a room theme – bathrooms, say – then cut out pictures of fittings in a number of styles. Play around with them, and see what appeals.

Keep an eye out for the way shops show off their merchandise. Many employ stylists to experiment with new looks. Think of retro Seventies interiors used as a background for modern high-street buys, or classic wallpaper patterns shown in an urban loft. Investigate, too, the new wave of antiques dealers. Many these days are putting fine old pieces into a super-contemporary setting. Others have an even trendier take, upholstering Victorian button-back chairs in Sixties-print Scandinavian fabrics, or displaying pretty 18th-century cabinets against funky painted walls.

Look, too, at the architectural character of your home. If the interior is bland and plain, then an exotic mix of decorative furniture styles will inject it with personality. A house with a warren of small rooms, by contrast, may actually suggest using the surprise of several contrasting looks. Buildings with an innate clash of architectural styles – a Victorian house with a Sixties extension, say – might inspire a deliberate combination of the two periods throughout.

Decoratively speaking, the simplest way to mix styles is to combine an unusual choice of furniture in a single space. Provided the decorative background is plain (white walls and stone or wood floor), there is great fun to be had from juxtaposing a French marble-topped commode with a pair of trendy acrylic chairs, or a sleek wood Scandinavian dining table with rustic timber benches. Once you are confident, go a step further by contrasting furniture with unexpected architectural detailing. Classic dark wood panelling, normally combined with period furniture, might look fantastic painted white and teamed with plum silk Thirties armchairs, for an Elegant Modern finish. Or install sleek, super-modern glass bowl basins in a Traditional Country bathroom.

It's much harder (though ultimately more satisfying) to successfully combine a string of rooms reflecting a number of different styles. Most commonly, we will go for modern bathrooms and kitchens, and want the living spaces and bedrooms to remain elegant and traditional. It's vital to pick one broad thread to draw everything together. You might use identical flooring throughout – stone and wood boards look good with old and new pieces – or wood veneer wall panelling as a linking factor. Alternatively, pick a cohesive decorative theme – a tightly controlled palette of three colours – to bind Vintage and Classic Period rooms together. Types of fabric (crunchy, smooth, abstract), or a preponderance of a furniture silhouette (cubic, curvy, retro), can unify varied styles.

For all the fun of mixing, there's also a word of caution. However good your 'links' from one style option to another, it's visually confusing to combine too many different influences. The results will be schizophrenic, both for you to live in and for guests to visit. Two or three key styles are sufficient. Sticking to the categories of

RIGHT AND FAR RIGHT: **In traditional houses, use subtle links to draw together varied styles. Fabric is a good choice, whether you use an identical print throughout, a fabric 'genre' such as toile de Jouy, or a textural theme. Here, mauve toile** (RIGHT) **is used with grown-up curtains and antique furniture, for a Classic Period look. Teamed with simple fittings, pink toile is just as appropriate a choice in a Traditional Country bathroom.**

BELOW: **Use characterful, bold accessories to introduce new styles into a simple room. Here, the giant plain clock delineates Modern Country** (LEFT), **while retro kettles** (RIGHT) **and big rough-hewn platters** (CENTRE) **are just enough to characterize Vintage and Natural styles.**

contemporary, country, or period styles can also be a useful guide. Once you have settled on the looks you want – Scandinavian meets Modern Country, say, or Elegant Modern with Sleek – concentrate on drawing out specific decorative elements from each. These will become key visual themes to reiterate from room to room. For Scandinavian meets Modern Country, for example, reference points might be blond woods and a clean silhouette. For Elegant Modern meets Sleek, it may be marble detailing and sculptural linens.

Remember that it is productive to dare to cross style boundaries. It can be reassuring to crystallize the key elements of each chosen look, and stick closely to them. But experiment a little, too. These days, we're used to seeing 20th-century classic furniture teamed with chintz, or urban lofts accessorized with vintage lighting. But that's only because a curious few, in the beginning, decided to shake up the design status quo. Try the same at home. By mixing unexpected styles today, you've got the makings of future trends.

contemporary styles

A modern look is no longer
just for the brave or the young.
Contemporary style has come
of age over the past decade,
and interiors have never
looked sharper or fresher.
What's more, there's enviable
choice. Whether you pick the
cutting-edge furniture and
glossy good looks of Sleek
style; the cool, comfortable
interiors of Mellow Modern; or
the tactile, muted surfaces of
the Natural look, rooms are
guaranteed to be pared down,
soothing, and easy to live with.

RIGHT AND BELOW: **With Sleek's** emphasis on open spaces and big windows, natural light becomes as much a part of the scheme as colour. A glass wall, floor-to-ceiling windows or glass bricks not only provide a sleek surface, but they encourage the play of light onto plain white walls. Pale floors, such as limestone or painted concrete, are equally reflective. A neutral colour scheme will enhance the nuances of light and shadow at different times of the day.

sleek

With its roots in minimalism, and at the cutting edge of modern, Sleek style is now the look of choice for trendy urbanites. Light-reflective surfaces, from sandblasted glass to limestone, cubic furniture, and generous lateral spaces are key, as is a sparkling palette of whites or neutrals, with a flash of contrast colour.

ABOVE AND OPPOSITE: **The Sleek** colour palette is neutral, but can go dark or light according to preference. Deep wood tones, from macassar ebony to walnut, look sophisticated in city apartments, and can be used as successfully in the kitchen as for grown-up wall panelling in the living room. Closer to minimalism are the uncompromising, pure whites or grey-whites of laminates, painted MDF or natural stone. They are beautiful to look at, but not for the lazy, as they must be kept spotlessly clean.

Once the preserve of architects and design aficionados, the Sleek look is now the acceptable face of modern style. Still minimalist in spirit, yet a softer version of late, it suits today's architect-designed spaces, with their dramatic floor-to-ceiling windows, open-plan living areas and seamless cabinetry. Yet if Sleek looks good in city pads, it now has its place in country homes, too. For a pared-down interior, what could be a better backdrop than a verdant view?

Space planning is crucial. This look depends on streamlined areas and the illusion of space, so it's vital to create new 'bones' for each room. That means built-in seamless storage, from floor-to-ceiling cupboards to simple wall alcoves, sliding partition doors for dividing open-plan spaces, and dual-purpose features such as a low stone bench-cum-modern hearth. You are aiming to create areas of uninterrupted space, so the more built-in features, the better.

Architectural detailing must be tailored to match. Traditional windows are fine, but Sleek style looks best teamed with new-build windows: steel-frame grid designs, floor-to-ceiling sliding glass doors or an entire wall of glass. Consider elongating internal doors to stretch from floor to ceiling, or install unframed glazed styles to aid light flow. Precisely because Sleek looks best against an unfussy

background, lofts, new-build homes and houses that have been stripped of architectural detailing create the perfect backdrop.

If fabric or pattern is core to traditional looks, hard surfaces are the backbone of Sleek style. So focus attention on flooring, worktops, wall panelling and partition walls. Pick materials that can be used in a slick, uninterrupted run: slabs of stone, from granite to limestone; cement cast in situ; stainless steel; or hardwoods, from ebony to oak. Surfaces should blend seamlessly, be that on a single, or on interconnecting, planes. So choose materials that can be used as effectively on worktops as on floors. They should also impart a glossy light-refracting sheen.

With all the attention on the hard surfaces, walls should be plainly painted, or with a subtle finish such as polished plaster. This is not the time for fussy window treatments. If you do choose curtains, pick a fabric that will fall into sculptural folds: crisp linens, wool or felt are ideal. Otherwise, stick to blinds, from plain roller and Roman designs to Venetian styles. If you're not overlooked, dispense with them altogether.

As for furniture shapes, look for purity of line. The outline matters, as pieces will be set amongst free-flowing spaces, often silhouetted against unadorned walls or windows. Go for a mix of linear, cubic pieces – the rectangular sofa is today's furniture classic – with softer organic curves mixed in. Upholstery should be plain, though textural: linen, wool, suede and velvet are all good choices. And keep accessories scaled up and minimal. Less, when it comes to the Sleek look, is always more.

OPPOSITE LEFT AND CENTRE: **Sleek is ideal for small rooms such as bathrooms, as a continuous surface across floor and walls makes a space seem bigger. Enhance the effect with glass dividing walls, or an unframed glazed door.**

ABOVE LEFT: **When planning, make the 'shell' of the room an interactive part of** the scheme, so that it can offer streamlined, built-in storage. Here, a box-style partition not only divides an open-plan space, but also offers attractive yet seamless alcove storage.

LEFT: **Think of surfaces as planes of colour and texture, then play with them across walls and floors to get the visual balance** right. Here, the chocolate of the flooring is repeated vertically as a bedhead, and the ensuing dark and light squares echoed, in little, on the bedcover.

ABOVE: **Use furniture in curved shapes, to mix in with the trademark boxy furniture lines. Lamps, cushions and upholstery should repeat the lean, unfussy outline.**

FAR LEFT: **This is a look that thrives on lightness and pale tones, so maximize it by making minor – yet highly effective – architectural changes. Add new glazed internal doors, or fit traditional styles with sandblasted glass panels, to bounce maximum light back into each room.**

LEFT: **Just because the look is relaxed doesn't mean it can't be elegant, too. Choose accessories, from vases to china, in sophisticated elongated shapes, so that a practical yet easy daytime dining room can be dressed up at night. Leather-upholstered dining chairs provide a linking thread, as they are both practical and luxurious.**

OPPOSITE AND BELOW: **An all-white kitchen always looks slick and fresh, but team it with the warmth of a wooden worktop or floor, to prevent it feeling clinical. Likewise, restrict stainless steel to decorative highlights: use it for a narrow run of splashback, utility lighting or as detailing on dining-room furniture.**

mellow modern

Based on a white-on-white palette, accented with flashes of steel, wood and translucent glass, the Mellow Modern look is the relaxed way to do contemporary. With its pared-down rooms and gently contoured furniture, it's comfortable to live with and easy on the eye, the perfect choice for busy family life.

For those who love the sleek lines of minimalism, but have neither the time nor the inclination to totally clear their clutter, this is a look made in heaven. It's casual and user-friendly – even looks good with a little mess – but it scrubs up well for entertaining. Mellow Modern offers sharp style, but with rounded edges. Eagerly adopted by those in country or suburban homes wanting a slicker take on traditional style, it's versatile enough for garden flats or city apartments. It's also highly achievable. With echoes of the pale, light colour schemes of Swedish and Long Island interiors, but the glossy surfaces of sleek city living, it combines a tranquil spirit with supreme practicality.

Precisely because the look is streamlined, clever space planning and great storage are key. You're aiming for rooms that look effortlessly tidy, so you need enough cupboards to conceal the average household's clutter. Concentrate on built-in storage, but design it to give the illusion of free-standing pieces. The trick is to wall-mount cupboards to maximize floor space, but choose panelled rather than flush doors for a classic mood, and raise them slightly above floor level to give the impression of traditional furniture. Adopt the same thought process for worktops or built-in tables: an unfitted look is easily achieved by teaming them with free-standing stools or benches.

BELOW: Use built-in storage to emphasize the Mellow Modern mood. These bathroom cupboards are inspired by architectural-style contemporary alcove shelving, yet the detail of rounded metal knobs gives a softer twist.

OPPOSITE: Intersperse sleek surfaces like wood veneer, marble and glass with wobbly, more organic textures. This bathroom feels more inviting because the vanity unit worktop and walls have been decorated with smaller-scale mosaic tiling. Small expanses of textured concrete or bumpy slate are good alternatives.

ABOVE: Concentrate on taking the hard edges off finishes and furniture, literally and visually. This bathroom is certainly slick, with its glossy ceramic tiles, but the worktop has been deliberately contoured into a gentle curve. The theme is reinforced with a round bowl-style sink and shaving mirror. A roll-top bath or curved shower enclosure will have a similar effect. Likewise, the all-white colour scheme has been softened with the introduction of a mid-toned wood shelf.

Generous expanses of quality, chunky surfaces create the requisite clean, simple outline, but for Mellow Modern go for a subtle sheen, not gloss. Stone such as granite or marble should be honed, rather than highly polished. In place of sophisticated wood veneers, choose oiled woods with a good natural grain, and steer clear of too much stainless steel, which can seem hard-edged and unfriendly. Laminate in pale tones is just as practical and easier on the eye. Combine your sleek horizontal surfaces (worktops, floors) with more traditional vertical surfaces on walls or cupboard fronts, to soften the look. Tongue-and-groove, MDF panelling in simple squares, or varnished plywood are all good choices.

A fresh, pale colour scheme is a must. Make whites your starting point, either pure brilliant white or softer versions, from milky tones to palest vanilla. Creams or shades of beige look too traditional, and don't sit so well with

contemporary furniture. Home in on the muted shades of natural textures for colour contrast, from the soft greys of stone to the honey or chocolate of wood, and steer clear of bright shades, which can look aggressive. For accents, pick leafy green (from the garden outdoors to the flash of a kitchen chair), or muted, off-pastels such as mushroom pink or Swedish grey-blue.

Make your design choices with one eye on practicality, the other on good looks. Quality, natural surfaces like stone or wood look all the better for a little wear and tear, whether as worktops or flooring. For the white finishes – from white-painted matt walls to white gloss floorboards –

RIGHT: **Modern bathrooms take on a more relaxed mood if sanitary ware is combined with traditional cabinetry.** By sinking the basin into a stone worktop, and adding discreet taps, this vanity unit looks more like a piece of unfitted furniture. Wall-mounting gives a particularly streamlined option in the small attic space.

BELOW LEFT: **Contrast smooth, sophisticated surfaces such as wood and mirror with curvy furniture, lighting and accessories,** to break up any hard edges and set a more intimate mood.

BELOW RIGHT: **Adding dense, touchy-feely textures softens Mellow Modern style:** a wool rug or deep-pile upholstery makes a sitting room more inviting.

LEFT AND BELOW: **Though matt white painted walls, or wood panelling, are the most obvious choices in the Mellow Modern interior, a paint finish can look equally good. When choosing suitable colours, take inspiration from the subdued tones of natural materials such as wood or slate, and keep the finish painterly and soft.**

take heart that they touch up easily, so keep a spare pot of the correct shade to hand. Glass and stainless steel, which are so high-maintenance when used in large quantities, should be used only sparingly for details such as low splashbacks, or an occasional tabletop, so will add sparkle rather than elbow grease.

For window treatments, the aim is to add softness, without fussy detailing. The crisp lines of plain roller or tailored Roman blinds are ideal. To play up the light, fresh look, choose them in simple yet textured fabrics, from loose-weave cotton to unlined linens, in whites, neutrals or greys. Curtains should be simply gathered from a metal or wood pole. If you want to maximize light play, then Venetian blinds or louvred American-style shutters work well with the Long Island influences, and cast pretty shadows.

Given the Mellow Modern look's careful mix of the sleek and the traditional, it's comparatively easy to blend different styles of furniture. Aim for some curvaceous pieces, such as a plump Howard-style sofa or bucket-style plastic dining chairs, teamed with contemporary linear furniture, such as a low and lean sideboard, and a modern dining table. This is a budget-friendly solution, as existing classic chairs can be reupholstered in textured neutrals or white cottons, then teamed with slick high-street modern buys, such as tables or storage units. Stick to tight upholstery, for a leaner line, or very plain loose covers with, at the most, a flat or box-pleated valance.

And don't forget the importance of ambience. Doors that open onto a relaxing, verdant outdoor space, an open fire, and an easy, informal furniture arrangement go a long way to reinforce this lightest and most practical of looks.

BELOW: The panelling in this room could look rather traditional, but by painting it a gentle, matt off-white the owner has brought it more up to date. The painting, lamp and display of accessories stick to a limited colour palette and simple geometric shapes, while the bold pink flowers add a touch of zing.

RIGHT: Everything has its rightful place in this style, and ease and comfort are just as important as smartness and sophistication. These furnishings may be elegant and attractive, but, crucially, the lamp gives good light for reading by, too, while the table is a convenient place to put down a drink or a book.

OPPOSITE: Elegant Modern requires good use of space, and this dining/sitting room has plenty of furniture without feeling cluttered. The fact that the two rooms can be open plan or closed off (with double doors) is nicely convenient. Notice details such as the stainless-steel dimmer switch and the subtly patterned blinds.

elegant modern

Not all contemporary interiors have to be funky and bright, or bare and minimalist. There is a certain gentle pleasure to be had from taking classic furnishings and combining them with neutral colours and well-thought-out modern detailing in order to create a style that is sophisticated, subtle and harmonious, with a mature and timeless appeal.

It is relatively easy to define the Elegant Modern style by saying what it is not. It is not ultra-fashionable, in the sense of the latest designer colours, furniture and accessories (and definitely not gadgets). Nor, however, is it in any way unfashionable. There is nothing passé or out of date here. For this look you need to be aware of trends yet also able to rise above them, creating rooms that are at once out of time but also very much of today, and that have the grace and harmony of the past combined with the functionality and aesthetics of the present.

Elegant Modern is equally adaptable to urban or rural living, though it has a sophisticated feel that is perhaps more of the city. Considered use of space is important, so that it is neither bare nor crowded. There is just the right amount of furniture for convenience (a side table next to an armchair, for example, providing a place to put down a drink and to stand a lamp for reading by). Be careful, however, because while this style is utterly comfortable, it is not particularly cosy. So no overstuffed sofas, riotous

ABOVE LEFT: A neutral carpet runs from the bedroom through to the bathroom, unifying the two spaces. The sense of flow from room to room is helped by a repetitive colour palette of taupes and browns.

LEFT: A combination of shades of milk and white chocolate gives this bedroom a restful, balanced harmony. The walls and floor are smooth and fairly bare, but the bed itself, with its woollen blanket and piles of pillows, looks welcoming and comfortable.

ABOVE: The concept of a washstand is pretty traditional, but this example, with its slender legs, chrome taps and backing of wall-to-wall wood and mirror, is entirely, yet subtly, modern.

OPPOSITE: Ease of use is vital to the Elegant Modern style. Here, a large work surface gives plenty of space for bathroom necessities (in matching storage), while a pair of pivoting mirrors provides all the reflections one could ever need.

patterns or cluttered ornaments, thank you very much. Beautiful upholstery is perfect, but deeply button-backed sofas and chairs are just too fussy. Pattern is minimal, and rather subdued – it could be simple abstracts or geometrics, or floral prints in just one or two colours, for example. And accessories are limited to beautiful pieces that enhance their environment, either reflecting it in terms of shape, colour or style, or bringing a dash of something fresh and vibrant in the way of form, texture or colour.

Colour, in fact, is key to getting this style right. The range covers the full gamut of neutrals, from whites and off-whites to chocolate and charcoal, with the occasional zing of a bolder shade such as citrus yellow or navy blue. And because Elegant Modern colours are, overall, fairly muted, texture comes into its own. Hard and soft, nubbly and smooth, coarse and shiny – a subtle mix will

make each room feel welcoming and look appealing. The key materials to look out for are beautifully grained and polished wood, soft linen and cotton, brushed steel, plush velvet and wool and gently worn stone.

Finally, make sure that details really count. You will feel neither elegant nor modern if your door handles are made of plastic or your carpets of acrylic fibres. There is a certain sense of luxury to this look, but it need not be hugely expensive. Blinds made from plain cotton, for example, could be given an unusual pull made of knotted cord or leather, or a cupboard made from painted pine could be transformed by new door knobs in patinated brass. Such attention to even the smallest elements of each room will ensure the quiet subtlety and mature co-ordination that are essential to achieving this look.

OPPOSITE: Though warm and mellow, all-over wood panelling can seem dark and overpowering. It works well in this cosy sitting room, because it has been teamed with broad, unadorned windows that let in plenty of sunlight. The pale linen upholstery also acts as a natural highlight.

LEFT: For a really modern look, pick natural surfaces with a glossier finish, and mix with streamlined Scandinavian-inspired furniture. The visual warmth of stone and wood can be further enhanced with underfloor heating, which will be particularly welcome in bathrooms and kitchens.

BELOW: A modern Natural look is just as effectively built around a few key pieces, such as a timber table and chairs, provided the whole palette is kept neutral and tightly controlled. In this streamlined sitting room, it is the natural colours and textures that hold together a variety of style influences, from the modern modular sofa to a rustic wood-burning stove and classic leather armchair.

natural

There is an enduring appeal to the Natural look. Wholesome and honest, with its rough-textured materials and neutral palette, it's easily paired with modern furniture for a chic yet cosy space.

In an age where modern style and the man-made go hand in hand, it's refreshing to see a contemporary take on natural looks. Pared-down style, with its white cotton covers and shabby-chic timbers, has evolved into a slicker configuration. The textural materials are still in evidence, but now they are teamed with sharper modern shapes and a hint of sophistication. So here is a style that looks as good in the city as in the country, as it has a foot in both camps.

Certain properties lend themselves particularly well to the look. Consider a country cottage, with its exposed beams or a flagged stone floor, or even an urban loft with bare brick walls. Modern buildings are easily adapted, too. Cladding a wall with timber or stone, or adding ceiling beams, is a great way to add architectural character. What you don't want is a pastiche of a Swiss chalet or American log cabin. The ideal mix is a combination of rough, pitted materials plus big, modern windows.

Many modern looks are built around natural components. What makes this style so different is that the textural balance has shifted. Instead of being a contrast material, stone or wood becomes the star of the show. Panelling may be taken across the ceiling, as well as used on vertical surfaces, or concrete moulded into a bath, or a worktop, as well as covering the floor. So research what looks good, and what will work. Check out whether a particular finish

RIGHT: **Just as you would compose a good colour scheme using two to three key shades, use only a few dominant textures to create a contemporary modern look. The oak panels used in this bedroom create a cohesive interior, as they are used, stained dark, on the wardrobe, and then again on the custom-made bed, which is simply accented with the white cotton bedding and monochrome art.**

BELOW: **Think of surfaces not just as a decorative element, but as a means to shape individual spaces. Continuing a given surface from one plane to another – floor to bath, as here, or wall to ceiling – makes a room seem bigger, and gives a sleeker finish.**

will physically work in your home. An upstairs floor may need reinforcing to take slabs of stone; plaster must be sound to hold wood panelling in place.

Focus on texture. You are aiming for interesting, slightly rough surfaces. If going for wooden floorboards, choose reclaimed flooring in place of super-polished hardwoods, or gently 'distress' existing boards with wire wool and a wax finish. Wall panelling may be wood-stained tongue-and-groove, or varnished plywood, which has pleasing honey tones. As for stone, slate, concrete and limestone are more heavily textured than highly polished variations like granite. Good Natural wall finishes include polished plaster and exposed brick.

Comfort is paramount, so combine those hard surfaces with heavy, satisfying textiles. With its ability to look homespun or chic, depending on how it is styled, linen is always a winner, but so too are hessian, wool flannel, denim, canvas and cotton. Any of these looks good hung simply as plain curtains, from iron rings and poles, or used for upholstery. Choose your fabrics in muted plains, so that the textural stories become the main theme, or combine with battered leather, or a flash of an animal-skin rug, for contrast.

Once the Natural 'shell' is complete, the modern finishing touches come from mixing in contemporary linear furniture, or 20th-century classic pieces, many of which were manufactured in wood veneers with metal. Keep your eye on trendier takes of modern crafts – ceramics or wood platters in generous and simple silhouettes – and the look will be complete.

THIS PAGE: **When picking natural surfaces, look not just at variations on colour (from pale to dark, muted to strong), but at the patterns caused by wood grain or pitted stone, and the tactile pleasure of the surface underfoot or on a worktop. Once key textures are in place, they can be accentuated with carefully chosen accessories, from hand-embroidered textiles to battered leather or foxed glass.**

RIGHT: **This 1950s Danish house was built to emphasize function and construction – nothing is hidden or disguised. The floorboards were whitewashed and left to age naturally, while the brick walls were given a thin whitewash simply to stop them from dusting, leaving the bricks still visible. The ceilings are timber-clad, and the windows are free of blinds or curtains.**

MAIN PICTURE: **In this sophisticated living room, classic stools designed by Alvar Aalto in the Thirties are combined with a long, comfortable sofa with simple upholstery. As is typical of this style, the floor is wood, the walls painted white, and the window treatments minimal. The use of soft fabrics with strong geometric patterns, and an eye-catching display of organically shaped ceramics, softens the look while keeping within the monochromatic colour palette.**

scandinavian

For those who enjoy simplicity and fuss-free living, the Scandinavian style is ideal. It is a look that has lasted more than five decades with little need for change – a look that combines designer furnishings with natural materials, and in which form, function and fabulous good looks are seamlessly, subtly integrated.

There's something paradoxical about Scandinavian style. It enfolds a puzzling number of opposites: comfort and minimalism, sophistication and simplicity, tradition and innovation, and vernacular and modernism. And yet, despite these apparently irreconcilable contrasts, this is a style that really works. For those who adopt it, it is less a style than a way of life, a means of surrounding oneself with unpretentious, practical and easy-to-live-with things that are quietly harmonious and subtly interesting.

The modern Scandinavian style arose between the two World Wars, becoming most popular in the Fifties – hence its rather retro look. Nevertheless, this is a style that has stood the test of time, and many of the furnishings designed in its heyday have become true classics, even more popular today than they were then. The look combined elements of modernism, which had swept across Europe and then the USA, with Nordic traditionalism, softening the occasionally harsh Modern Movement style by using natural materials and more organic, curvaceous lines. Simple, functional shapes were the key – nothing garish, jarring or difficult, just well-designed, beautifully constructed pieces in

TOP: **This dining area demonstrates the way in which Scandinavian style combines simplicity with designer classics: the plainest of tables is surrounded by a set of Wishbone chairs by Hans Wegner.**
ABOVE: **White units and a black splashback give the kitchen an air of sleek sophistication.**
RIGHT: **Another simple colour scheme: black Series 7 chairs by Arne Jacobsen around a Tulip table by Eero Saarinen.**

LEFT: This very modern Stockholm apartment has all the basic elements of Scandinavian style, such as a wooden floor, simple colour scheme, pared-down furnishings and plain, clean lines, while subtly updating it for the 21st century.

BELOW LEFT: Beautiful blond birch dominates this Finnish interior. The open-plan kitchen/sitting room is incredibly airy and bright, with minimal window treatments and a plain rug on the floor. The furniture is equally simple, including a pair of K 65 stools designed by Alvar Aalto in the mid-Thirties, and two Series 7 chairs by Arne Jacobsen.

which form and function came together in the best-quality materials. Important designers then, and now, included Alvar Aalto, Georg Jensen, Arne Jacobsen, Poul Henningsen, Finn Juhl, Eero Saarinen and Hans Wegner.

When considering Scandinavian style, remember the importance of the forces of nature in the northern nations of Sweden, Norway, Finland and Denmark. Extremes of landscape and climate are the norm, from snow-capped mountains to boiling geysers. And, while this may be the land of the midnight sun, in the long winters daylight is a fleeting pleasure. So, unsurprisingly, making the most of warmth and light features heavily in the priorities of any Scandinavian interior. Another factor is the pre-eminence of wood as an architectural and furnishing material – plentiful and inexpensive, it tends to dominate the look, though sophisticated rooms combine it cleverly with other natural materials such as cane and rattan, wool, cotton, glass and ceramic. The typical Scandinavian room, then, will have a wooden floor, perhaps with timber-clad walls and ceiling, too, or else pale, plain paintwork. Light fittings, though understated, will be carefully designed and positioned for maximum effect, and textiles will be warm and cosy, often in natural colours but sometimes in bright and cheery shades, with simple stripes or bold, geometric patterns. Window treatments are either non-existent or barely there, enhancing light rather than blocking it out. And furniture is generally made from blond wood, steamed and bent into fluid, interesting shapes, with minimal upholstery. There is a general air of fuss-free relaxation, of uncluttered living that is easy, elegant and enormously appealing.

country styles

It's a mistake to think that country style should be confined to homes in the country. It works well in less grand town houses, too. And, of course, there is a huge choice of countries to emulate, from the West Country thatch to the Provençal *mas* to the Tuscan farmhouse. Generally, the style mixes antiques, comfortable furniture and fabrics and lots of natural materials.

OPPOSITE: **Simple, handwoven textiles are very much used in today's Traditional Country look. Watch out for old French cot covers, curtains and bed hangings. Early fabrics used vegetable dyes, which means that the colours fade elegantly and that all complement each other. This room takes on the red and white mixture and plays about with different scales of checks and patchwork.**

LEFT: **Toile de Jouy is a sure-fire winner for a rural look. It can be mixed with similarly coloured plain cottons, ginghams or ticking.**

traditional country

Don't rest on your laurels when taking on Traditional Country style. It is as much controlled by current fashions as the sleekest cutting-edge design. Watch the trends in more obvious areas, and then adapt them to suit your taste.

It is a fallacy to assume that, because a style is traditional, it cannot also evolve with fashion. If you were to look at fashionable cottage design in, say, 1890 or 1930, you would find two very different takes on the same theme and you would, equally, be able to spot roughly when they were designed. It is just like fashions in clothes – you can always spot the real Victorian women from someone dressed up in 19th-century costume. Thus Traditional Country style in the early 21st century is quite different from even that of the Eighties, when the trend for opulence and excess filtered down even to the interior design of the cottage.

Now, the trend for authenticity, for neutral colours and for minimalism produces a style that is very up to date, even though it appears traditional. In designing your rural interior, always follow the trends that are emerging in more modernist styles, then adapt them to suit your idyll. For example, lampshades are constantly changing (and lots of table and hanging lamps are very traditional and rural), so if you hang on to one of an outdated shape, colour or fabric, your designs will immediately look weary or misplaced. Curtains are another area to consider carefully: while the Eighties were all about immense quantities of

RIGHT: **Even traditional styles move with the fashion. The current obsession is for mixed and matched neutrals, where the main interest comes from texture. This fireside corner includes a woven basket, bobbly throw on a smooth velvet chair and a natural floor covering.**

BELOW RIGHT: **Flea-market finds like an old milk box make good storage for kindling by this working log fire. The old oriental carpet has just the right faded look to combine with the built-in and glazed cupboards in each alcove.**

fabric, lined, interlined and hung from ornate poles, in this new century curtains are much more restrained. They are generally of plain natural cotton, linen or wool, simply patterned with checks and stripes, and hung from unadorned wooden poles. Even more simple are the woven slubby old French linen sheets, hung so that the light shines through them. Translucency is very smart at the moment.

Furniture fashions are also on the move – and just as well, because the need for grand and expensive antiques is less important today. While a fine piece of heavy old oak is a wonderful addition to the scheme (and you only need a single piece), it's just as effective to use painted furniture in traditional styles. Watch out for well-proportioned chairs, tables and cupboards, no matter how broken-down or how ugly the colour of the wood. These can be painted in layers of differing shades, then distressed with sandpaper so different colours and hints of wood appear in such well-handled areas as chair arms and cupboard handles. Then wax the whole to antique it.

Floors should remain natural. Don't bother with the expensive Eighties option of French limestone; use English flags, Suffolk terracotta pamments or red and black quarry tiles. If these are still too expensive, painted concrete, seagrass or sanded boards are equally good options. Faded oriental rugs will cosy these up. Finally, add quirky ornaments – Cornish carved lighthouses, old photos of yachts, home-made herb cutters. The trick is to have lots of each.

TOP: The neutral decor of this bedroom allows the geometry of the solid oak beams and the curves of the iron bed to make the patterns.

ABOVE: A faded patchwork quilt is the main feature in this bedroom.

LEFT: The heavy shelf above the Aga is stacked with old-fashioned glass storage jars and an old ceramic pestle and mortar.

OPPOSITE: **Everything in this working kitchen has been chosen to suit the room – the black cupboards with their steel handles complement the black and metallic stove. Quantities of kitchen utensils, every one of them in steel or white enamel, hang like sculptures above the working areas. The floor is a touch of genius, pulling together the monochrome decor.**

LEFT: **What makes this charming eating area Modern rather than Traditional Country? It is the final touch of the industrial hanging lamp in steel, rather than brass. Without this, the room would have a simple cottagey look.**

BELOW: **An old-fashioned Windsor three-seater has been painted for effect and its broad back packed with cushions. Apart from the fact that they are essential for comfort, the feeling is generous. Such cushions can be tweaked by sewing on stripes or sections of different fabrics in complementary colours.**

modern country

The inspiration for this style is elegance of line, craftsmanship and a spare touch. It needs an eye for detail and an ability to see beauty in mundane objects. This look can't be left alone: it is all about tweaking objects, texture and colour and watching trends.

Modern Country is a most enjoyable style to create, because in it you will mix all the latest fashions, colours, technology and cutting-edge design with centuries of tradition. You can use woven osiers (willows), which have been around since the Stone Age, with medieval horsehair-based lime plaster and then add to it a perfect Sung pottery bowl or one, very similar indeed, by such cult potters as Rupert Spira or Edmund de Waal.

The Modern Country stylist is after the same effect: the idea is to worship simplicity, elegance of line and worldwide craft techniques such as weaving baskets, throwing clay or knotting carpets. Thus, a good eye is all-important: you must be able to spot beauty without pretension, and to let it speak for itself. Once you can do this – the watchword is to avoid all fuss or unnecessary ornament – then you will have the pleasure of mentally travelling the world and taking time to create your look.

The other major element is the use of surprise. The otherwise traditional kitchen suddenly switches to sombre black cupboards and steel instead of brass. Farmhouse tables are coated in a thick layer of matt white paint, and the chairs alongside have woven raffia cushions. Tweeds are used instead of ginghams. The use of modern art is another pointer to Modern Country.

Modern Country style is not, as you might think, intended for rural homes

ABOVE: **The positioning of this old roll-top bath is what makes the room feel new. Instead of being put against the wall, it is placed centrally. The plain shower curtains, hung from a giant clothes horse, give a feeling of privacy as well as controlling the spray from the giant showerhead. The addition of a huge, textured basket and a willow log basket used for laundry is very much in the Modern Country style.**

BELOW: **This bedroom is reminiscent of a monk's cell, it is so sparse: no bedhead, no paintings and precious little colour. However, the room's ceiling angles and the sturdy oak chair make this a rural scheme, not an urban one.**

OPPOSITE: **The neutral simplicity of colours and form give extra importance to the luscious black glazed pottery plates and amusing spoon and fork hangings. The basketwork accessories add a rural touch.**

alone. It works just as well in urban spaces. It is, for example, particularly well suited to the modern fashion for warehouse and industrial conversions and, indeed, obsolete industrial artefacts such as iron staircases, steel shelving and old cogwheels will fit into the style. Similarly, it suits all attic spaces where the roof beams slope to the floor and where there are struts and beams to give the rooms a background geometric grid.

This is a highly fashionable style and, for that reason, if you adopt it you must keep up with the fashion in design as it moves along. Also, if some object or treatment is starting to become a cliché, then you should consider dropping it. But don't feel you have to change some well-loved corner just for the sake of it; a cliché kept long enough will suddenly become the next best thing. People will marvel that you have something so precious and authentic. It is, however, important to keep an eye open

for small changes that can make a room look tired. Lighting is crucial because the technology moves fast and, because of their nature, lamps attract attention. Watch out, too, for the paintings and prints on your walls – are the frames becoming boring, should the mount be changed in colour (bright ones are out) or should the mount be dispensed with altogether? Is the hang right? Is it old hat to prop pictures on shelves? Are mirrors – another attention-seeker – also in need of up-to-date frames? If you adopt a modern style, you need to check such details constantly. Usually, small tweaks and changes are not too expensive, especially if you can learn, for

RIGHT: **Classical symmetry in what is clearly a country bathroom gives it a modern gloss. The two chunky ladder-like towel rails are just propped against warming radiators. The tones of the wooden floor are echoed in the plain Roman blinds.**

BELOW LEFT: **Only the chair, of a glowing wood, has colour in this all-white bathroom. The mirror is without ornament and the heavy towels are pure white. This allows the shape of the basin and the planked wall behind to provide texture and form.**

BELOW RIGHT: **An old orchard ladder comes in handy for hanging the towels.**

LEFT: **Horizontal planks are a major decorative element in a simple, plain white bedroom with warming red covers on each bed.**

BELOW LEFT: **The modern classic Tizio bedside light and slatted blinds add a Modern Country touch to an ancient building.**

example, to adapt existing frames and cut mounts yourself. Watch to see what young artists are doing to their frames. Even a coat of paint will transform them.

Another good wheeze is to look critically at the arrangement of objects in a room. You have found a wonderful old library ladder, painted and distressed it. And you have put it in the living room to hang magazines from. That's now getting a bit dated, so just move it to the bathroom and use the rungs to hang towels to dry. Bored with that? It will fulfil the same need in the kitchen. You can move your lovely pottery bowls from garden room to kitchen and fill them with lemons; you can take your tweed cushions and give them an extra broad band of ribbon or plain fabric or, indeed, pile them up in complementary heaps by the bedhead. The whole point is to be unpredictable, to keep on changing so that your carefully chosen objects never become invisible because you no longer notice them. Pieces can be stored away and new objects found to take their place, then the whole reshuffled again. Don't just pile them up all together. Another element of Modern Country is a certain spareness.

By using practical objects as an element in the design, you will automatically achieve this look, because well-chosen work surfaces, storage, furniture and kitchen pans are things of beauty in themselves. Those which are not can be hidden in your simple cupboards which, of course, have cleverly chosen knobs or handles. Modern Country is a style that always needs your full attention. Keep everything calm, keep it controlled, keep it carefully considered.

period styles

Choose a style that takes beautiful designs from the past and updates them for the present. Whether you prefer Classic Period style, with its elegant, considered, sometimes formal approach, or Vintage and Retro, which is more casual, individual and dashing, you can create a look that will suit you and your home in a way that has lasting, timeless appeal.

FAR LEFT: **Heavy and luxurious dark curtains frame a large Georgian-inspired window. Though the table and daybed are more 19th century in feeling, they are overpowered by the sweep of the fabric and the formality of the tie-backs.**

LEFT: **These curvy dining chairs are inspired by Greek shapes designed before Christ. The windows and honeysuckle iron balcony beyond are pure Palladian in style.**

BELOW: **A good fireplace is a necessity for this style. This one gives the room focus and symmetry, while the dark floorboards and central picture are also classical in feeling. The snakeskin stool and sheepskin rug are a playful take on this style.**

classic period style

To create rooms in Classic Period style, you need only pore over grand 18th-century houses and the carefully drawn designs of architects such as Wren and Hawksmoor and furniture makers like Hepplewhite and Sheraton. You need to be a purist to capture the classical period at its best, from using authentic paint colours to splashing out on genuine antique furniture.

OPPOSITE: **The classical style doesn't need only period furniture; it needs a good knowledge of how 18th-century rooms worked. This drawing-room corner, with much later furniture and lighting, is pulled together by the firmly 18th-century curtain treatment. The generous, if plain, curtains hang from a formal pelmet and are held below centre with formal tie-backs.**

At first glance this style seems to be pure 18th century but, in fact, in Britain the movement to follow classical Greek and Roman proportions actually began in the 17th century, with Inigo Jones's Queen's House at Greenwich. And that copied the work of Andrea Palladio (1508–80), who was inspired by Vitruvius, who took Roman buildings as his models. This is a strictly defined style with, outside, windows clearly proportioned so that the smaller ground floor is succeeded by the larger *piano nobile* and, further upwards, smaller bedroom windows on the third and fourth

floors. Inside, the large sash windows have glazing bars which decrease in width as the 18th century progresses. Inside, too, are formal cornices, skirtings, door surrounds and ceiling roses, which use the classical orders – Ionic, Corinthian, Doric and Tuscan – to inspire their ornament.

Of necessity, Classic Period style rooms are formal, symmetrical and dependent on versions of classical furniture. Greek chairs with sabre legs and heavy, moulded backs evolved in the 18th century to Chippendale, Sheraton and Hepplewhite versions, which are still changing with the work of modern

designers. Wrought- and cast-iron balconies, door furniture and internal banisters make use of classical ornaments such as acanthus leaves, honeysuckle flowers, ivy and fig foliage. Meanwhile, the main decor remains in the 18th century, with traditional Georgian furniture mixed with classical urn and obelisk table lamps and plaster casts as decoration, along with formal bird's-eye-view black-and-white prints of 17th-century gardens, etchings of classical sculpture and architectural details such as those drawn by Piranesi. These should be hung symmetrically, in big groups. The subject matter or quality of the print is less important than the severe black frames and lack of any mount.

In this style, furniture and fabrics need to be formal, plain and not over-coloured. Ideally, furniture should be displayed symmetrically and only rearranged for meals. Fireplaces need cast-iron register grates with yet more classical ornament, surrounded by marble, slate or wood mantelpieces, preferably with a plain but important mirror or picture displayed above. Panelling is always acceptable, as are plain wooden floorboards covered with oriental carpets or rugs.

Classical rooms should be painted in authentic 18th-century colours, readily available from heritage paint suppliers who copy colours from original paints found in period houses. It's also an idea to use 18th-century paint techniques here – scumbling, dragging, sponging and the like. Skirtings can be marbled and doors and other woodwork given added emphasis by using two tones of the same colour.

This is an easy look to copy – it needs no input from you – but it does require both a knowledge of classical motifs, 18th-century interiors and, ideally, at least a few pieces of good 18th-century furniture.

THIS PAGE: **Though the patterns of the curtains and wallpaper, derived from French toile de Jouy, would not have been used together in the 18th century, the formality of the decor is pure Classic Period style. Added to this is the extremely grand four-poster bed, a mahogany antique dating from the last years of that century. It does not have overpowering drapes but, instead, the quality of the wood has been emphasized by a similar-coloured cover, mirrored in the border of the curtains.**

ABOVE LEFT: **Rooms inspired by the classical period were sparing in their use of colour and more interested in the natural shades of tropical hardwood such as mahogany and rosewood, as shown in these bedposts.**

ABOVE RIGHT: **Georgian-style panelling and 18th-century windows with light glazing bars and integral, internal shutters were originally intended for a grander room than a bathroom.**

RIGHT: **Even though the bath is Victorian, the panelling and plaster cast put this room firmly in the 18th century.**

vintage & retro

For those who want to bring the past into their homes but who are
not fans of formal antiques, the Vintage and Retro style is ideal.
Casual and individual, this is a style that demands nothing more
than that you go with the flow, mixing and matching patterns, shapes
and colours with dash and panache.

Poised somewhere in the grey area between fine antiques and
modern furniture comes Vintage and Retro – a look that is all
about easygoing comfort and which often involves mixing the old
with the slightly less old, plus a bit of new. This style has generous
boundaries. It might, on the one hand, include casual, pretty
collectables such as Cornishware crockery or French chandeliers or,
on the other hand, involve eye-catching mid-century modern chairs
or vivid Sixties colours. It's up to you which way you choose to take
it. If you tend towards the Vintage aesthetic, it is slightly more cosy

and relaxed, with a general feel that is gently unmodernized and
contains nothing too expensive, rare or special. It might mean, for
example, ginghams and washed-out chintzes, simple wooden
chairs, old sofas re-covered in canvas or ticking, curly iron
bedsteads, hinged-arm metal lamps and cream-painted Shaker-style
kitchen units. For a more consciously Retro look, however, you
might select designer plastic chairs and colourful lights, boldly
patterned textiles and, in general, pieces that make a little more of
a statement. This look tends to follow decades, so you might

OPPOSITE LEFT: **A modern, chocolate-brown wallpaper has subtle Retro overtones, while the hinged-arm lamp brings character to this comfortable corner.**

OPPOSITE RIGHT: **The introduction of suitable prints and colours, especially in the form of this striking painting, goes a long way towards setting the scene for the Vintage and Retro style.**

LEFT: **In this period house, the eclectic mix of old and new furnishings gives a relaxed, retro-chic look.**

ABOVE LEFT: **Spindly-legged Retro chairs fit perfectly into a Georgian interior which has been decorated in modern, neutral tones.**

ABOVE: **A striking 1962 Arco lamp and barely-there wire chairs by Harry Bertoia, designed in the late Forties, add enough Retro flavour to a modern kitchen to give it an appealingly individual aesthetic.**

TOP: **Colour and pattern combine here with a funky Retro kitchen unit, giving the room a laid-back and eclectic character.**

ABOVE: **A pretty painted chair can usually complement the furnishings in any room.**

RIGHT: **These bathroom fittings can be sourced as antiques or modern replicas – the point is that they create a coherent style, with a suitably functional feel.**

LEFT: **These shades of beige and brown normally suggest the Seventies, but here they have been teamed with a Thirties-style pedestal basin – a daring decision that has paid off.**

BELOW LEFT: **This room has plenty of functional, industrial chic, softened by the use of pink and the feminine touch of a floral-printed bed throw.**

decide to pick Thirties Deco, Fifties post-war chic, Sixties pop or Seventies cool.

Modern reproductions are often a vital part of Vintage and Retro, whether a Belfast sink or a drawer handle, a corner cupboard or a curvy tap. In fact, the delightful thing about Vintage and Retro style is that it is just as effective whether you use junk-shop finds, salvaged furnishings, carefully chosen high-street buys or eye-catching pieces for which you hunted high and low. The key is to be relaxed, whether you choose to mix and match in an ad hoc way or decide to create a more coherent, overall look.

Vintage and Retro works well throughout the house, and is as successful in a bathroom or a kitchen as it is in a bedroom or living room. Involving nothing more complex than a lick of paint, colours can often set the tone, and pattern, too, is a great scene-setter. While you could go to town choosing appropriate furnishings down to every last detail, it is equally possible to create the look relatively easily, quickly and cheaply. It can consist simply of the pleasure that comes from the introduction into an otherwise contemporary room of, say, a gathered curtain made from pink gingham, a hanging rack of pots and pans, a display of pressed glass or a spindly Fifties pendant lamp. Remember that this is not about perfection, but enjoyment of gradually creating an individual look from diverse sources, so your finished effect can be as laid-back or as impressive as you like, as long as it gives you the greatest possible pleasure.

the rooms

kitchens & eating areas

A major influence in current kitchen design is that of the professional chef's kitchen. It is bringing a minimalist edge even to country-style interiors. Steel is mixed with black, surfaces are empty and necessary cooking tools and crockery are of white, glass and yet more steel. Yet even in the most modern scheme, naturals such as wooden floors, marble and granite are very important.

sleek

Cutting-edge kitchens need sleek surfaces and flush cupboards, dressed up with the gloss of granite, steel and glass. High-maintenance and sophisticated, these are statement rooms, with state-of-the-art appliances to match. Keep detailing minimalist, the palette neutral and tidy as you go. In the Sleek kitchen, everything (from saucepans to jam pots) must be hidden away.

Inspired by the clean lines of the truly minimalist kitchen, yet nowhere near as severe, today's Sleek cooking zones are temples of discipline and sparkle. Gorgeous when tidy, disastrous strewn with last night's supper, they must provide a place for everything – even the kettle. Perfect for organized cooks, style aficionados and city slickers, they make life easy, provided you follow the minimalist mantra.

Space configuration is key: these kitchens need to look (and be) streamlined. Particularly effective are banks of units down one wall, galley-style, or cupboards aligned opposite one another, with an island unit. For a really pared-down look, incorporate major appliances and worktop space onto an extra-large island, and 'lose' remaining storage in flush floor-to-ceiling cupboards. If you're incorporating a dining area, think about extending the worktop into a breakfast bar; more streamlined than filling space with a dining table.

These kitchens mean hiding clutter, so the amount and style of cupboards is vital. Plan sufficient variety – tall cupboards for the ironing board, shallow shelves for food storage, and so on. Pick opaque fronts to look calming and smart, even if there's a jumble behind. Good choices include

OPPOSITE ABOVE LEFT: **Storage needn't be kitchen cupboards on the wall. Consider bespoke joinery, so shelving can be made to your requirements: cover with sliding, or flush, doors for a sleek finish.**

OPPOSITE ABOVE RIGHT: **A slick island unit can divide the kitchen and living space. This one has a minimalist breakfast bar one side, and access to the hob on the other.**

OPPOSITE BELOW LEFT AND CENTRE: **As accessories are kept to a minimum, attention is focused on** fittings, so pick good-looking, yet highly functional extras like modern spout taps and stainless-steel rail storage.

OPPOSITE BELOW RIGHT: **In a kitchen/ diner, carry the Sleek theme to the eating area, and keep the table as minimally styled as the worktops.**

BELOW: **Pay attention to cooking utensils and tableware, as they should be as smart and glossy as the kitchen itself: stainless-steel pans, white china, and catering-quality implements all look good.**

KEY FEATURES

▮ HARD WORKTOPS, FROM GLOSSY GRANITE AND MARBLE THROUGH TO HARDWOODS, CORIAN, OR RESTAURANT KITCHEN-STYLE STAINLESS STEEL.

▮ BANKS OF FLUSH DOORS, OPENED WITH MAGNETIC SPRING-CATCHES, DISCREET STAINLESS-STEEL KNOBS, OR LONG D-HANDLES. DRAWER DETAILS SHOULD MATCH.

▮ ULTRA-MODERN STAINLESS-STEEL APPLIANCES, INCLUDING GENEROUS RANGE-STYLE COOKERS, SIX-BURNER HOBS, EYE-LEVEL BUILT-IN MICROWAVES AND GIANT AMERICAN FRIDGE-FREEZERS.

▮ SLEEK HARD FLOORS, FROM LIMESTONE AND TIMBER BOARDS TO SLATE OR STAINLESS STEEL.

▮ STREAMLINED FURNITURE IN ICE WHITES OR BRIGHT CONTRAST TONES, SUCH AS BREAKFAST-BAR STOOLS, DESIGNER DINING CHAIRS, OR A GLASS-TOPPED TABLE.

laminate, wood veneers, stainless steel, or painted MDF – not glass, unless you are tidy. Doors should be flush, or with discreet handles, and consider sliding doors or roll-down steel shutters to mix in.

Choose worktops, splashbacks and flooring to enhance purity of line. So avoid tiled areas, or highly patterned natural materials, which will jar with flush-fronted cupboards. Extend splashbacks from worktop level to the base of wall-mounted cupboards, and plan for an uninterrupted run of worktop. A sink and drainer 'moulded in' to stainless-steel or stone surfaces looks very sleek.

Go for as much gloss or high sheen as you can: steel, granite and marble are particularly reflective.

As for furniture and accessories, keep things minimal. Dining furniture should be modern, either in the neutral tones of the natural surfaces, or with vibrant splashes of colour, from lime to electric blue. Appliances on show should be in gleaming steel. Acceptable extras include cube storage jars, a plain glass vase, and pure white platters for fruit. Don't forget lighting, tailored to play up gleam. A mix of under-cupboard lights and low-voltage halogen spots over a central island creates all the drama you need.

FAR LEFT ABOVE AND BELOW: **Appliances must blend seamlessly with the cupboard fronts, so plan them at the start. If a vast fridge-freezer is a priority, then consider stainless-steel units to match. Always choose the full-fascia panel option for appliances like dishwashers, so that even the controls are concealed.**
ABOVE LEFT: **In small kitchens, where space is at a premium, a small, wall-mounted worktop can double as a breakfast bar. Choose minimalist stools to match.**
BELOW LEFT: **Be realistic when picking glossy surfaces. All-over stainless steel looks fabulous and withstands wear and tear, but shows up every fingerprint.**
ABOVE AND OPPOSITE: **Choose open shelving or glass-fronted cabinets with care, as they only look good if filled with plain tableware, arranged in perfect order. Stainless-steel detailing goes with every surface, from wood to marble.**

STREAMLINED CHIC STYLE STUDY

Composed around a muted, neutral colour scheme, mixing textures from smooth marble to knobbly mosaics, warm wood to cool stainless steel, this is a user-friendly yet sophisticated kitchen. The cooking zone is tightly planned, with all appliances close to hand, while the dining area has ambient lighting, chic furniture and softer, more mellow detailing.

This room seamlessly links alcove space and a larger, open-plan area. By squeezing all appliances and storage into floor-to-ceiling units on two walls, and adding a slim island unit as a barrier between cooking and eating zones, the living space remains tranquil and uncluttered by kitchen things. The central positioning of the cooker hood draws the eye to the attractively tiled wall, rather than the cupboards either side.

There's a confident mix of surfaces, whose subtle, neutral tones hang together visually. The two major links are the honey-coloured oak floorboards and stainless steel, on appliances, stools and for kitchen tools. By keeping the kitchen surfaces pale, from the sandblasted cupboard fronts to the mosaic tiles, it's easy to introduce softer, creamy tones in the dining zone.

Lighting is active in making two separate areas feel streamlined. There are four low-voltage halogen spots above the cooking area, for practicality and drama, while the dining zone is softly candlelit. Textures move from the wobbly and organic surface of the tiled wall, to more streamlined fabric bench upholstery, and finally to the tailored, yet soft, tight upholstery on the dining chairs.

WHY IT WORKS ISLAND UNIT CONCEALS MESS FROM THE TABLE ■ FLOOR-TO-CEILING STORAGE ■ SLEEK, FLUSH DOOR AND DRAWER FRONTS ■ PALE, SOPHISTICATED COLOURS

OPPOSITE ABOVE AND BELOW: If kitchen and dining area are to be combined, it's vital to choose a table and formal chairs to suit the mood, though not necessarily the surfaces, of the units. It's often best if the dining furniture does have a more sophisticated finish, so it's suitable for dinner parties,

but make sure it is practical, too. Chair upholstery should be at least spongeable, and tabletops easy to clean. Here, the wood frame and laminate tabletop are warm to the touch and look suitably grown-up, as well as being easier on the eye than a table with aggressive stainless-steel detailing.

THIS PAGE: If space is tight, build in as many appliances as possible, including the microwave or coffee machine. This way, worktops remain clutter-free, and all appliances are close to hand. Pull-up or roll-down door fronts or shutters at worktop height (LEFT) conceal everyday gadgets.

ABOVE FAR LEFT AND CENTRE: **Eating zones should be styled to match the kitchen, melding clean lines with fresh whites. Greenery instantly lifts the core palette, so this look works well in a garden extension. A mix of chairs and bench seating is a streamlined compromise in narrow spaces.**
ABOVE, TOP RIGHT AND TOP CENTRE: **Use stainless steel to accent, rather than dominate, the kitchen. A steel splashback, cooker hood or handles all echo the theme.**
FAR LEFT: **Pick natural surfaces with low sheen, which also look and feel warm to the touch. Solid wood, stone and Corian make good worktop choices, and polished plaster provides a soft, pretty alternative to white walls.**
LEFT: **Mix in occasional unfitted extras, such as a wheeled trolley.**
OPPOSITE: **This kitchen brilliantly combines casual free-standing pieces, such as a plain rustic dining table, with sleek fitted cupboards and wall-mounted shelves.**

mellow modern

Combine a fresh, white palette with warm-looking natural surfaces, from solid wood to chunky honed stone, for this contemporary–classic kitchen style. Hovering between the streamlined discipline of Sleek, and a more relaxed, practical mood, the Mellow Modern kitchen provides a welcoming, sociable backdrop to the busy, family home.

KEY FEATURES

▌ MATT OR GLOSS PLAIN-PAINTED WALLS IN EVERY SHADE OF WHITE, FROM SPARKLING ICE TO MILK-WHITE, OFF-WHITE OR SOFT GREYS.

▌ PLENTY OF WOOD DETAILING, FROM PALE OAK TO WARM CHERRY, USED FOR KITCHEN SURFACES, ON FURNITURE AND AS HARD-WORKING FLOORING.

▌ A MIX OF MODERN LAMINATE AND STEEL FURNITURE, WITH SOFTLY CURVED RETRO CHAIRS, OR TRADITIONAL 'DISTRESSED' TIMBER TABLE AND STORAGE UNITS.

▌ STAINLESS-STEEL ACCENTS FOR APPLIANCES AND ACCESSORIES, TEAMED WITH SANDBLASTED GLASS ON CUPBOARD FRONTS OR SPLASHBACKS.

▌ A COMBINATION OF STREAMLINED BUILT-IN STORAGE CUPBOARDS AND MORE RELAXED, EYE-LEVEL SHELVING.

The Mellow Modern kitchen is a clean and contemporary take on the easy, rustic kitchen. The mood is sociable, the surfaces practical, and the style upbeat and young, but with enough sophistication for kitchen-table entertaining. It's the perfect look to mix with traditional architecture, yet is equally at home in a modern garden extension.

Space planning is important because you are aiming for streamlined storage, teamed with a sociable focal point – somewhere for all to gather and eat. If there's room, an island unit is ideal: designed with an overhanging worktop on one or both sides, it reduces the need for a separate dining table. In small rooms, arrange units on two or even three walls, so that a small table may be placed centrally.

If kitchen units are sleek and flush, then introduce some friendlier curves with retro plywood chairs or high stools. Alternatively, tongue-and-groove or plainly panelled cupboard doors may be mixed with sleek contemporary furniture. The key is to combine modern and traditional in almost equal quantities. The new take on the rustic, country dresser is open shelves, but keep this storage perfectly ordered, with plain white or glass containers and tableware.

RELAXATION CLASS STYLE STUDY

With its mix of pristine white and honey-toned wood, this
kitchen is light, fresh and easy to live in. Yet it is highly
practical, too. Everyday foodstuffs are neatly arranged on
eye-level shelves, and there are easy-grip D-handles and
an island unit with yet more open storage. Contrast colours
of olive green and black add a comfortable new twist to
the Mellow Modern palette.

This young, modern kitchen bridges the style gap between high-maintenance all-white surfaces and a too-rustic wood finish. The white laminate and stainless-steel units look pristine and workmanlike, and can be tidied up for entertaining. Yet the addition of wood, from worktops to flooring, stops the overall finish looking too clinical.

In a relaxed, working kitchen, some food, storage jars and tableware will need to be out on show. This has been carefully planned for here. Custom-built shallow wall shelving means key items are neatly arranged and easy to see. Because food packaging is colourful, deep colour accents have been cleverly added into the decorative scheme, so they don't jar with too much white. The olive green of the shelves, and the black of the leather chairs, have provided just enough contrast colour.

There is a studied mix of furniture styles, from the ultra-simple table to retro dining chairs and the wall-mounted wooden plate rack, so it was easy to combine textural surfaces, contributing a relaxed mood. While the stainless steel and laminate are shiny and practical to match the glass tabletop, the matt woods, blackboard surfaces and leather add a softer, lived-in finish.

OPPOSITE LEFT AND TOP AND CENTRE RIGHT: **The open-shelf style still looks streamlined because it has been carefully planned. Tableware and cooking utensils are sorted by size and colour, and – though casually hung – there is a designated place even for the broom and the tea towel.**

By keeping foodstuffs on upper shelves only, balanced by the pure white cupboards below, a sense of order is maintained.
ABOVE: **Mellow Modern is all about mixing curved and straight silhouettes, so the rectangular table and blackboard cupboards are softened by the retro chairs.**

LEFT AND RIGHT: **To achieve a relaxed-looking kitchen, storage must be minutely planned. This kitchen works because there is an excellent mix of options, from lots of drawers and open shelves to conventional cupboards and floor-to-ceiling storage behind the blackboard fascias.**

WHY IT WORKS LOW AND HIGH EASY-ACCESS STORAGE ■ WARM WOODS LINK FLOOR AND SURFACES ■ PRACTICAL YET SMART STAINLESS STEEL, LEATHER AND BLACKBOARD

elegant modern

For those of us who desire the functionality of ultra-modern appliances but do not necessarily admire their avant-garde looks, there is a middle way. An Elegant Modern kitchen subtly incorporates good-looking kitchenware into a timeless environment, creating a mature and sophisticated yet still comfortable and contemporary space in which to cook and eat – either en famille or more formally.

The Elegant Modern kitchen gives you the best of two worlds: the simple pleasures of traditional features and the convenience of today's technology. Both, however, are restrained rather than obvious – traditional does not mean olde worlde, while technology does not scream 'look at me'.

Kitchen storage mixes flush-fitted cupboards with plain open shelving, glass doors and the occasional, neat, hanging rail or rack. This way beautiful things can be displayed, or everyday items kept close at hand, while clutter – the secret enemy of this look – is hidden well out of sight.

Add cookers, microwaves and other appliances that are quietly sophisticated in styling, and you are halfway there. Keep colours muted and textures varied, including durable, attractive materials such as natural wood, polished or patinated stone and the occasional touch of stainless steel with, perhaps, a woollen rug or a linen blind for softness. Make lighting efficient yet understated – spotlights inset into the ceiling or under wall units, supplemented by lamps in convenient places, will do the trick. For dining, a classic wooden table is ideal, with a set of matching chairs in a relatively plain, timeless style.

KEY FEATURES

▌ STORAGE THAT COMBINES FITTED CUPBOARDS WITH OPEN SHELVING – BUT KEEP IT NEAT OR THE SENSE OF HARMONY SO VITAL TO THIS LOOK WILL TURN TO DISORDER.

▌ A PLAIN COLOUR SCHEME THAT COVERS THE RANGE FROM WHITE TO CHOCOLATE OR CHARCOAL IS THE IDEAL BACKDROP, WITH SURFACES MADE FROM POLISHED WOOD, STONE OR STAINLESS STEEL. AVOID MAN-MADE MATERIALS FOR WORKTOPS.

▌ FLOORS SET THE SCENE, AND SHOULD BE DURABLE AND TIMELESS. WOODEN FLOORBOARDS, CLASSIC STONE FLAGS OR AN ELEGANT VINYL WILL ALL WORK.

▌ TECHNOLOGY WITH SIMPLE, APPEALING FEATURES, AND ZILLIONS OF FUNCTIONS.

OPPOSITE LEFT: **A classic wooden dining table (this one has a hint of modern styling), plus a set of matching chairs, is a key ingredient.**

OPPOSITE RIGHT: **This kitchen/eating area features a well-co-ordinated mix of stripes and plains, with a good combination of hard and soft textures.**

THIS PAGE, CLOCKWISE FROM ABOVE: **A touch of stainless steel can update any kitchen, especially when combined with neutral walls and flooring. Traditional wicker chairs in a cream-coloured room have timeless charm. Simple blinds allow in plenty of light without distracting from a clean-lined look. Open shelving looks gorgeous, but must be kept tidy. Wooden floorboards are elegant whether in a kitchen or dining room. A mix of glass and solid doors means that all sorts of storage is catered for.**

SUBTLE HARMONY STYLE STUDY

The Elegant Modern kitchen is beautiful to look at, efficient in the way it works and harmonious in feel. It is the mix of technology with tradition that gels these items together, and the owners of this kitchen have thought through all the details to ensure that their room has a timeless appeal without compromising on function.

The main components of this kitchen are the striking surfaces: a gleamingly polished stone floor, a more matt stone worktop, dark-wood cabinetry, a stainless-steel cooker and extractor, and white-tiled and painted walls. They are classic materials used in a contemporary way, and they work within the very limited colour range of metallic grey, chocolate, beige and white, emphasizing a sense of careful order and sophistication. Although these are all hard surfaces, some are more shiny and reflective than others, thus varying the textural range, while a little softness – vital if the room is not to seem cold – has been added via fabric chair covers, a wirework basket and stacked-up cookbooks. The result is a room that exudes subtle harmony and calm efficiency.

The free-standing range cooker is a typical example of a great mix of old and new. Classic styling combines with all the latest features; its air of understated professionalism is just right for this look. Like the fitted cupboards, it stands on neat metal legs, making it appear less bulky and emphasizing the sense of space. Plenty of units hide clutter, while more attractive items live on open shelves: a neat solution for a kitchen with quiet character.

WHY IT WORKS A STRICT COLOUR PALETTE ▪ SUMPTUOUS MATERIALS USED IN A SIMPLE WAY ▪ EFFICIENT TECHNOLOGY SOFTENED BY RELAXED DETAILING ▪ WELL-PLANNED STORAGE COMBINING OPEN SHELVING WITH CUPBOARDS

ABOVE, FROM LEFT TO RIGHT:
Ceramic and stone are traditional materials, but here they have been used in a contemporary way, smooth, plain and ultra-crisp. A free-standing range cooker typifies the mix of classic styling with new technology that makes an Elegant Modern kitchen work. It might be a designer tap, but its simple curves give it a gracious, timeless air. Open shelving, often found in more traditional kitchens, is appropriate here because of its neutral styling and the neat arrangement of its contents.

LEFT: **A colour scheme that varies from white to chocolate, with stainless steel and stone thrown in for good measure, has an efficient harmony.**

RIGHT: **The relaxed features of this breakfast bar – simple wooden stools with white fabric covers, a floral painting and rise-and-fall lamp – are pleasantly traditional but have modern good looks.**

KEY FEATURES

▮ ALL-ENVELOPING WOOD SURFACES, ON DOORS, WORKTOPS AND FLOORS, WITH HARDWOODS FROM SYCAMORE TO OAK, CHERRY TO ELM.

▮ A SUBTLE, MID- TO DARK-TONED PALETTE FOR WALLS, SOFT FURNISHINGS AND ACCESSORIES, RANGING FROM CHARCOAL TO MUSHROOM PINKS OR PALEST GREY.

▮ HONED STONE SURFACES, EITHER ON FLOORS, OR WORKTOPS AS WELL, INCLUDING LIMESTONE, GRANITE, CONCRETE, SLATE AND MARBLE.

▮ CLEAN, LINEAR SHAPES ADD A MODERN SPIN TO RUSTIC NATURAL MATERIALS.

▮ TACTILE MATERIALS, INCLUDING LINEN, CALICO, SCRIM AND COTTON.

▮ GENEROUS, NO-NONSENSE APPLIANCES, INCLUDING CHUNKY RANGE COOKERS, CAPACIOUS STAINLESS-STEEL SINKS AND CATERING-STYLE HOBS.

OPPOSITE ABOVE LEFT: **In an open-plan space, which includes a seating area, dining zone and kitchen, tie in soft furnishings with practical utility surfaces. Extend the theme of wood, stone and metal with rough-textured fabrics for sofas and curtains, from loose-weave linen to bouclé wool or chenille. A neutral palette works best.**
OPPOSITE ABOVE RIGHT: **White tableware may be too stark a contrast against muted woods and stone. Investigate textural options, from wood platters to modern ceramics in muted shades.**
OPPOSITE CENTRE AND BELOW: **Although the overall finish should be modern and streamlined, pick open-plan or flush storage according to whether you want a slick, or relaxed, kitchen.**
BELOW: **As the colours and textures of the surfaces provide the strongest design story, play down accessories and keep outlines smart and rectangular. The occasional organic-shaped item, from a sculpted wood bowl to a simple lampshade, adds essential contrast.**

natural

The antithesis to the clear-cut freshness of Mellow Modern, the Natural kitchen relies on muted, sombre tones. Look for natural textures with accentuated colours or designs: the rich grain of walnut or burr oak, or the gentle self-patterns of a concrete floor or worktop. To add a contemporary spin, mix them with utility metals, modern flush doors and an accompanying neutral palette.

Wood and stone have always been core kitchen elements; the earliest kitchens boasted a wooden table and flagstone floor. These days, the same natural components make a utilitarian but sophisticated look to enjoy for its textural good looks and practicality.

To give maximum visual impact, check out specialist kitchen companies to find a decorative wood with a pleasing rich grain. Show it off as a run of cupboards, or panel a wall. Muted stone worktops or a stainless-steel splashback will make a good colour and textural contrast to the vertical wood surfaces. If mixing a timber floor with wood cupboards, either go for a deliberate contrast (dark with light, say) or keep to similar tones; otherwise the effect will look muddled. Avoid mixing painted woods with natural grains.

Given the subtle textures of natural materials, mix kitchen surfaces with subdued wall finishes, as bright white walls create too much contrast. Choose plain matt paint, in off-tones from mushroom pink to taupe, or go for a textured finish, from polished plaster to a paint effect. Pick window treatments that play up moody lighting, from Venetian blinds to sandblasted glass.

NATURALLY COMPACT STYLE STUDY

Proof that a contemporary Natural scheme can look as good in a small, urban apartment as in a modern country house, this efficiently designed alcove kitchen looks warm yet smart. Although the space is clad in honey-toned wood from floor to ceiling, slick stainless-steel appliances and well-planned lighting add clever contrast.

Planned to fit neatly into a small space with no natural light, this kitchen benefits from the contemporary Natural look. For a start, the muted, warm colours work particularly well with electric light. And, as the palette is a tight mix of pale wood, silvery metal and white accessories, it accentuates, rather than closes down, the already small space.

The wood grain is a direct inspiration for the kitchen design. Its distinctive straight lines are echoed in the wall cupboards, which have a very tall, thin outline. The stainless-steel strips on the opening edges accentuate the grain further. The narrow, streamlined kitchen style visually pushes up the ceiling height, turning an unremarkable space into a well-defined work zone. The horizontal drawers and open shelves also make the room seem wider.

While the power of a Natural kitchen lies in its soft, muted colours, it also needs a touch of brightness. In a room where there is no sunlight, well-planned wall-washing lighting creates natural highlights, and bounces off the stainless-steel appliances below. The white accessories, glasses and catering-style saucepans are deliberately on display, to provide extra sparkle.

WHY IT WORKS CLUTTER-FREE WORKTOPS ■ IDENTICAL WOOD SURFACES THROUGHOUT ENLARGES SPACE ■ METAL CUPBOARD AND DRAWER DETAILING ■ SLEEK APPLIANCES

OPPOSITE MAIN PICTURE: **The small proportions of the kitchen work in its favour, as all appliances, including a convenient eye-level built-in microwave, are easy to reach. Worktop space is very restricted, so a flush electric hob and inset stainless-steel sink provide the most seamless finish.**

OPPOSITE TOP: **In a small space like this, with a limited colour palette, it is in keeping for small appliances to be in smart, shiny chrome.**
ABOVE LEFT AND CENTRE: **To maintain the slick spin on natural finishes, stainless-steel appliances are invaluable, as they look smart, as well as being practical.**

ABOVE: **Open-plan shelving looks especially neat if lined with a wood to match the cupboard fronts.**
BELOW LEFT: **This kitchen looks so cohesive because every detail has been thought out. Plenty of drawers take everyday necessities off the worktop and seamlessly out of view.**

KEY FEATURES

▌ A SENSE OF ORDER – THIS KITCHEN SHOULD BE WELL PLANNED FOR EFFICIENT USE, BUT STILL HAVE A RELAXED AND WELCOMING AIR.

▌ WOODEN FLOORS, PERHAPS WITH RUGS FOR COMFORT UNDERFOOT.

▌ FUNCTIONAL, FITTED CUPBOARDS, WHICH COULD FEATURE BEAUTIFUL WOODEN FRONTS, OR BE COMBINED WITH OPEN SHELVING FOR ATTRACTIVE DISPLAYS OF GLASS OR CERAMICS.

▌ PLAIN WALLS – CLAD IN TIMBER, OR SIMPLY PAINTED WHITE.

▌ AN EYE-CATCHING DINING TABLE AND CHAIRS BY ONE OF THE BIG-NAME SCANDINAVIAN DESIGNERS; EITHER ORIGINAL OR, SINCE MUCH OF THEIR WORK IS STILL IN PRODUCTION, NEW.

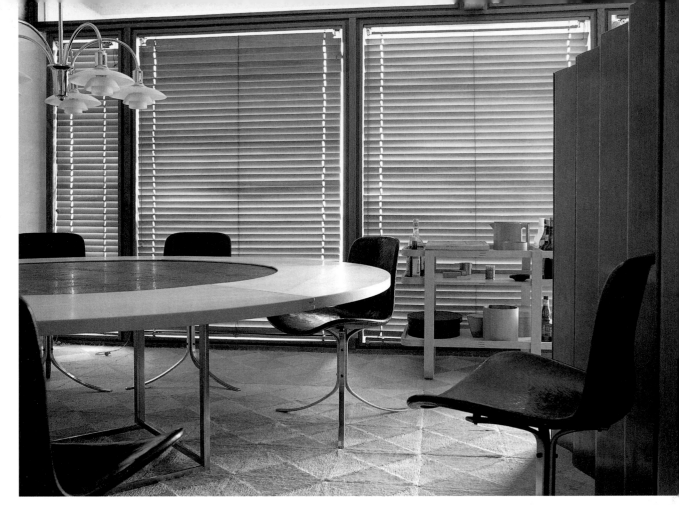

RIGHT: **In this sophisticated dining room, the table and chairs were designed by Poul Kjærholm in the late Fifties and early Sixties, while the striking pendant light is by Poul Henningsen.**

OPPOSITE TOP ROW, FROM LEFT TO RIGHT: **Sleek, fitted cupboards are functional, especially in shiny white with recessed handles. Open shelving adds a more relaxed look. A soft rug underfoot makes the room feel more cosy.**

OPPOSITE CENTRE ROW, FROM LEFT TO RIGHT: **A simple, open design makes this kitchen very appealing. In an industrial-style space, wooden cupboards add warmth and character. An all-white kitchen is softened by timber detailing.**

OPPOSITE BELOW: **These 1958 Cherner chairs are the focal point of an otherwise subtly plain and neutral kitchen/diner, in which the principal ingredients are timber and matt, white emulsion.**

scandinavian

Good looks and practicality go hand in hand in the Scandinavian kitchen and eating area. The neutral palette and the sense of clutter-free order that are so important to this style are emphasized in a way that is both effortless and elegant.

There's no doubt that ease of use is paramount in the Scandinavian-style kitchen. But that is not to say that warmth and comfort should be sacrificed. As is typical of this look, efficiency should be combined with a relaxed simplicity that makes this room as pleasant to sit and chat in as it is to prepare a family meal. Units, for example, may be fitted wall to wall for convenience and to make the most of space, but they can be fronted with beautiful, tactile, natural wood, or combined with open shelving on which attractive storage jars, glassware or crockery are displayed.

Wooden floors are, of course, ubiquitous, but could be topped with the occasional rug (preferably washable) for cosiness, while splashbacks and walls are kept plain and minimal. Window treatments, too, are either banned or barely there, while lighting is invisibly functional. The exception is over the dining table, where you may wish to hang a striking pendant. And with the dining table and chairs comes your chance to show off some gorgeous mid-20th-century designer furniture, in the form of curvy, fluid designs by Jacobsen, Aalto, Wegner and other major names.

MODEST CHIC STYLE STUDY

Warm wood, simple forms and plain colours combine in this attractive kitchen. The open-plan house was designed in the Sixties, and many of the furnishings also date from the mid-20th century, yet this room does not look old-fashioned. Instead, with its typical Scandinavian blend of comfort and usability, it has as much appeal today as it ever did.

This kitchen is unpretentious and practical. It belongs to a designer of furniture and ceramics, and her professional concern with simple, good-looking functionalism shines through in her home, too. While the hard-working part of the room consists of plain fitted units, the ultimate in modest chic, an efficient shelving system displays the owner's ceramics, as well as food, gadgets and other kitchen kit. The result is that typically Scandinavian mixture of pragmatism with a dash of decorative flair.

Sheer floor-to-ceiling curtains block out harsh sunlight without interfering with the visual subtlety of the dining area, while wooden flooring flows throughout the open space, emphasizing its bright, airy feel. The simple furniture – which looks contemporary but was designed in 1944 – is curvy and comfortable, in blond wood and wicker, its round shapes a pleasing contrast to the strong horizontals and verticals of the kitchen system. Perhaps most eye-catching of all, however, are the light fittings – a brass pendant designed by the owner, and a PH 5 by Poul Henningsen. Distinctive looks belie its clever construction, which distributes light evenly without glare.

OPPOSITE ABOVE: **The owner designed this stainless-steel cutlery for Georg Jensen in 1991.**

OPPOSITE BELOW: **This classic lamp, the 1958 PH 5 by Poul Henningsen, is so popular that one is said to hang in half of all Danish homes. Its striking circular forms repeat those of the table and chairs below and the ceramics behind. Amazingly, the table and chairs were designed, for the Danish Consumer Co-operative, in 1944.**

ABOVE LEFT: **The brass lamp is the owner Grethe Meyer's design. Its inverted bowl shape echoes the forms of her ceramics, seen behind.**

ABOVE RIGHT: **Efficient, plain white units hide boring kitchenware, while an elegant, functional shelving system, designed by Grethe Meyer with Borge Mogensen, displays a collection of her work, from teacups to large bowls in a range of colours.**

WHY IT WORKS FUNCTIONAL UNITS PLUS A GREAT DISPLAY OF CERAMICS ∎ EYE-CATCHING LIGHT FITTINGS ∎ MONOCHROMATIC COLOUR SCHEME ∎ UNPRETENTIOUS FURNITURE

KEY FEATURES

▋ A GENEROUS FARMHOUSE TABLE, PAINTED, STRIPPED OR WITH A CLOTH, AT THE KITCHEN'S HEART. THIS IS WHERE FAMILY AND FRIENDS ALL MEET AND EAT.

▋ A MINIMUM OF FITTED CUPBOARDS. OPEN SHELVES, DRESSERS AND TABLE DRAWERS DO THE BUSINESS INSTEAD.

▋ KITCHENWARE AND CROCKERY, CHOSEN FOR ITS GOOD LOOKS, ON DISPLAY.

▋ ANTIQUE KITCHEN UTENSILS, STORAGE JARS AND A CLOCK ARE ALL KEY DECORATIVE FEATURES.

▋ A BUTLER'S SINK, WITH OLD-FASHIONED TAPS, IS WHERE THE WORK IS DONE. IF NOT, THE DISHWASHERS AND WASHING MACHINES ARE EITHER HIDDEN OR PUT IN ANOTHER ROOM.

OPPOSITE ABOVE LEFT: **The dramatic roof structure is emphasized by built-in dressers holding equipment used as decoration.**
OPPOSITE ABOVE RIGHT: **Even the smallest room has space for an intimate round table, with farmhouse chairs, to dine at.**
OPPOSITE CENTRE LEFT: **This cool blue and white cooking area has a traditional French stove as its centre. Displayed near it are French enamelware and pottery.**
OPPOSITE CENTRE RIGHT: **Garden flowers may be the only non-culinary element in the room. They should look just picked.**
OPPOSITE BELOW: **Mixed country chairs are painted to match the plain farmhouse table and the shelves, dresser and cupboards around the walls.**
BELOW, FROM LEFT TO RIGHT: **This relaxed corner is completed with a simple fabric cover to the shelves below. A butler's sink is essential, even if the dishwasher is hidden underneath. The curving legs of a compact round table and the two country spindle chairs are set against a window to take advantage of their silhouettes.**

traditional country

Surprisingly, this is a look which is just as popular with townies as real country folk. The reason is that few town houses have enough room for a dining room, so a homely, welcoming area in the kitchen suits modern entertaining ideas. Rather than chilly minimalism, old country looks are ideal for relaxing.

Traditional Country style must have a generous space. This look will never work in a narrow galley kitchen or a meagre corner. But it is perfect for a large basement in town, or for family kitchens in any cottage or farmhouse. The essential element is the central table, where all meals are eaten: the bigger, the better but (if space is limited) a cloth-covered round table in a corner will easily seat four. Light this well, perhaps with a hanging brass chandelier. Antique country chairs – don't bother to match them – add the final touch and can be painted to tone with your colour scheme.

With this style, the kitchen itself is all on view, so it's important to ensure that everything is vaguely colour co-ordinated. Ensure that all crockery is white, all pans and utensils steel, and be aware that even Yorkshire pudding tins can look decorative hung on walls. Old dressing-table mirrors also make good displays. Pick up these and other antique pieces from car boot sales and house clearances – it's surprising what you can find. Then add a plain linen tablecloth or patchwork throw, generous vases of flowers and potted plants, and the look is yours.

RURAL RESTRAINT STYLE STUDY

A great deal has been shoehorned into this room to make
a serious working kitchen that is also spacious, welcoming
and stylish. Virtually nothing in the room is for display alone.
The owners have managed to resist the temptation to fill the
high shelves near the ceiling with dust-collecting tat. Instead,
the shelves act as a decorative cornice.

This is a Traditional Country kitchen created by a proper cook. There is no evidence of gadgets, but rather a chef's array of practical tools, from classic toasters and scales to a hanging array of matching utensils, pots and pans, placed where they are most needed. Above the trademark butler's sink, a traditional plate rack is filled with plain china. The professional-looking cooker is neatly put into an old chimney breast, which also houses a strong ventilator – very necessary if the room is also used for family meals and entertaining. Although there are plenty of fitted

cupboards with drawers below eye level, they are as unobtrusive as their traditional design and handles allow, as is the glass-fronted fitted dresser used for keeping cookbooks tidy and grease-free. All is in a creamy neutral shade, including the 18th-century country chairs, the old farmhouse table and the tongued and grooved backing behind the butler's sink.

Though the room has all the elements of Traditional Country style, the owners have been extremely disciplined. Nothing but a vase of flowers is purely decorative; even the impressive old clock has its use.

OPPOSITE ABOVE: **Matching hooks hold a perfectionist's array of stainless-steel tools. There's not a gadget in sight. Where necessary, awkward and ugly pieces can be confined to cupboards.**

OPPOSITE BELOW: **The whole kitchen is virtually monochrome, with the walls a retiring cream and the utensils acting as the only ornaments. The gingham tablecloth ensures the central table is warm and welcoming.**

ABOVE LEFT: **It takes discipline to achieve such order from so many disparate shapes, but clearly cooking comes first.**

ABOVE RIGHT: **A traditional dresser is built in next to the heavy-duty cooker, but the high shelves above remain carefully uncluttered. It's important that such a room is always immaculately clean, and objects at this height would cause problems.**

WHY IT WORKS NO COLOUR BUT THE GINGHAM TABLECLOTH ▌ ALL UTENSILS MATCH
▌ USE AND DECORATION ARE COMBINED ▌ NOTHING IS INCLUDED FOR DISPLAY ALONE

modern country

The difference between Traditional and Modern Country
kitchens is, in both senses, minimal. Both have chunky
farmhouse tables, both rely on plate racks and quirky
displays, but the Modern version tends to ditch the antique
decorative touches for contemporary statements, though
these can be as old as Bauhaus, along with the patina of
terracotta tiles for black and white geometrics.

Assuming your kitchen is big enough to
become a family dining room or a place
to entertain friends in candlelight in the
evening, then the possibility of a Modern
Country kitchen is yours. You don't have
to live in the country – it may be better to
think of this style as *rus in urbe* – but you
need to import the generous space and
light that come naturally to the heart of
the farmhouse, the accessible room where
everyone eats, cooks and slumps. A good
leafy view would also be helpful.

The difference between traditional and
modern takes on the farmhouse kitchen is
that the modern style has a strong element
of minimalism about it, even if there's
plenty on display. First, all colour is kept
under strict discipline: where units are built
in, they match the walls; where furniture is
painted, it matches them, too. Any fabrics,
from blinds to tea towels, are in similar
shades and extremely unobtrusive. This
even goes for the kitchen tools and the
crockery. John Pawson, the minimalist
architect, decrees that food should be
eaten and served from white plates, and
the Modern Country stylist agrees. But,
while Pawson hides everything behind
closed doors, the Modern Country cook

KEY FEATURES

▌ A MODERN TAKE ON OLD VALUES, THIS STYLE DEPENDS ON NATURAL MATERIALS, ESPECIALLY WOOD.

▌ STEEL COOKERS AND RANGES, THOUGH THE AGA RETAINS A PLACE.

▌ THE MAIN FEATURE OF THE ROOM IS STILL A FARMHOUSE TABLE, GENEROUS, WELCOMING AND DESIGNED FOR FAMILY MEALS.

▌ USE FITTED UNITS TO UPDATE THE LOOK, GIVING TRADITIONAL PANELLING AND FITTINGS A TWIST.

▌ KEEP COLOUR TO A MINIMUM. THIS WAY MINIMALISM MEETS ROMANTICISM.

OPPOSITE LEFT: **Glowing wood warms this scheme of stone-coloured walls teamed with steel equipment.**
OPPOSITE RIGHT: **This style needs lots of space, light and, preferably, a good view. The white chairs are characteristic of the modern take on old values.**
TOP LEFT: **The inverted pyramid glass light here lifts a traditional scheme into the realms of today. The chairs, too, are an update of an old pattern.**
TOP CENTRE: **A traditional kitchen would have open cupboards; a minimalist one, no handles on the doors. This compromise characterizes the style.**
TOP RIGHT: **A chunky table and modern chairs in front of a farmhouse dresser show how to get the look.**
ABOVE, FROM LEFT TO RIGHT: **The black-and-white tiled floor brings country style into town. Hanging tools and rail are chosen for their stark outlines and steely metal. The square-section ceramic table light and classic photographs are typical of the look.**

likes them neatly serried on a practical plate rack above the draining board and the always functional utensils in matching steel hanging where they are most needed.

Restraint is also needed in your choice of accessories. There is no space in this style for 'design classics' such as Bovril jars and baked bean tins to be quirkily on display. Indeed, quirkiness is not an option, though at a pinch chrome, steel and enamel storage jars and bins may be used to hide the Fairy Liquid bottles and Bero flour bags. Nor is this the place for 18th-century paintings of fat cows, but rather classic photographs in black and white. But remember: one or two impressively modern touches are needed – a steel chandelier, a studio pot or an African hanging – to focus attention on contradictory elements.

Yet, if this sounds starkly clinical, the Modern Country style is not. By using textures and shapes instead of colours, it continues to be generous in spirit. Modern takes on Windsor chairs add curves to the strict geometrics of tongue-and-groove and glazing bars on cupboard doors; naturals like woven willow and hand-loomed pots relieve the uniformity and, finally, the traditional use of brass for cupboard door handles, hanging lamps and chunky cookers is translated into steel. These variations on a traditional style encompass the entire look of Modern Country.

ABOVE: **Sandwiched between glazed cupboards with unusual glazing bars is a state-of-the-art steel cooker.**
ABOVE RIGHT: **The crockery on show behind doors fronted with chicken wire is predominantly white.**
BELOW RIGHT: **Steel handles update the cupboards below the traditional butler's sink.**

OPPOSITE ABOVE LEFT: **Blowsy roses and a fine view add romance to a strictly neutral eating area.**
OPPOSITE ABOVE RIGHT: **Decorative touches are achieved by Japanese-inspired ceramics, basketwork and jelly moulds.**
OPPOSITE CENTRE RIGHT: **Agas are so much kitchen classics that they will fit in virtually any scheme. The**

white enamel, however, is good in modern rooms.
OPPOSITE BELOW LEFT: **The white-painted beams, classic photograph and tongued and grooved walls are offset by a fine Windsor chair.**
OPPOSITE BELOW RIGHT: **Decorative touches of an old table and rusty old park chairs relieve this kitchen's severity.**

MODERN ROMANCE STYLE STUDY

Cleverly, the owners have turned a working kitchen into what appears to be a romantic dining room by filling every available surface with pots and vases of flowers. Even more cleverly, this room can be completely altered in a moment: change the flowers for multiple candles, African sculptures or decoy ducks and the whole is transformed.

This Modern Country kitchen could not be more neutral as a backdrop. There is no sign that it even is a kitchen, because all large kitchen appliances are hidden away in elegantly panelled cupboards, whose diamond pattern is echoed by the softly coloured diamonds on the floor. In addition, the neutral colours of the units, tables and chairs mean the room is infinitely adaptable and can be dressed with accessories, as here, to create new looks. Terracotta pots of blooming flowers are grouped throughout and the theme is echoed by two large botanical prints on an uncluttered wall. A flowery linen table runner is covered by flowering tulips. Even the red wine in large glasses matches the cloth and adds an air of festivity. Yet, at night, gleaming mirrors on the walls and candlelight on the table would completely change the atmosphere, as would autumn berries, throws and spicy pomanders, or in winter, piles of lemons, carrots and red cabbage, teamed with poinsettias or Christmas cactus. This is a backdrop for infinite change.

WHY IT WORKS COMPLETE ABSENCE OF KITCHEN REFERENCE – EVEN THE SINK RECALLS A FLOWER ROOM ■ UNUSUAL DIAMOND-PANELLED CUPBOARD DOORS ■ NEUTRAL COLOURS ALL THROUGH ■ ATTENTION TO DECORATIVE DETAIL

OPPOSITE ABOVE: **Two large botanic prints hang together above a useful serving surface.**

OPPOSITE BELOW: **The palest cream paint covers walls, cupboards, chairs and table. Even the floor is painted to match.**

ABOVE LEFT: **True attention to detail matches an embroidered table runner with the red of the wine and the overall flowery decor.**

ABOVE CENTRE: **Food can be extremely decorative, and here it provides the only splash of colour in a neutral scheme.**

ABOVE RIGHT: **An outside view helps, but even with plain blinds, plant pots give that country look.**

RIGHT: **The diamond patterns on the floor turn up again in the unusual panels of the cupboards. All attention, however, centres on the antique terracotta pots.**

KEY FEATURES

▪ TRADITIONAL REBATED PANELLING ON ALL CUPBOARD DOORS, ESPECIALLY THOSE BUILT IN.

▪ ARCHITECTURAL FEATURES PRESERVED AND EMPHASIZED – CORNICES, DOOR SURROUNDS, SKIRTINGS.

▪ USE OF ANTIQUES, ESPECIALLY FURNITURE, THROUGHOUT, INCLUDING DINING CHAIRS, OLD MIRRORS AND EVEN SCULPTURE.

▪ WOODEN FLOORS IN WORKING AND EATING AREAS. THESE SHOULD BE WAXED AND COVERED WITH ORIENTAL RUGS.

▪ KITCHEN UTENSILS SHOULD VEER TOWARDS CLASSIC COPPER RATHER THAN STEEL; COPY RESTAURANT KITCHENS.

classic period style

Imagine a working kitchen and dining room in a Georgian town house and you'll get the idea of this style. There are numerous examples to copy, from the back regions of National Trust houses to adventurous designers currently transforming old houses in areas like Spitalfields in London. Of course, you need modern equipment in this 18th-century setting, but make it as unobtrusive as possible.

OPPOSITE ABOVE LEFT: **The practical working kitchen in the foreground leads into the more formal dining area beyond. This configuration is typical of town houses.**

OPPOSITE ABOVE RIGHT: **Classical Greek-style chairs are formally arrayed around a table, whose lines are hidden by matching felt. The upholstery's strong stripes are crucial to this scheme.**

OPPOSITE BELOW LEFT: **Period light fittings enliven a working area.**

OPPOSITE BELOW RIGHT: **Old-fashioned taps from a salvage yard look authentic.**

ABOVE LEFT: **This dining area can be transformed into a hall simply by moving the cloth and chairs.**

ABOVE CENTRE: **The fashionable faux 18th-century style relies on authentic antiques.**

ABOVE RIGHT: **Old panelling on the walls is painted in soft white to complement the traditional table linen and decanters.**

Classic Period style needs care if you are to combine both kitchen and dining room in a single area. The kitchen needs to be practical, with hidden fridges and so on behind handmade period doors, while the dining area is as formal as they get. Happily, many houses combine two rooms in one with wide, ever-open doors joining them, while also acting as a barrier. Even without this, the two spaces can be delineated with a change of flooring or a complementary colour on the walls. The formal end needs antique chairs, though a modern table can be hidden with traditional white napery spread over a neutral backing of felt. As in all classical settings, go for symmetry of pictures or old mirrors and use ornament to emphasize the classical basis of the whole. Marble busts, urns and obelisks are excellent here. Lighting can even take in brass chandeliers or classical table lamps shaped like columns or obelisks. With a few good antiques, it's possible to create a feeling of opulence by adding old but cheap black-and-white prints, hung symmetrically, or mirrors in old frames. The best background to all this is a soft, old white, giving the impression of layers of dulled limewash.

PUTTING ON THE RITZ STYLE STUDY

The restaurant kitchens of grand hotels have changed little over the centuries and it's possible to imagine this stylish reworking is at the back of the Ritz or Georges V in Paris. This is why the owners have perfected the Classic Period style in their smaller space. The configuration of worktops, central island block with unobtrusive sink, and heavyweight equipment is both good-looking and extremely practical.

This is the room of someone who takes cooking seriously (it contains an industrial-sized range cooker and fridge, plus separate pantry) and is willing to combine form and function seamlessly. It can only work, however, if every part of the whole is top-quality.

The large collection of pans that hangs above the central worktop is of the best-quality copper and contains enough sizes to satisfy a chef; the hanging rail is professional, as is the huge, though recessed and therefore unobtrusive, fridge-freezer in the background. Cleverly, its colour is copied in the cupboards under the central block. Similarly, the wood of this is similar to that of the floor, so the island block is much less bulky in appearance than in fact. Glazed wall cupboards are underlit, giving a good working light to the surrounding worktops and interesting shadows and pools of light. Elsewhere, industrial top lighting housed in Art Deco-style shades ensures good working conditions everywhere. Where not covered with cupboards and work surfaces, the walls are tiled in white: an excellent and practical surface behind cookers – and, of course, typical of grand hotel kitchens.

WHY IT WORKS COPPER PANS ▮ GLAZED WALL CUPBOARDS ▮ NEUTRAL WOODEN TOPS ▮ RESTAURANT KITCHEN LAYOUT WITH CENTRAL BLOCK ▮ INDUSTRIAL COOKER AND FRIDGE

OPPOSITE ABOVE: **This array of copper pans is large enough to delight a chef. They all hang on S-hooks and a purpose-built rack.**

OPPOSITE BELOW LEFT: **Painted cupboards with understated but traditional handles hide further, more practical, drawers.**

OPPOSITE BELOW CENTRE: **The kitchen has two sinks. This butler's version is large enough to clean vegetables or soak big pans.**

OPPOSITE BELOW RIGHT: **The second sink, on the island block, has lever taps that can be turned by dirty or greasy hands.**

ABOVE: **Everything in this kitchen is intended for serious use, from the hanging pans to the large fridge-freezer and cooker. To achieve the look, top quality in everything from pans to flooring is essential.**

vintage & retro

Going back to the days when kitchens were not the all-singing and dancing, professional-standard creations of the 21st century, the Vintage and Retro kitchen has a functional appeal all of its own. Utility meets good looks in the form of open shelving, unfitted furniture, hanging racks and accessories, which can range from casual collectables to groovy American-style appliances.

To create a Vintage and Retro kitchen it is vital to avoid rows of modern, boxy, fitted units. There should be nothing too sleek and clever here; instead the look is all about simplicity and charm. Walls with tongue-and-groove panelling or white ceramic tiles make a great background, while floors covered in quarry tiles, stone flags, wooden boards or black-and-white checked vinyl will look suitably traditional.

For storage, aim for a mix of free-standing pieces such as old butcher's blocks, dressers, chests of drawers and hanging racks that share a similar aesthetic: plain or painted wood in simple forms and with unfussy knobs and handles. Open shelves are a great way to display collections such as Cornishware, pressed glass or jelly moulds, while less attractive kitchen kit can be hidden in cupboards with frosted-glass doors or doors fronted with gathered fabric panels. Don't go overboard on the country look, however. This is more practical than pretty (think enamel jugs rather than chintz-printed teasets), and you can add into the mix a lip-licking selection of retro appliances such as toasters, blenders, coffee makers and even fridges, all with heavy-duty styling and utilitarian good looks.

KEY FEATURES

▌ UNFITTED FURNITURE – OR AT LEAST A MIX OF FITTED AND UNFITTED – WHICH MIGHT INCLUDE BUTCHER'S BLOCKS, DRESSERS, CHESTS OF DRAWERS AND HANGING RACKS.

▌ ATTRACTIVE KITCHEN PARAPHERNALIA ON UNSTUDIED DISPLAY.

▌ TONGUED AND GROOVED OR CERAMIC-TILED WALLS, CO-ORDINATING WITH A SOFT COLOUR SCHEME SUCH AS CREAM, PALE GREEN OR BUTTERMILK.

▌ PRACTICAL FLOORING IN TRADITIONAL MATERIALS, SUCH AS STONE FLAGS, QUARRY TILES, WOODEN BOARDS OR BLACK-AND-WHITE CHECKED VINYL.

▌ GORGEOUS RETRO APPLIANCES, FROM JUICERS AND BLENDERS TO FRIDGES AND OVENS.

OPPOSITE LEFT: **A tongue-and-groove wall is the perfect base for this look. Here, it is matched with a free-standing chest and open shelving.**

OPPOSITE RIGHT: **Vintage and Retro does not have to be too traditional or cosy. Introducing some gorgeous American-style accessories will add zing.**

THIS PAGE, CLOCKWISE FROM ABOVE: **Fitted cupboards can be given the Vintage and Retro treatment by combining them with open shelves, hanging racks and a free-standing range cooker. Utilitarian chic in the form of a wood-and-metal work surface, an old-fashioned fridge and racks of enamel jugs. Retro prints can enliven an all-white kitchen. Cornishware is a lovely Retro accessory. A black-and-white floor is a great base for this look. Hanging pans make an ideal display, both eye-catching and practical to use.**

ABOVE: **American diner-style chairs bring the Retro look to this kitchen.**
ABOVE RIGHT: **The use of a sharp green and orange recreates the ambience of a Sixties room.**
RIGHT: **This 1957 Tulip dining set has a wonderfully retro effect in a stainless-steel and white kitchen.**
BELOW, FROM LEFT TO RIGHT: **A casual dining area combines floral with industrial. Buttermilk paint has a typically vintage feel. Fabulous prints set the Vintage and Retro**

scene. **Funky looks in the form of a retro light and Bauhaus-style chairs. A modern table combines perfectly with a set of retro dining chairs. Slatted wood introduces an unusual texture into a plain and simple dining area.**
OPPOSITE ABOVE LEFT: **Pale blue paintwork gives this wooden unit a charmingly Retro look.**
OPPOSITE ABOVE RIGHT: **Just one item of furniture, such as this storage unit, can be a kitchen's focal point.**

In dining rooms and kitchen eating areas, the Vintage and Retro style comes into its own: it's straightforward to create and hugely effective. There are almost unlimited permutations of the simple concept of a dining table and a set of chairs. You could choose mismatching old wooden chairs (painted or bare, with wicker seats or backs, or maybe even salvaged church pews), American diner-style chrome and bright vinyl, Fifties elegant bentwood, Sixties curvy plastic or Seventies wicker. The table itself, small or large, could be made from polished wood, a sassy laminate or battered old pine. Reclaimed doors or railway sleepers also make great, solid surfaces from which to eat that would look perfect in a room of this style. A boring dining table could be covered in a Fifties geometric print, faded chintz or a polka-dot oilcloth, co-ordinating with the colours of the room itself – whether soft pastels for a more relaxed, Vintage feel, or bolder shades for a striking, 20th-century Retro ambience. Meanwhile, overhead you could add a pretty (not too grand) chandelier, a more utilitarian spun aluminium pendant or an eye-catching mid-century modern lamp.

SIMPLY BEAUTIFUL STYLE STUDY

This functional, attractive kitchen/dining room has been designed with great care to be plain and simple, but certainly not boring. Reclaimed dining chairs, glass-fronted cupboards, a deep, square sink and basic pendant lamps are all key ingredients, with a Vintage vibe that is quietly casual, easygoing and utterly unselfconscious.

There is a fine line between simple-and-beautiful and simple-but-boring; the way to achieve the former rather than the latter has to do with using appealing materials, subtle colours and understated but intriguing furnishings with subtlety and flair – there is just as much planning involved in creating simplicity as there is in putting together a scheme that appears more complex.

This Vintage kitchen/dining room is all about simplicity. Yet look closely and there is a sophisticated layering of materials, in the form of wood – both bare and painted – and metal. This is the backbone of the scheme, to which have been added soft paint shades of buttermilk and dove grey, creating a harmonious ambience. The ethos of Vintage is everywhere, from the old fold-up chairs to the aluminium pendant lights, from the deep, square Belfast sink to the plain-fronted cupboards. The large, free-standing cupboard, battered and worn, is a lovely piece, while the uneven dining table, made from old wooden boards, is useful and attractive. As a great quirky touch, the English Delft tiles used as a splashback are perfect. This room seems neither modern nor dated, just charmingly timeless.

WHY IT WORKS BARE WOODEN FLOORBOARDS COMPLEMENT THE DINING TABLE AND CHAIRS ▪ SOFT, INTERESTING COLOURS ▪ MIX OF FITTED AND FREE-STANDING CUPBOARDS, ALL SIMPLE ▪ CLEVER LAYERING OF MATERIALS AND TEXTURES

OPPOSITE ABOVE: **The uneven nature of the dining table – made from reclaimed timber – only adds to its charm. The folding wood-and-metal chairs look like they came from a school, while the simple pendant lights are timeless.**

OPPOSITE BELOW: **The mix of buttermilk and dove grey is a subtle choice.**

ABOVE, FROM LEFT TO RIGHT: **Natural light floods into the kitchen via a pair of French doors. A deep, square Belfast sink is typically vintage in feel. The battered old salvaged cupboard works beautifully in this casual scheme, and is capacious enough to hold all sorts of kitchen paraphernalia.**

RIGHT: **Plain-fronted cupboards combine with a wall cupboard that has glass doors and an open plate rack, providing a useful, visually interesting range of storage.**

living rooms

Most stylish living rooms, even
those designed on traditional
or rural lines, are currently
decorated in a finely balanced
mix of neutral colours. As life
outside gets ever more hectic,
the main area for relaxation
in the house is becoming
increasingly calm and
ordered. Work with a pale
neutral palette and many
natural materials, with only
single bursts of colour.

KEY FEATURES

▮ CHOOSE LEAN RECTANGULAR SOFAS AND BOXY ARMCHAIRS, WITH SMALL METAL LEGS. COFFEE TABLES, SIDEBOARDS AND STORAGE UNITS SHOULD HAVE LOW-SLUNG SILHOUETTES TO MATCH.

▮ TIGHT UPHOLSTERY, IN PLAIN BUT TEXTURED FABRICS, SHOULD HAVE MINIMAL DETAILING (SO NO FRILLS OR PLEATS). GOOD FABRICS INCLUDE CHENILLE, BOUCLÉ WOOL, VELVET, FAUX SUEDE AND BRUSHED COTTON.

▮ GO FOR MINIMAL SCATTER CUSHIONS AND VERY SIMPLE WINDOW TREATMENTS, FROM CURTAINS IN SCULPTURAL FOLDS TO PLAIN ROLLER OR ROMAN BLINDS.

▮ CHOOSE A CONTEMPORARY HOLE-IN-THE-WALL FIREPLACE OR A BOXY, PLAIN FIRE SURROUND.

▮ PICK HARD FLOORS, FROM LIMESTONE TO TIMBER, WITH A 100 PER CENT WOOL RUG FOR SOFTNESS, PLAIN OR IN A CONTEMPORARY DESIGN.

▮ WALLS SHOULD BE IN SOOTHING NEUTRALS, EITHER PLAIN-PAINTED, OR WITH SOPHISTICATED FINISHES, FROM POLISHED PLASTER TO WOOD-VENEER PANELLING.

OPPOSITE ABOVE LEFT AND RIGHT: **Make spaces sociable by arranging furniture close together, for easy conversation. Consider a mix of a low sofa and a daybed, positioned opposite each other, or use modular seating units to create L- or U-shapes.**
OPPOSITE CENTRE LEFT: **Furniture should also be arranged to maximize a great view or natural sunlight: keep window treatments ultra-simple to maintain simplicity of line.**
OPPOSITE CENTRE RIGHT: **Pick storage units with cupboard doors or sliding panels, so clutter is easily concealed. Sandblasted glass and perspex are light-reflective and look modern.**
OPPOSITE BELOW: **The classic rectangular sofa looks best without cushions to spoil the linear silhouette. But a cashmere or silk throw, crisply folded, is an attractive extra.**
BELOW, ALL PICTURES: **Lighting and, if possible, firelight are vital to create ambience, and to bring visual softness to the Sleek style's angular lines and hard surfaces. Consider unusual options, such as floor lighting or wall-washers.**

sleek

The modern living room is chilled out and sophisticated, a place for soothing your soul while home alone, or for welcoming guests. In today's busy world, ambience is key. So for open-plan living areas – which may lack atmosphere – promote it by arranging furniture in intimate corners, then pay attention to mood-inducing lighting, a wonderful sound system and sleek, lounge lizard-style furniture.

Unashamedly design-conscious, the Sleek living room demands visual self-control and a reasonably elastic budget. Squashy sofas will ruin the purity of line, so you must be prepared to start afresh with contemporary furniture. The look is pared down, but you won't sacrifice comfort. The new sofas are long enough to stretch out on, not to mention the accompanying daybeds and floor cushions.

A neutral palette is de rigueur, because it guarantees a Zen-like calm, and creates a wonderful backdrop for modern art or a single piece of bright furniture. Pure whites in the living room can seem chilly, so go for milkier tones or pinky greys, to add atmosphere. Use upholstery colour as a tool with which to balance up, or blend in, chosen natural surfaces, then concentrate on texture. An overlap of rough with smooth, cool with warm, adds visual interest.

Banish clutter from the room, so the overall effect is streamlined. Everything from books to the stereo must be hidden in built-in cupboards or in a free-standing sideboard. If technology is on view, make it super-modern, and choose a mix of low-voltage spots and statement modern side lamps (on dimmers), to promote ambience.

TRAFFIC CALMING STYLE STUDY

Spanning the full depth of a modern, open-plan city house, this large white-on-white living room has several seating zones, yet remains visually cohesive. With its mix of pale tones, from bleached wood boards to white leather, and contrasting linear and curvaceous furniture silhouettes, it is both comfortable to relax in and soothing to the eye.

This living room works successfully in a large open-plan area, because the furniture is carefully grouped into several intimate zones to fill the space. At one end, two cubic armchairs sit opposite a curvy chaise longue, while at the other there's a parallel arrangement of a leather daybed and rectangular sofa. Floor space next to the staircase is kept free for human traffic, for easy access to the desk and garden.

Despite the mix of contrasting curvy and linear sofa styles, the seating looks pulled together and sophisticated. All upholstery is in pale tones, and all furniture heights low,

with neat, exposed legs. As a deliberate link, hewn-timber occasional tables are dotted between the seating zones.

Throughout the room, there's an ongoing contrast of angular with round, sleek with organic. The boxy silhouette starts with the armchairs, and is echoed in the abstract art on the wall, the hole-in-the-wall fireplace and the shapes of the simple, glossy coffee tables. Yet there are curves in the daybed bolster, the ostrich eggs on the table and the cylindrical lampshades. The tension of the two contrasting silhouettes creates drama, as well as adding softness.

OPPOSITE ABOVE: **Graphic or floral patterns would be anathema to the cool plains in this room. Silk cushions, adorned with organic wavy lines, add interest without overpowering.**

OPPOSITE MAIN PICTURE: **The room has modern architectural detailing, so it makes sense to choose cubic furniture in the same vein. Its linear outlines overlap visually with the squares of the windows and the dropped ceiling of the mezzanine level.**

ABOVE LEFT: **Rugs are cleverly used to delineate individual seating areas, but because they are in pale, creamy tones they don't detract from the tranquil bleached tones of the timber floor.**

ABOVE RIGHT: **Just as a dark scheme needs natural highlights, so a white-on-white scheme needs sombre tones to delineate shapes and add interest. Here, the glossy coffee table works hard to impart a touch of drama.**

WHY IT WORKS WHITE-ON-WHITE COLOUR SCHEME ■ SYMMETRICAL SEATING ■ TEXTURAL BLEACHED TIMBERS ■ SIMPLE, BEAUTIFUL ACCESSORIES ■ LUXURIOUS UPHOLSTERY

ABOVE FAR LEFT: **Comfort is key, so pick good-quality feather scatter and upholstery cushions.**

BELOW FAR LEFT: **Match your furniture to the architecture of the room. In this modern loft with square window panes, a cubic armchair and rectangular stool made sense. The choice of crumply linen loose covers softens the look.**

LEFT: **Lamps and shades are an inexpensive, instant way to inject fluid, organic shapes into a contemporary living room.**

CENTRE, TOP AND MIDDLE: **Have fun choosing contrast textures, but use for occasional pieces (from stools to cushions) rather than on major pieces of furniture. The buttoned leather stool and silk cushions here add touches of luxury to a casual sitting room.**

ABOVE, TOP AND MIDDLE: **There's an enduring freshness to an all-white scheme, so use white for walls, painted floors and loose covers.**

OPPOSITE, ALL PICTURES: **Bespoke architectural features, from window frames to a stone hearth, need to combine clean lines with the warmth of natural materials.**

mellow modern

Decked out in enticing white and vanilla tones, and awash with natural light, Mellow Modern living rooms are sociable and relaxed, a world away from the formal sitting rooms that once dominated our homes. Fill with plenty of cosy seating, occasional tables for drinks, and lots of user-friendly storage, then sit back and enjoy.

KEY FEATURES

▮ CHOOSE DEEP, PLUMP SOFAS WITH RECTANGULAR OR CURVY CONTOURS, AND FAT, FEATHER-FILLED CUSHIONS. GO FOR TIGHT OR LOOSE COVERS IN CRUMPLY LINENS, COTTON OR WOOL.

▮ COMBINE SOME STREAMLINED BUILT-IN STORAGE WITH FLOOR-TO-CEILING, CHUNKY SHELVES TO HOLD NEATLY ALIGNED BOOKS, CDS AND MAGAZINES.

▮ LOOK FOR SIDE LAMPS, WITH PRETTY CARD OR FABRIC LAMPSHADES, TO IMPART A SOFTER LOOK THAN ANGULAR CONTEMPORARY LIGHTING.

▮ A LIGHT, FRESH COLOUR SCHEME, BASED AROUND SOFT WHITES AND BLEACHED NATURAL SURFACES, IS RELAXED AND EASY TO LIVE WITH.

▮ CONCENTRATE ON A MIX OF SURFACES, FROM SMOOTH STONE OR WOOD FLOORS AND FIRE SURROUNDS TO DIMPLED LEATHER UPHOLSTERY.

This is the living room style we all dream about. It can be cosy and atmospheric in winter, with flickering firelight and creamy soft upholstery, yet in summer it's fresh and light, with windows flung open and cool stone floors. If it seems out of reach for a busy household, given the light colours, think again. Loose covers can be washed, hard floors mopped, and white walls easily touched up.

As this is a relaxed living zone, the mood and feel of upholstered furniture is key. You need a giant sofa to lounge on, preferably with an accompanying footstool – or choose an L-shaped modular seating unit so two people can lie down at once. A couple of armchairs are also vital, but choose a rounded silhouette with deep seats.

When selecting surfaces and fabrics, create a mix of relaxed, crunchy textures, spiced with sleek and smooth accents. That might mean linen upholstery teamed with silk cushions, or a timber floor with sandblasted-glass cupboard doors. The contrast is deliberate, so the room can be casual by day and dressed up for entertaining.

A neutral palette is important, because it looks both fresh and classic. While major surfaces should be in white, or tones of white

ABOVE LEFT: **For an elegant take on Mellow Modern, concentrate on creating fluid lines and contours. In this living room, off-white linen curtains have been gathered to fall into sculptural folds, and the sofa has been encased in a crisp, tailored loose cover.**

ABOVE RIGHT: **Plan a scheme that will feel and look cosy at every hour of the day. Although very simple, with its grey sofa and minimal detailing, this living room basks in sunshine from overhead skylights, yet is lit by flickering firelight in the evening.**

BELOW: **The more curved silhouettes there are, the softer the finish. With its winding staircase and bucket-style armchairs, this room is both elegant and relaxed.**

OPPOSITE: **At the sophisticated end of the Mellow Modern style, darker tones hold sway, from stone and darker woods to slate and animal skins. Use flashes of white to add essential highlights.**

(think of walls, upholstery, cupboard fronts), inject these with warmer overtones. You have only to think of the honey tones of oak flooring or the mellow shades of sandstone to see how to extend the core white palette. Variations on these might be taupe or biscuit for upholstery or pinky polished plaster for walls. If you want colour for accessories, add subtle ice-cream highlights, like soft lilac, pink or ice-blue.

As you're aiming for a relaxed mood, this is a living room to fill with favourite treasures, from books and music to paintings and family photographs. But it's crucial to plan enough storage to hold everything neatly, otherwise the room will look messy. Devise a combination of built-in cupboards with opaque doors so unsightly clutter is kept from view, and generous open shelves. Shelf fronts should be thick and simple, either filling an alcove or 'floating' in the centre of a wall. Pay attention to stacks of books or magazines; align them neatly for a streamlined finish.

The emphasis is on cosiness, but remember to add modern, angular shapes to play up the contemporary mood. A painted MDF sideboard, with a low, lean outline, or a white laminate side table with stainless-steel detailing, can be just enough to tip the balance.

REPEAT TO FADE STYLE STUDY

Streamlined and sophisticated, with its low, linear furniture and modern hearth, this is nevertheless a very comfortable family living room. Its cosiness and interest lie in the design's abundant use of texture. Rough, honest concrete is contrasted with soft faux suede and linen, while smooth timber is juxtaposed with sparkly ceramic tiles.

This living room works so well because surfaces, furniture and architecture comprise one cohesive whole. Faux suede cushion fabrics recur as upholstery for doors, abstract pattern is repeated from small surfaces (scatter cushions) to one large surface (double doors), and textures veer from rough to smooth, but are all realized in matching, pale tones. For example, the hearth and the daybed are almost identical in shade, but very different in feel.

Most obviously, it is the rectangular silhouette that is echoed and repeated on every surface. By elongating the doors, and tiling long thin vertical panels above the hearth, the designer of the room has

started to play with an oblong theme. The shape is then echoed horizontally in the long, lean sofas and the built-in hearth stone, and even repeated in little with the thin, tall vase.

Yet, although the shapes throughout are angular, the living room manages to look tactile and cosy. The key is a muted, even pretty, colour palette. Instead of white, upholstery textiles are a mix of oatmeal, cream and aubergine, and walls are finished in pinky polished plaster to tone in. The honey shades of the solid oak floor warm the scheme still further. The final softening touch is the use of a printed linen, with an organic yet graphic motif, and fresh flowers.

OPPOSITE FAR LEFT: **Flashes of white in the lampshade and vase, and sparkly glass on the table, create natural highlights to gently lift the muted colour scheme. So, too, do the pale, creamy ceramic tiles above the hearth. They are particularly effective when lit by firelight.**

ABOVE CENTRE: **A sociable furniture arrangement has been effected by placing two sofas at right angles to one another, to allow for easy conversation. Yet individually each has its own focus: the daybed is close to the fire, whereas the far sofa takes in the pretty courtyard views.**

ABOVE RIGHT: **The use of touchy-feely texture on the main door, as well as cupboard doors, adds a mellow new dimension to an essentially modern room.**

RIGHT AND FAR RIGHT: **Key colours are confidently used for wildly different details, from a print on a scatter cushion to the polished plaster on the wall.**

WHY IT WORKS SOFT PALETTE OF NEUTRALS AND PINKS ▮ STREAMLINED FURNITURE SHAPES ▮ MIX OF NATURAL LIGHT AND FIRELIGHT ▮ LIGHT-REFLECTIVE GLASS AND TILES

elegant modern

Translating the graciousness of the past to a modern setting is not as difficult as it might sound. This style allows for a combination of antique furnishings with contemporary pieces, as long as neither is overtly 'old' or 'new' – timeless harmony is the aim. Calm colours and natural, tactile materials add to the mix, resulting in a room that is as ordered as it is comfortable.

The secret of Elegant Modern living is the same as it has always been: unfussy, effortless relaxation, with everything in just the right place. William Morris said, 'Have nothing in your house that you do not know to be useful or believe to be beautiful,' to which we may add, 'Have nothing that stands out too much, that is jarring or clashing, or that is surplus to requirements.'

Lighting is the great disguiser and emphasizer in any room – use it cleverly to hide flaws and make the most of attractive features, combining ceiling lamps (if you have a central pendant, put it on a dimmer) with understated wall, table and floor lamps. Choose a restrained colour scheme that concentrates on taupe, ivory, cream and stone, with perhaps a dash of a stronger colour to give it a boost, and flooring either of polished wood with a lovely rug or a natural-coloured carpet. Sofas and chairs, in simple shapes and with unfussy upholstery – which includes antique and modern pieces – should be placed so that conversation, reading and watching TV are equally pleasant. Finally, go easy on accessories. Carefully chosen vases, pictures, sculptures or candlesticks add interest, but too many will dominate and upset your careful balance.

KEY FEATURES

▌ CALM COLOURS – EMULSION IN OFF-WHITE, TAUPE OR STONE, OR PERHAPS SUEDE-EFFECT PAINT FOR SUBTLE TEXTURE. WALLPAPER IN UNDERSTATED PATTERNS.

▌ VERSATILE LIGHTING THAT CAN ILLUMINATE THE WHOLE ROOM OR SPECIFIC AREAS, BE DIMMED EASILY, AND BRIGHTEN UP A CORNER FOR READING OR WRITING.

▌ FURNITURE THAT MAY BE EITHER OLD OR NEW, BUT THAT IS SIMPLY SHAPED, WITH COMFORTABLE BUT NOT OVER-THE-TOP UPHOLSTERY, AND IN PLAIN FABRICS.

▌ A LAYOUT THAT IS NEITHER TOO CLUTTERED NOR TOO SPARSE, ALLOWING FREEDOM OF MOVEMENT, CONVERSATION AND RELAXATION.

OPPOSITE LEFT AND RIGHT: **Antique and modern pieces sit comfortably side by side in this harmonious living room, aided by a soft colour palette of creams and chocolate.**

THIS PAGE, CLOCKWISE FROM ABOVE: **Books** really do furnish a room, especially when they are as well organized as this. One strong shade can give a boost to an otherwise muted colour scheme. Upholstery should be plain and simple, with window treatments to match. The repetitive geometric shapes of the furnishings in this room are calm and soothing. Fitted cupboards keep clutter out of sight. Balance is important for this look, so a symmetrical arrangement of objects, such as these slender lamps, can be highly effective.

CLASSIC WITH A TWIST STYLE STUDY

The rule of decorating is that there are no rules – just an individual sense of taste, style and what suits you best. So, while the typical Elegant Modern living room might consist purely of restrained colours with a subtle dash of something stronger, this one has injected a zingy, bright shade that brings an otherwise relatively plain scheme bang up to date.

Taking the style to its limits, the owners of this living room started with a neutral, classic scheme of dove-grey walls, taupe curtains and ivory upholstery, and added a frisson of citrus colour that is both contemporary and highly individual. The result is still relaxed and comfortable, with a good use of space and a versatile lighting scheme. Storage is very open – everything is on display – but well organized, with carefully chosen ornaments in monochromatic tones.

The starting points are the largest surfaces – the floor and walls, both exceptionally plain. The fireplaces, too, are sculptural but not showy, generously sized and create attractive focal points, one at each end, for the room. Painted white, they co-ordinate with the white lampshades, pale fabrics on the armchairs and white-framed pictures. The sizeable coffee table seems light and delicate, thanks to its slender frame and glass top. Made of wood, it complements the slim bookshelves that line the chimney alcoves. Though there are a fair number of things going on in this room, such attention to detail ensures that no single element is overwhelming, and pulls the scheme together in a subtle but successful way.

WHY IT WORKS COMFORTABLE FURNITURE IN CLASSIC SHAPES ■ BOLD COLOURS UPDATE THE LOOK ■ NEATLY ARRANGED ACCESSORIES ■ A SENSE OF ORDERED COMFORT

OPPOSITE ABOVE: **A bunch of flowers in a co-ordinating colour can help unify the different elements of a decorative scheme.**

OPPOSITE BELOW, FROM LEFT TO RIGHT: **Next to an enormously comfortable armchair and ottoman, in plain, pale upholstery,** are a couple of spindly lights that make reading more pleasant. Coloured cushions on the sofa complement the orange velvet-covered chair: this look is neither old nor new, but simply timeless.

ABOVE: **The dove-grey walls of this living room are interesting but still** neutral, and complemented by the simplest of gathered curtains at the window. Open shelving provides space for carefully chosen and neatly arranged ornaments and books, while the seating is both comfortable in itself, and comfortably and sociably arranged.

KEY FEATURES

▌ BIG, COSY ARMCHAIRS AND SOFAS ARE KEY. CHOOSE DESIGNS WITH ROUNDED CONTOURS AND PLUMP SEAT CUSHIONS, THEN UPHOLSTER WITH SHABBY-CHIC FABRICS, FROM BATTERED LEATHER TO COSY VELVET OR WOOL.

▌ GO FOR TEXTURED WALLS, CLAD IN ANYTHING FROM TIMBER TONGUE-AND-GROOVE OR PLYWOOD PANELS TO EXPANSES OF NATURAL STONE.

▌ HARD FLOORING SETS THE RIGHT TONE, FROM RECLAIMED TIMBER BOARDS TO SLATE TILES. THE ODD RUG, SUCH AS SISAL, ANTIQUE TURKISH OR WOOL, ADDS SOFTNESS.

▌ MIX TOGETHER OLD AND NEW FURNITURE, FROM JUNK-SHOP ANTIQUE PIECES TO THE OCCASIONAL 20TH-CENTURY CLASSIC.

▌ DISTRESSED SURFACES ARE A MUST, SO FOXED MIRRORS, CRACKED LEATHER, SCRUBBED PINE AND TEXTURAL PAINT FINISHES ARE ALL OPTIONS.

natural

With its warm tones and heavily textured surfaces, the Natural living room is an all-enveloping space, a place where you can hunker down and gather with friends. Such a high comfort rating means it works as well in a tiny cottage parlour as in a city loft space, imparting an effortless, cosy ambience. Kit it out with squashy furniture, cocooning textures and soft lighting for the ultimate chill-out zone.

The Natural sitting room is a breeze to copy, because it's casual in mood and layout. It's the look to pick if you own distressed antiques and modern pieces, and want a strong theme with which to draw them together. Exploit its chameleon-like potential. Accessorize it with stone and dark greys, and it becomes gritty and masculine. Dress it with wools and creamy colours, and it is tactile and cosy.

Don't confuse this look with country style. It may be big on natural textures and neutral tones, but there isn't a rose-print in sight. Far more important is the emphasis on nubbly fabrics like loose-weave linens for drapes, or calico or canvas for tight upholstery. And there is a distinct absence of country clutter. Accessories should be minimalist and eye-catching, such as a plain pottery platter, letting the eye concentrate on the grain and texture of the natural surfaces.

Play up the casual mood with relaxed furniture arrangements: set pieces at an angle or back to back, rather than symmetrically. Overlap textures: stone tiles adjacent to timber boards, wool cushions against leather upholstery, and so on. The more unrefined and interesting the mix, the more impact the living room has.

LARGE-SCALE LIVING STYLE STUDY

Crammed with an eye-catching combination of textures, yet planned around a creamy palette, this living room is welcoming and tranquil. The architectural shell is modern and pared down, with a double-height living space and simple glass doors, yet the mood remains intimate. The secret lies in a combination of scaled-up squashy furniture, which adds cosiness, and pale neutrals, for a soothing finish.

It's not easy to create an intimate living area in a double-height, open-plan space, yet this one is a triumph. It helps that there are good, natural bones: there are two sets of French doors leading onto the garden, and the space is flooded with sunlight from upper-level windows. And, because it is dramatically clad in stone, the fireplace wall is a welcoming focal point.

The mix of natural textures and surfaces is particularly accomplished. Timber is the recurring theme: the floor, walls, door frames and overhead beams are all fashioned from the same bleached wood,

creating a warm-looking canvas. Yet, to break up the smooth finishes, the stone cladding adds a raw, rough note. Even the furniture is used to weave in fresh textural stories. While the sofa is covered in sophisticated cream linen, the rocking chair and nearby stool introduce a woven finish.

Furniture and accessories are arranged with a light touch, to create a casual, unfitted look. Framed black-and-white photos are propped up on shelves, as are the rustic baskets on the mantelpiece. While the sofa is drawn up cosily to the fire, the occasional chairs and stools offer flexibility.

OPPOSITE ABOVE: **It can be tricky to accessorize a very large space, but here clever use of scale provides intriguing focal points. It's brave to mix tiny ceramic pots against the vast scale of the stone-clad chimney breast, but it works.**

OPPOSITE BELOW: **Placed directly beneath the flow of light from upper windows, the cream sofa brings a natural highlight into a very muted, natural colour scheme. The broad white photograph mounts have a similar effect.**

ABOVE LEFT: **Accessories should be simple, and in keeping with the natural theme. Giant wooden or ceramic platters, pottery bowls or woven containers look good, but choose versions with a simple, modern shape.**

ABOVE RIGHT: **The architecture provides a modern take on an old rustic theme. The near-vertical stairs remind of a ladder, leading to a garret, yet have the room's minimal detailing.**

WHY IT WORKS STONE CLADDING CREATES A FOCAL POINT ▪ COSY, TRADITIONAL FURNITURE ▪ WARM CREAM-AND-GREY PALETTE ▪ BOLD MONOCHROME ACCESSORIES

LEFT: **This is a classic Scandinavian combination of old and new furniture. The chairs are by Poul Kjærholm, from the middle of the 20th century, but the sideboard, sofa and rug are much more recent. A monochrome colour scheme helps to pull the look together.**

OPPOSITE LEFT: **Scandinavian designers occasionally ventured into plastics. The Ball chair, designed by Eero Aarnio in 1966, is one such example. Note how well it fits into the typical Scandinavian living room with natural colours, simple window treatments and loads of light.**

OPPOSITE ABOVE RIGHT: **Interesting forms provide variety here, while a pair of cushions adds a subtle dash of vibrant colour and pattern.**

OPPOSITE CENTRE RIGHT: **Much of this furniture was designed in the late Fifties or early Sixties, but its good looks stand the test of time.**

OPPOSITE BELOW RIGHT: **A mix of square and round forms results in understated sophistication.**

scandinavian

With practicality and comfort as priorities, the Scandinavian living room is an eminently easy to live in, attractive place. A sense of space and light is paramount, and there is a relaxed mix of soft, pale colours, the gentle tones of timber and the interesting textures of natural fabrics. The chances are you will never want to leave.

The colours of nature set the scene in the Scandinavian living room – predominantly blond and mid-tone woods, unbleached cotton and linen, parchment, stone and frosted glass. It's a sophisticated, subtle look, which you can take in all sorts of directions, from retro to highly contemporary, fairly minimal to cosy and comfortable, as long as the result has that combination of warmth, practicality and relaxed easiness that so defines Scandinavian style.

These are uncluttered spaces in which light – such a precious commodity in these northern countries – is maximized, often via

large glass windows with almost invisible or non-existent curtains or blinds. A sheer panel of voile, some plain gathered fabric hung from a concealed track, wooden slatted blinds or vertical louvres are really all you can get away with here. Floors are inevitably covered in timber, either boards or parquet; sometimes walls and ceilings, too, while furniture is composed of wood, occasionally combined with clean-lined upholstery in black or tan leather or a simple, hard-wearing fabric. Remember that anything fussy or ornate should be avoided at all costs – forms are based on simple,

KEY FEATURES

■ ANYTHING THAT WILL MAXIMIZE LIGHT, INCLUDING PALE, PLAIN WALLS AND MINIMAL (IF ANY) WINDOW TREATMENTS. THESE COULD BE SHEER PANELS OF VOILE, GATHERED COTTON, WOODEN SLATS OR VERTICAL LOUVRES.

■ FURNITURE ARRANGED TO ENHANCE THE SENSE OF SPACE, THOUGH WITHOUT LOOKING SPARSE OR MINIMAL.

■ SIMPLE, CLEAN-LINED FORMS, OFTEN GEOMETRICALLY INSPIRED BUT NOT HARD OR HARSH.

■ RUGS, CUSHIONS AND OTHER TEXTILES IN UNDERSTATED SHAPES AND PATTERNS THAT SUBTLY ENHANCE RATHER THAN INTRUDE UPON THE VISUAL STYLE.

■ BEAUTIFUL, POLISHED WOODEN FLOORS, EITHER BOARDS OR PARQUET.

ABOVE LEFT: **In a converted Stockholm office building, the unadorned upholstery of this comfortable armchair gives it a look that is absolutely timeless. Without the unnecessary addition of a cushion, it has a fresh, clean air that complements the drum-shaped parchment lampshade with its simple base.**

ABOVE RIGHT: **A curving birch ceiling is a dramatic feature of this Finnish house. Awesomely spacious and light, the living room features simple furniture, in timber and black leather, and the ubiquitous PH 5 pendant lamp.**

OPPOSITE: **Polished parquet flooring is a gorgeous highlight of this Stockholm living room. Though the walls and upholstery are plain, there is a tangible sense of warmth and comfort here, which is due to the use of natural materials, an ordered layout and the subtle variations in colours and textures.**

geometric shapes, perhaps with neat detailing such as piped edging for tidiness, but certainly no button-backs, fancy pleats or frilly edges. Even cushions should be used with care: keep them basic and simple or they will seem out of place. Rugs, too, are lovely for adding warmth on a hard floor, but should be quite plain in order to enhance the look. And, while furnishings and accessories don't exactly have to be minimal, they should be chosen and placed with care, so as to give the impression of a practical, liveable room that is comfortable rather than crowded.

When you have large expanses of wall that require painting, the ideal colours are pale, light-reflecting and harmonious. White is fine, though it can look rather stark; better, maybe, would be cream, stone or ivory. You do not have to exclude pattern entirely, but, where you do introduce it, do so carefully. Chintzy florals, obviously, are out, but stripes, checks and bold geometrics, in small doses, can look fabulous. This is not, after all, a lesson in dull plainness, but a way of living that eschews frippery in favour of functionalism and pared-down good taste.

DESIGNER SHOWCASE STYLE STUDY

It may be packed with 20th-century designer furniture, but there is nothing
pretentious about this Danish living room. Instead, practicality and comfort
are key, while the scheme sticks to a simple mix of clean-lined furniture,
natural, tactile materials and monochromatic colours. The result is warm
and welcoming, unstudied, subtle and timelessly appealing.

WHY IT WORKS LIMITED COLOUR PALETTE ▮ INTERESTING BUT UNPRETENTIOUS FURNITURE
▮ MIX OF MATERIALS AND TEXTURES ▮ FUNCTIONAL BUT ALSO COMFORTABLE DESIGNS

OPPOSITE: **The room counterpoints strong horizontal and vertical lines with fluid curves and, although the colours are within a strictly limited range, there is an appealing mix of textures, from wood and wicker to leather and glass, to bring interest and variety.**

ABOVE LEFT: **Poul Kjærholm designed the adjustable PK 24 chaise longue. In wicker on a delicate stainless-steel frame, it is typically uncompromising in terms of quality and function.**

CENTRE AND BELOW LEFT: **The PK 0 chair, made from black, moulded wood, was never mass-produced. Its form makes it almost as much a sculpture as a piece of furniture.**

BELOW: **The glass-and-steel coffee table is another Kjærholm design. Though slender and minimal in style, it has great character.**

Natural colours and materials dominate this living room, which belongs to the widow of Poul Kjærholm, one of Denmark's most eminent furniture designers of the Fifties and Sixties. It combines comfort with a strict functionality – Kjærholm was uncompromising in his attention to detail.

Structurally, the whitewashed walls and robust wooden ceiling beams provide a grid-like background to the room. And, with a monochromatic colour scheme, the outlines of the furnishings take over, creating flowing patterns of counterpointed curves and straight lines. Textures, too, are intriguingly varied. So, in the foreground sits a wicker and stainless-steel chaise longue by Kjærholm, with a similarly organically shaped screen in the background. The black, moulded wood PK 0 chair is sculptural, while the leather sofa is simply elegant and inviting. This is, effectively, a showcase for Kjærholm's most striking work, yet it is also a living, breathing room, with a comfortable sofa, a soft rug and practical lighting. Ultimately, Scandinavian rooms tend not to make too much of their designer pieces, but simply include and use them in a mix both practical and attractive.

KEY FEATURES

■ SQUASHY SOFAS ARE ESSENTIAL. THEY SHOULD BE WELL USED, EMBEDDED WITH UNREGIMENTED CUSHIONS AND SOFTENED WITH THROWS.

■ WHERE WOULD THE LOOK BE WITHOUT A LOG FIRE? THE FIREPLACE, SURROUNDED BY BASKETS OR HEAPS OF LOGS, IS THE CENTRAL POINT – EVEN IN SUMMER, WHEN THE LOGS SHOULD BE LAID BUT NOT LIT.

■ COLOUR IT NEUTRAL. THERE'S MASSES OF CHOICE AMONG THE WHITES, GREIGES, BEIGES AND CREAMS, BOTH IN PAINTS AND FABRICS.

■ KEEP EVERYTHING NATURAL, FROM WOOD OR TILE FLOORS TO LINEN OR COTTON FABRICS.

■ ANTIQUES ARE ESSENTIAL: A WINDSOR CHAIR, BATTERED ENAMEL JUG, RAG RUG OR PATCHWORK QUILT SAYS IT ALL.

traditional country

This look is deeply and unashamedly romantic. Not hearts and flowers, but designed to fulfil a fantasy of rural life far removed from the muddy reality. It should conjure up pussy willows, birdsong and snuggling in a cashmere throw in front of a scented fire. To achieve the look, everything must be natural, at ease with itself and apparently effortless.

Traditional Country style has evolved over the centuries, from medieval castles furnished with oak chests and stick stools to Victorian farm workers' cottages where economy was turned into beauty. Thus, the look needs a clear eye for simplicity allied with elegance. There is no room here for gilded French chairs or swagger portraits – more for three-legged cricket tables, rag rugs made from cast-off clothes and naive portraits executed by travelling painters. But, behind the defining features, a feeling for comfort is essential and this is achieved by adding plenty of squashy chairs and sofas (all

well used), by light and airy colours and expansive windows, by using natural materials from wood to stone and by the essential glowing fire.

Rural style adapts with the seasons – a feeling for the countryside in all its moods defines the look. It's easy to achieve. Pick the first wild spring catkins and stuff them in a jar, collect smooth pebbles and skeleton leaves, pile old bowls with fir cones or gourds and, best of all, always fill the room with the scent of blossom, smoking applewood logs or spicy pomanders. If you live in a town, ring seasonal changes with flowers and fruits.

OPPOSITE ABOVE LEFT: **The long, low stone mantelshelf is the focus of this uncluttered room, and the fireplace has been emphasized by a large wooden log basket and carefully placed light. The line is continued at right angles with a wide shelf, made welcoming with a padded seat and cushions.**

OPPOSITE BELOW LEFT: **Ginghams, tickings and neutrals are all important to the style. Here, the furniture is cream-painted to merge with the woven flooring, which emphasizes the generously checked tie-on cushions and striped padded table mat.**

OPPOSITE ABOVE RIGHT: **The palest of shades – even the flowers are muted – gives a feeling of comfort and calm.**

ABOVE LEFT: **Wood is a key element, from banisters to floor to piles of logs in willow baskets.**

ABOVE CENTRE: **While old beams are a constant element of the style, they should be underplayed rather than blackened.**

ABOVE RIGHT: **Summer fireplaces can be turned into artistic firewood storage space.**

GLOBAL GATHERING STYLE STUDY

It would be hard to guess in which country this serene room is found, for so many provincial and unassuming furnishing elements are used together. The reason the whole works so well is partly the owner's eye for elegant simplicity, but also because rural living, wherever it is, creates its own demands.

ABOVE: **A modern painting hangs above a traditional French marble fireplace. An antique Provençal chest takes up the French theme. Everything in the room, from willow basket to brass lamps and fireguard, is of a natural material.**
RIGHT: **The curving legs of an antique wooden side table are** emphasized against an all-cream background, including a painted old corner cupboard.
OPPOSITE LEFT: **With half a decent view, bay windows should always be given comfy window seats. A nearby antique desk has matching paintwork and old-fashioned keys in its locks.**

OPPOSITE ABOVE RIGHT: **A heavily glazed French earthenware dish – its chips deliberately on view – has been filled with matching, smooth ornamental balls.**
OPPOSITE BELOW RIGHT: **A single floral cushion is centred against a plain cream sofa. Its embroidery mirrors the flower arrangments.**

Analysing the qualities of this room – and every decorating enthusiast should do so – results in an overwhelming feeling of calm, despite there being a fair amount of clutter. This is down to the colours used: every single element is neutral, with a preponderance of milky beige. Pattern is largely kept to geometric checks and stripes, with a single floral cushion and pottery lamp echoing the casual flowers found throughout.

The fireplace and Provençal chest alongside are clearly French, as is the arrangement on the mantelshelf; but the window treatment and colour scheme are Scandinavian. Meanwhile, the hanging lamp is Indian and the choice of squashy sofas pure English. The way the light from several large windows is maximized harks back to Scandinavian style – light is precious up north. Two deep windows remain uncurtained, while the bay window, with window seats on a white painted base, has translucent blinds. Though this scheme appears very pulled together, it's easy to achieve with painted furniture and loose covers on the chairs in understated fabrics. It is the antithesis of opulence.

WHY IT WORKS CONTROLLED COLOURS ▪ EVERY ELEMENT IS NATURAL ▪ VERY LITTLE PATTERN APART FROM GEOMETRICS ▪ LIGHT IS MAXIMIZED ▪ COMFORT IS PARAMOUNT

modern country

There's a fine line between a traditional rural look and its updated, modern version, and much of the difference is in the choice of decorative objects. Sir Terence Conran pioneered our current thirst for old farming tools and industrial relics such as cogwheels, and the love affair has lasted 40 years. The look also has elements of Shaker, American naive and English eccentric, but the whole is achieved with careful discipline. One wrong move and its appeal would be lost.

Even the Modern Country living room needs plenty of comfort to create the romantic fantasy of barefoot picnics and winter mulled-wine parties. This is as strong in this style as in its more traditional cousin. The use of old farmhouse painted cupboards with distressed paintwork, milking stools from the byre and old French peasants' sheets breathes a nostalgia for times when linen was handwoven and furniture well used. We are using objects from a pauper's past to relive a dreamlike rural idyll in a more comfortable future.

What makes the difference between Traditional and Modern Country styles is the latter's irreverence. Bauhaus meets bodger in a single room; a junky metal Fifties kitchen cupboard becomes a living-room chest and a stick-leg seat is transformed into a coffee table. This is a style which has its own wry humour.

Nor does Modern Country see any need to confine itself to a single tradition – French cabriole-leg chairs jostle Russian wooden benches, which are in turn busy with African weave cushions. Metallic modern sculpture vies with country Chippendale mirrors and anglepoise lights. When you get the knack, it's a hugely enjoyable look to put together.

KEY FEATURES

▌ MINIMALIST WHITE PALETTE IN WHICH THE VARIOUS SHADES OF WHITE ARE EXPLOITED AGAINST EACH OTHER; NATURAL MATERIALS CHOSEN FOR THEIR TEXTURE.

▌ UNUSUAL SCULPTURAL OBJECTS, ONCE PRACTICAL, USED BOTH AS ORNAMENTS OR FOR DIFFERENT PURPOSES, SUCH AS A LADDER FOR FABRIC DISPLAY.

▌ UNEXPECTED EXPLOITATION OF ARCHITECTURAL FEATURES – WHITE-PAINTED BEAMS, TONGUED AND GROOVED TEXTURES, EXPOSED CHIMNEYS.

▌ THOUGHTFUL MIXTURE OF MODERN AND ANTIQUE OBJECTS AND FURNITURE, WITH THE EMPHASIS ON COMFORT. EASY CHAIRS, SOFAS AND CHAISES LONGUES BORROWED FROM TRADITIONAL COUNTRY STYLE.

OPPOSITE LEFT: The inspiration in this plain grey and white living room comes clearly from Scandinavia. The planked panelling, windows on each side of the fire and the slight 18th-century feeling are all typical.

OPPOSITE RIGHT: Because the effect is simple and neutral, a large number of different styles sit happily in this living room. Colouring beams is always effective.

THIS PAGE, CLOCKWISE FROM ABOVE: Fabrics such as tweeds and checks can be stolen from tailors. Quirky, reworked and distressed antiques are typical of Modern Country. A monochrome room depends on angles and shapes for its interest. As you can see, wickerwork is extremely comfortable. A comfy sofa covered in white is inviting beneath the windows. Though in a town house, the combination of open fire and squashy sofa is rural.

IN THE FRAME STYLE STUDY

The owner here has understood the built-in benefits of this living room – its huge windows and outside door, both with rural views – and taken full advantage of them. Though the scheme appears, at first glance, to be minimal, it is far from it. But the decorative objects are chosen to be muted, at one with their surroundings.

This utterly 21st-century room shows all the characteristics of Modern Country style. While the palette and the use of pattern and texture are firmly controlled, the overall effect is still romantically harking back to a past when handmade objects were used every day. To us, such things are luxuries, and this is how the room deploys them. For instance, a painted, well-worn wooden paddle stands like a sculpture beside a wonky, white-painted Windsor chair, which looks as if it were put together by bodgers deep in the woods. Both are treated with reverence. So, too, are the gleaming and mid-toned wooden floor and the ceiling beams, which run transversely to the boards beneath. Neither is over-emphasized, but their texture and integral pattern are brought out by the simplicity of the decor. The sofas are used to add softness and pleasure to an otherwise hard-edged look, which includes a lack of curtains at the windows and a contemporary glass-topped coffee table. The cushions, all in shades of the same neutral, are chunky, handwoven and piled on a soft sheepskin; a heavily tasselled throw adorns a white, loose-covered arm.

OPPOSITE ABOVE: **Old everyday objects are treated with reverence. A wooden paddle and wonky Windsor chair become sculptures against a pale wall.**

OPPOSITE BELOW: **Light from large and deep windows and an open door is used to create interesting silhouettes from the rocker and glazing bars. The flowers in an old jug are a traditional touch.**

ABOVE LEFT: **Don't be ashamed of ancient sofas in well-laundered covers. They exude comfort.**

ABOVE RIGHT: **Any comfy old sofa can be transformed by the addition of a pale loose cover chosen to fit the decor. Here, an added creamy throw picks up the colours of the cushion on the sofa beyond.**

WHY IT WORKS HARDLY ANY PATTERN ANYWHERE ▪ PREDOMINANCE OF NEUTRAL COLOURS ▪ THE INTEREST LIES IN TEXTURES ▪ WINDOWS ARE LEFT UNCURTAINED

classic period style

Classic here means 18th century, when the architectural values of Greece and Rome were everywhere applied. If you start with a room of that period, the look is easy, but even a modern box can be given applied ceiling roses, panelled doors and generous skirtings. Find them at builders' merchants and architectural salvage houses. Panelling can be copied from the old craftsmen's pattern books.

Given enough spending power, this is an easy look to achieve. Though the Classic Period style is ideal in a Georgian town house, it can still be workable in a garret or country farmhouse. The secret is to take symmetry as the most important value: furniture should come in matching pairs, black-and-white etchings be hung in tiers and balanced, and large classical objects like urns or even lamps made from Ionic columns are best matched on each side of the fireplace, console table or window. Colours can be deep and strong, though preferably not used in smaller rooms or those with bad light. It's also an idea to limit patterns to a few 18th-century-style fabrics. Toile de Jouy is ideal, because the designs are loose but the colour is monochrome. Choose a shade which complements others in the room. Though leather club chairs and sofas are basically 19th century in inspiration, they are fine here – especially as you'll want something more comfortable than an 18th-century hardback chair to lounge in.

OPPOSITE ABOVE LEFT: **Good architectural features do help: the arches, dado, door surrounds and a glimpse of 18th-century banisters elevate a neutral decor.**

OPPOSITE ABOVE RIGHT: **Classical themes can take emphatic colours in the Pompeiian mode. Strong red and the heavy iron fire surround are relieved by a dainty cornice.**

OPPOSITE BELOW LEFT: **Toile de Jouy – here as a loose cover – makes the perfect foil to the severe classical look. And it's authentic.**

OPPOSITE BELOW CENTRE: **A gothic mirror is placed directly over a tiered wooden box to give a sense of symmetry.**

OPPOSITE BELOW RIGHT: **Club sofas are not strictly 18th century, but this deep-buttoned leather Chesterfield is perfectly at ease in its surroundings.**

BELOW: **Symmetry is an important ingredient of this look. A pair of identical easy chairs, with identical throws and cushions, makes sense of a difficult space.**

KEY FEATURES

▪ A SENSE OF SYMMETRY IS VITAL. USE PAIRS OF MATCHING CHAIRS, MIRRORS OR ORNAMENTS TO BALANCE EACH OTHER IN IMPORTANT POSITIONS.

▪ ARCHITECTURAL FEATURES: IT'S NOT POSSIBLE TO CREATE THE STYLE WITHOUT DECORATIVE CORNICES, DOOR JAMBS AND SKIRTINGS, BUT THEY CAN EASILY BE ADDED TO DULL SPACES.

▪ CLASSICAL ALLUSIONS WILL POINT UP THE LOOK. TRY URNS, OBELISKS AND CLASSICAL PRINTS.

▪ AN IMPORTANT FIREPLACE, MARBLE, IRON OR CARVED WOOD, MAKES A GOOD STARTING POINT.

▪ DISCIPLINED USE OF STRONG EARTH-BASED COLOURS – OCHRE, TERRACOTTA, SIENNA – IS TRADITIONAL IN 17TH- AND 18TH-CENTURY SETTINGS AND HELPFUL IN REVEALING THE ARCHITECTURAL BONES.

FORMAL INVITATION STYLE STUDY

This room shows Classic Period style to perfection – but the whole is made up of potentially jarring elements. The parquet floor is French, as is the heavy marble fireplace, while the curtain treatment and use of squashy sofas is more English in feeling. But the importance of symmetry, a good fireplace and strong touches of colour form the overall signature.

TOP RIGHT: **An amusing doggy silhouette is juxtaposed with a dog painting above the fireplace.**

ABOVE LEFT: **18th-century rooms often lead from one to another. Note the carefully placed vases.**

ABOVE RIGHT: **A heavy marble French fire surround is the main feature in this room, emphasized by the strong monochrome painting (surprisingly unframed).**

OPPOSITE: **The formality of the window treatment, with its 18th-century console table emphasized by both orchids and leafy mirror, is softened by the random placing of the furniture in front.**

The skill in using this very popular style, as the owners of this room clearly recognize, is to balance the grandeur and formality implicit in it with a sense of pleasure and comfort. This has been achieved with a background formality that is quite imposing. The huge windows are given important, if translucent, curtains, in a rainbow fabric leading with strong orange, which provides the strongest colour in the room. The rug and walls are in paler, neutral tones of its shades. In front of each stands a large Chinese vase and between them is a formal console table holding a classical statue in front of an ornate mirror. The imposing fireplace in heavily carved white marble is made the focus of attention by putting a stark monochrome (and modern) oil painting above it, interestingly without a frame. Symmetrical candle holders are made of ornate bird statues. Then everything relaxes: the white squashy sofas are extremely inviting and given random comfortable cushions; the oriental rug and embroidered stool (doubling as coffee table) are endearingly worn. Even the silhouette on the mantelshelf is carefully placed to mock the big dog above. Note, too, how the more formal armchair and ornate table lamps are placed deliberately to break the formality of the background.

WHY IT WORKS FORMAL BACKGROUND FEATURES ALLIED WITH LOOSE PLACING OF FURNITURE ■ SYMMETRICALLY PLACED URNS AND CANDLESTICKS ■ CLASSICAL STATUES

vintage & retro

Once you have chosen to ignore fads and fashions, you really can go your own way, creating a Vintage or Retro living space that is furnished with comfortable, good-looking pieces you really love, whether they were picked up from a junk shop, found in a skip or bought at great expense from a specialist dealer.

OPPOSITE ABOVE LEFT: **Metal shelving salvaged from an office clearout provides Vintage chic in an otherwise modern, though understated, room.**

OPPOSITE ABOVE RIGHT: **Tongue-and-groove cladding, plus a mix of patterned textiles, gives this room an informal and welcoming air.**

OPPOSITE BELOW, FROM LEFT TO RIGHT: **A bench-style sofa and bentwood dining chairs are simple Retro additions to a modern**

scheme. **Open shelving and an old sofa disguised with a huge, plain throw have a casual, Vintage feel. Curly metal is a repeated motif in this living room, offset by its plain walls and floor.**

BELOW: **In the huge space of a loft apartment, special pieces such as a vintage leather sofa and armchair can be shown to their best advantage. The completely plain walls and flooring enhance their impact further, and the cowhide rug is a rustic touch.**

The Vintage living room has an eclectic, relaxed and comfy feel. It may be that nothing matches, but as long as nothing jars either, what does it matter? This style gives you great freedom of design. Floors, for example, could be carpeted, in traditional wool or natural matting, or covered in wooden boards (perhaps reclaimed), plus a decorative rug or two, while walls could be painted, clad with simple tongue-and-groove, or even wallpapered. Colours can be fairly varied. Using vintage finds inevitably means some mixing of colours, and the key to getting this right is to unify them with a careful choice of harmonious paints and textiles.

One of the most essential ingredients for this look is a squashy sofa, in a style that is neither obviously antique nor highly contemporary. Cover it with a throw if necessary, or have loose covers made. An armchair or two, perhaps upholstered in ticking or unbleached linen, or, if you are lucky enough to find one, in subtly worn leather, will be useful, together with lots of soft cushions. Open shelving suits this look, displaying books and ornaments in careful profusion, while lighting could vary from inexpensive paper shades to hinged-arm lamps or simple chandeliers.

KEY FEATURES

■ AN ECLECTIC MIX OF ATTRACTIVE OLD PIECES THAT ARE NEITHER FINE ANTIQUES NOR OBVIOUSLY CONTEMPORARY.

■ A MIX OF HARMONIOUS COLOURS THAT PULLS THE WHOLE SCHEME TOGETHER.

■ A COMFY SOFA AND CHAIRS, PERHAPS WITH LOOSE COVERS OR THROWS, AND PILES OF CUSHIONS. AVOID TASSELS, BRAIDING OR ANY OTHER FUSSY DECORATION.

■ OPEN SHELVING ON WHICH TO DISPLAY BOOKS AND ORNAMENTS THAT SUIT THE STYLE.

■ VINTAGE ROOMS ARE MORE COSY AND RELAXED; RETRO ROOMS A TOUCH MORE CONTROLLED.

■ WALLS, FLOORS, LIGHTING AND WINDOW TREATMENTS SHOULD BE SUBTLE AND MINIMAL, UNLESS YOU HAVE SPECIAL PIECES THAT WILL ENHANCE THE LOOK.

The Retro living room is more poised and deliberate. Here is a chance to show off special pieces, whether a large leather sofa, a pair of mid-century chairs, some unusual fabric or an eye-catching lamp. Colours set the scene for this look, and they tend to be bolder than in a Vintage living room; perhaps Fifties pastels, Sixties brights or Seventies muddy shades. Pattern, too, may be more obvious – a small dose can really go a long way towards establishing the right tone.

A room such as this could be a completely authentic recreation or simply a modern space to which has been added one or two retro pieces, whether junk-shop finds or rare and sought after. How far you want to take it is up to you. As with the Vintage living room, accessories are important, though bear in mind that too much clutter will only obscure the style rather than enhance it. Similarly, with so much going on, the background features of walls, floors, window treatments and lighting all tend to be subtle and minimal, with the exception of carefully chosen retro pieces that really promote the look, such as a groovy shagpile rug, patterned glass shades or a fabulous printed hanging.

LEFT, CLOCKWISE FROM TOP LEFT: A retro sideboard and chair sit quietly in one corner of this light, bright living room. In a scheme based around shades of chocolate and cream, an old leather club chair is an imposing addition. Fifties furnishings such as these are eye-catching and unusual. This spindly-legged table is typical, and would be just as suitable for an otherwise modern room as in a totally authentic scheme.
ABOVE: This no-holds-barred Retro living room with its range of key pieces makes a strong impact.
OPPOSITE ABOVE: Retro colours, geometric prints and a cool shagpile rug are the scene-stealers in this Retro room.
OPPOSITE BELOW, FROM LEFT TO RIGHT: Formal simplicity with a pair of period chairs. A good use of lighting enhances this living room. A quiet background makes this Eames plywood chair stand out.

POISE AND PANACHE STYLE STUDY

It can be hard to combine a variety of vintage and retro finds in one room, but this living space demonstrates how to do it very successfully. Here, the utilitarian mixes with the decorative, and pieces from different eras sit happily side by side, thanks to a carefully chosen colour palette and a delicate sense of order, space and restraint.

This gorgeous living room, despite being somewhat spare in terms of its furnishings, somehow manages also to convey a sumptuous feel. It has a lovely mix of old and new with, on the whole, a plain and utilitarian feel, lifted by a statement piece – a huge giltwood mirror – and a range of luxurious textures. These range from wood and wicker to silk, flokati and jumbo cord; hard and soft, shaggy and smooth, creating an ambience that has an elegant cosiness.

As a starting point, the warmth of the polished wooden floor is backed up by soft paint colours in stone and cream. The sofa is a modern reproduction of a traditional style, while the armchairs, covered in white cotton, could, underneath, be any cheap finds. The curtains and pendant light are utterly restrained, but subtle character has been added by the addition of vintage pieces – a floor lamp, a wicker basket chair, a bentwood chair, the mirror and a small dressmaker's dummy – that add instant flair without being overpowering. This is a room where an individual taste for vintage items has been exercised with great restraint, resulting in a coherent, calm and interesting space which has both poise and panache.

WHY IT WORKS RESTRAINED USE OF RETRO AND VINTAGE FINDS ∎ A PLAIN SETTING PROVIDES A GOOD BACKDROP ∎ SOFT, CALM COLOURS ∎ A RANGE OF VARIED TEXTURES

OPPOSITE BELOW, FROM LEFT TO RIGHT: **When furnishings that share a similar, simple and elegant aesthetic are put together they tend to look harmonious, even when they date from very different eras. The huge, ornate giltwood mirror is a statement piece that acts as a focal point in** the room. Contrasts of texture, here in the form of soft and shiny silk against plush jumbo cord, give the room a tactile appeal.

OPPOSITE ABOVE: **A plain fireplace is an ideal display area for some intriguing retro pieces. Though disparate in style, they share a** certain witty character, and have been well arranged; neither too cluttered nor too sparse.

ABOVE: Subtle, plain paint colours and a polished wooden floor act as a sophisticated backdrop to this inviting room. One window is bare, thus avoiding visual clutter.

bathrooms

Today's bathrooms serve a
dual purpose. They are places
for indulgent pampering as
well as quick and efficient
workday washing, and they
have to look good, too.
Whatever style you choose, a
practical layout with hard-
wearing materials, stylish
sanitary ware and great
lighting, combined with some
luxurious accessories, are
bathroom fundamentals.

sleek

Artfully planned to deliver a short, sharp sluice or a luxurious, deep wallow, today's cutting-edge bathrooms are temples of efficiency and calm, the perfect place for pampering. Equipped with gleaming hard surfaces, from limestone to glass, state-of-the-art fittings, from power showers to built-in music, and realized in slick, contemporary designs, they have become the new status symbols in our homes.

Bathrooms have undergone something of a design revolution in the last decade. Never have they looked quite so contemporary, nor been such a barometer of changing fashions. Influenced in part by the cool modern bathrooms we saw in designer hotels, and by our ongoing love affair with spas and gyms, the bathroom has become a new focus at home. Once just a place to wash and go, now it is viewed as a valuable new zone to chill out in, as well as a place to make a design statement.

Streamlined hard surfaces form the core of the Sleek bathroom. You are aiming for a look that covers the horizontal and vertical planes of the room with one cohesive finish, so it's vital to choose a surface that works practically as well as looking good. Versatile examples include limestone, marble, slate and tiny mosaic tiles. Stone is expensive to use in large quantities, so if your budget is tight consider a stone floor and a run of worktop, with plain painted walls. Consciously use accent surfaces to add sparkle, such as hotel-style wall-to-wall mirrors, or stainless-steel storage units.

As for bath panels and splashbacks, these need to blend seamlessly with adjacent surfaces. Options for baths include stone slabs, cast concrete, or backlit sandblasted

KEY FEATURES

▌ PRACTICAL AND SLEEK-LOOKING SURFACES SUCH AS LIMESTONE, MARBLE, SLATE OR CONCRETE, USED LIBERALLY FOR WALLS, FLOORS AND A BATH SURROUND.

▌ CLEAR OR SANDBLASTED GLASS, STAINLESS STEEL OR GLASS BRICKS ADD TRANSLUCENCY AND SPARKLE.

▌ A PALE, NEUTRAL COLOUR PALETTE, TO DRESS UP WITH WHITE OR MUTED TOWELS.

▌ ULTRA-MODERN TAP SHAPES, WALL-MOUNTED FOR A STREAMLINED FINISH.

▌ BOWL-STYLE OR RECTANGULAR SHALLOW SINKS, WITH BUILT-IN STORAGE.

▌ CAPACIOUS BATHS, OR WET-ROOM-STYLE POWER SHOWERS SET THE RIGHT TONE.

OPPOSITE, BOTH PICTURES: **Stick to two or three key surfaces for a pure look: this bathroom has been entirely kitted out with limestone, glass bricks and mirrors, with a glass sink.**

TOP LEFT: **Mix practicality with style. Countertop basins should be fitted with a steel rail for towels.**

TOP CENTRE: **For a more elegant take on Sleek, include an upholstered stool or an armchair, so that there's somewhere relaxing to sit.**

TOP RIGHT: **Wall-hang sanitary ware where possible, for a space-saving and sleek look.**

ABOVE LEFT: **Big ceramic tiles look out of place in modern bathrooms, but mosaic tiles are the exception, because they meld into a unified, textured surface.**

ABOVE CENTRE AND RIGHT: **Many bathrooms suffer from limited natural light, so sandblasted glass fittings, from basins to shower doors, can be an excellent light-reflecting choice.**

glass, while more stone, glass tiles or stainless steel makes for a sleek splashback.

Modern sanitary ware is pared down. Bowl and rectangular sink styles are now de rigueur, either wall-mounted or sitting casually on a run of worktop. In a big bathroom, double sinks look particularly luxurious. We've come a long way from white ceramic basins. Now there's a huge choice, from smooth or rough stone to sandblasted glass or ultra-slick stainless steel. The up side is that these sinks look fantastically glamorous. The flip side is that they are a nightmare to keep clean.

Team them – and the bath – with wall-mounted modern spout-style taps.

Make a conscious decision to kit out the bathroom with either a big luxurious bath or a fabulous shower, rather than trying to combine a shower over the bath (it doesn't look very sleek). If space is tight, consider a wet-room shower, with a ceiling-mounted rose and drain in the floor. In a big bathroom, team a separate shower with the bath, imaginatively screened with a sandblasted glass door, a glass brick partition, or a curved and mosaic-tiled wall.

TOP LEFT: **Make a dramatic feature of the bath by choosing a generous size, and placing it in a prominent position. Provided the surround is elegant and sleek, the bath inside can be a bargain buy.**
TOP RIGHT AND ABOVE: **Check that trendy basins are deep enough for a decent wash, and that there is a sufficiently broad surround for storing soaps and jars.**
ABOVE LEFT AND RIGHT: **Plain, pared-down surfaces throw attention onto bathroom fittings, so pick dramatic showerheads and spout taps. Some styles require a pump to up the water pressure.**
OPPOSITE ABOVE RIGHT: **Build in as many fittings as you can, from a wall-mounted shaving mirror to ceiling music speakers.**
OPPOSITE BELOW LEFT: **If a great shower is a priority, consider an extra-large custom-made shower tray and glass door, teamed with sparkling chrome fittings.**
OPPOSITE BELOW RIGHT: **In a big bathroom, add storage underneath the vanity worktop, so that all paraphernalia is cleared away.**

LUXURY AND GLAMOUR STYLE STUDY

Flooded with natural light, and enhanced by sophisticated surfaces from sandblasted glass to marble, this is a Sleek bathroom par excellence. With taps and controls pared down to the minimum, floor-to-ceiling windows, and glamorous mirror panels, it has the dramatic impact of a hotel en suite, but in the comfort of a home.

Here is an en suite Sleek bathroom detailed to work with modern architecture. Its greatest asset is a fabulous amount of natural light, flooding in from two floor-to-ceiling windows. But the space is generously proportioned, too. Consequently fittings are luxurious: twin basins are arranged far apart on a free-standing plinth, and there's a shower enclosure fitted with a marble bench.

While the expanses of stone look streamlined and cool, the veined marble adds bite to the scheme, as does the texture on the frosted-glass bowls. The organic mood of both ties in nicely with the vegetation spied in the garden beyond. With its undulating curves, the low armchair is also in keeping with the organic theme, yet is uncompromisingly modern, to match the bathroom fittings. The warm purple adds a flash of contrast to the cool, neutral palette.

Finishing touches have been planned with glamour in mind. Walls are panelled with floor-to-ceiling looking glass, and there are make-up and shaving mirrors close to the natural light. Tall heated towel rails and sophisticated lighting are also key. Yet, most of all, this Sleek bathroom exudes the sense of a private, luxurious space. With no blinds at the windows, no door on the shower, and one step from the bedroom, it is the ultimate grooming zone.

OPPOSITE LEFT: **The master bedroom and en suite bathroom look very cohesive, so there is no need for a door between the rooms. The same pale neutral colour scheme has been used throughout, and a stone floor seamlessly links the two together. Underfloor heating warms the stone underfoot.**

OPPOSITE RIGHT: **Luxurious marble has been used for the shower. The minimalist designer controls do not detract from the natural veined beauty of the stone.**

ABOVE: **The clever mix of floor-to-ceiling windows, with matching mirror panels, creates a trompe l'oeil effect, making the space seem bigger than it already is.**

ABOVE RIGHT: **To look at its best, this bathroom must be kept rigorously tidy; capacious storage elsewhere holds bathroom essentials.**

RIGHT: **The twin circular basins realized in translucent frosted glass, have been elevated to a decorative accessory, as well as practical necessity.**

WHY IT WORKS ORGANICALLY SHAPED BOWL BASINS AND CHAIR ▮ LUXURIOUS MARBLE AND LIMESTONE FINISHES ▮ ROOMY EN SUITE LAYOUT ▮ LIGHT-ENHANCING WINDOWS AND MIRRORS

KEY FEATURES

■ LOOK FOR SANITARY WARE THAT OFFERS A MODERN TAKE ON TRADITIONAL SHAPES, OR BLEND A ROLL-TOP BATH WITH MODERN TAPS.

■ KEEP TO A CRISP, FRESH COLOUR PALETTE WITH WHITE AT ITS CORE, ACCENTED WITH WARM WOODS, COOL STONE OR A SPLASH OF PASTELS.

■ STORAGE SHOULD BE BUILT IN OR WALL-MOUNTED, FOR A STREAMLINED FINISH, BUT DESIGNED WITH A FREE-STANDING LOOK IN MIND.

■ WALLS MAY BE PLAIN-PAINTED, PANELLED WITH TONGUE-AND-GROOVE, OR TILED FLOOR TO CEILING FOR A PRACTICAL YET COHESIVE FINISH.

■ STICK TO HARD FLOORS, FOR PRACTICALITY, BUT CHOOSE SATISFYING TEXTURES SUCH AS WOOD BOARDS, LINOLEUM, RUBBER OR LIMESTONE.

mellow modern

Expertly blending the traditional curves of the classic bathroom with today's sleek, smooth surfaces, the Mellow Modern version offers the best of both worlds. Sanitary ware is pristine and white, but textures are comforting and warming, ranging from matt ceramic tiles to wood veneers. The look is relaxed and unfitted, perfect for a home blessed with big windows and sunlight.

For those who see the bathroom as a room to retreat to, rather than a splash and dash washroom, this is the style to follow. While finishes are ultra-practical (it's a great look for a family bathroom), the decorative accent is on comfort and tranquillity. Here is a room to furnish with fluffy towels, bath potions and a transistor radio perched on a stool.

Begin with the sanitary ware. The contours are all-important, as you want fittings that are softly rounded, but without any fussy Victorian detailing or pedestals. Wall-mounted basins and toilets save floor space and look modern. Either team with a

plain bath, in a surround to match the finish on the wall, or – even better – a curvaceous roll-top bath. The roll-top is a fail-safe design choice. Painted all white, with trendy taps and modern block legs, it can look fabulously contemporary. In black, with traditional fittings, it is elegantly classic.

Do pay attention to storage, as this is a look that relies on clean, uncluttered surfaces. For the most streamlined solution, choose a vanity unit style to go beneath the basin, and kit it out with cupboards, drawers or open shelves. Alternatively, choose a wall-mounted or floor-standing stainless-

OPPOSITE ABOVE LEFT: **It's fun to team modern sanitary ware with the more graceful outlines of classic chrome fittings. This shower has the best of both worlds, as there is a generous traditional showerhead, combined with a wall-mounted modern spray.**

OPPOSITE ABOVE RIGHT: **Bespoke storage means there is a place for everything: sometimes, a series of tiny drawers is more useful than one big cupboard.**

OPPOSITE BELOW: **Provided sanitary ware is streamlined, a relaxed look can be achieved by accessorizing a bathroom much as you would a sitting room. The big, wood-framed mirror here is both elegant and practical.**

ABOVE LEFT: **A wall tiled with tiny mosaics looks decorative and has more textural interest than plain ceramic tiles. Choose tiles in three or four complementary shades, to mimic the tones of natural stone.**

ABOVE CENTRE AND RIGHT: **In a small bathroom it's vital to keep fittings very streamlined, but you can still soften the look by adding a circular mirror and spout taps.**

steel or glass-fronted cabinet. Use baskets or glass jars to organize smaller bathroom essentials on shelves, to maintain the pared-down look.

Choose surfaces to promote a warm, cosy ambience. You can still include practical stone, but restrict it to floors and as a solid, chunky surface for basins. The same goes for stainless steel or sandblasted glass: use it sparingly for splashbacks or as a bath surround. The best classic, streamlined surfaces are choices like painted tongue-and-groove, sparkly white metro-style ceramic tiles, or painted walls, teamed with wood-veneer storage units. For worktops or bath surrounds, laminate, mosaic tiles and concrete are also good options. Warm flooring choices are wood, from painted boards to parquet, linoleum, or even cork.

Stick faithfully to a clear, fresh palette, to make your bathroom an energizing room by day. If there is good natural light, then emphasize it with a crisp scheme of white-painted walls and white sanitary ware. If the room is dark, stick to mellow woods or muted stone finishes, teamed with white. Use mirrors to bounce light around, teamed with white towels, and add flickering candles at night.

OPPOSITE: **If space permits, a central bath sets a chilled-out mood, especially if placed at a rakish angle.**

TOP LEFT: **Play up the comfort angle by including an armchair and – if there's room – a dressing table, elevating a plain bathroom to the status of dressing room.**

TOP CENTRE: **Teamed with a black rubber floor and neutral ceramic tiles, even period bathroom fittings can look modern.**

TOP RIGHT: **For the most relaxing soak, the roll-top bath should be fitted with central taps, or a plain spout at one end, so there's somewhere comfortable for one (or two) people to lie.**

ABOVE LEFT: **Provided there isn't too much splashing, wood makes a warm and smart floor in the bathroom. Elevate the bath on a raised platform for a truly indulgent mood.**

ABOVE RIGHT: **Classic, yet always fresh, tongue-and-groove can be used on walls, bath surround and on cupboards. Give it a new look by laying boards horizontally.**

WHY IT WORKS NEAT, SHALLOW STORAGE ■ SPARKLING WHITE COLOUR SCHEME ■ LIGHT-REFLECTIVE STAINLESS-STEEL FITTINGS ■ ROUNDED CONTOURS ■ COHESIVE TILED SURFACES

ECONOMY OF SCALE STYLE STUDY

Fresh, cool and very pretty, this beautifully conceived bathroom makes the most of its compact surroundings. Clever space planning is key. This isn't a big room, yet the generous contours of the bath and its central position on the wall make the space seem much larger. A luxurious white-on-white colour scheme pushes back the walls and enhances natural sunlight.

OPPOSITE: **With a little forward planning, it was possible to incorporate niche wall storage, providing a streamlined solution for bath oils and soaps.**
TOP: **Basin-mounted taps, styled with a modern spout, are a good solution if it isn't possible to plumb in wall-mounted fixtures.**
ABOVE LEFT: **Panelling one section of wall with mirror, above the basin, also makes the room seem bigger. The chunky hardwood worktop to either side of the basin looks sophisticated and adds visual bite to the all-white scheme.**
ABOVE RIGHT: **Open shelves look contemporary and slick finished off with broad shelf trims and a decorative selection of containers.**

Small, but perfectly formed, this elegant bathroom has been planned for maximum comfort. The first design choice was to pick a generous bath to set the luxurious tone, regardless of a tight floor plan. The big bath tricks the eye into thinking the rest of the room is spacious and light. In reality, those inches have been 'borrowed' from elsewhere. The rectangular basin is scaled down to compensate, and storage is neatly fitted into an alcove and a niche above the bath, using no precious floor space.

Though it looks enviably frivolous, the pure white colour scheme is immensely practical. Everything can be wiped down, and there are no textiles likely to mark. Even the towels are sensible soft grey. As storage is all on view on open shelves, bathtime treats have been chosen for their plain glass containers, or teamed with white ceramic pots.

Clever use of scale in the tiling tricks the eye. Although the matt ceramic tiles are square and white throughout, they are medium scale at floor level, then tiny mosaics on the vertical planes. This makes the floor area look bigger. Sensibly, floor tiles are grouted in black, so the floor won't look grubby over time. The bath surround and splashback, however, are finished in white, making a seamless transition from tiled surface to plain painted wall.

elegant modern

Because it is all about creating spaces that function effortlessly, look beautiful and feel harmonious, this style is absolutely ideal for a bathroom. Picture your ideal hotel bathroom and you have probably got the idea: sumptuous fittings, well-planned storage space, good lighting and an overall style that is neither bland nor jarring, just sophisticated and serene.

In an Elegant Modern bathroom, planning is vital: there can be no half measures. Sanitary ware, for example, may be as simple as you like, but should be generous in size and sophisticated in design. This could be anything from an Edwardian roll-top bath to a 21st-century spa bath, but free of unnecessarily ornate or fussy details. Coloured or plastic suites are banned, too – they just don't have the right classic feel. Instead, concentrate on beautiful, luxury materials such as limestone, marble, wood, ceramic, glass and chrome, all as tough and durable as they are attractive. Though classic, they can be used in a simple, modern way.

If you have space, install a pair of basins, for ease of use when you and your partner are rushing to get ready. Mirrors should be as large as possible, and storage designed to take everything but the bare essentials – there is nothing less elegant than a display of old flannels, spare toilet rolls and bottles of cleaning fluids. Finally, install lighting that highlights the mirrors, basin and bath (if you like to read in the bath, the latter is essential), but which can be dimmed when a cosy atmosphere is required.

OPPOSITE ABOVE LEFT: **A classic pedestal basin has been combined with simple, modern fittings, including a pair of built-in, vertical cupboards that have been screened with frosted glass.**
OPPOSITE ABOVE RIGHT: **There's a fabulous sense of space here, thanks to the expanse of floor area, in beautiful stone, that has been left clear. The sunken bath adds to the feeling of opulence.**
OPPOSITE BELOW, FROM LEFT TO RIGHT: **Installing a pair of basins is** wonderfully indulgent, but also practical in a busy bathroom. Storage can be built around and under a basin for maximum efficiency; this dark-wood unit stands on slender legs and thus increases the perception of space. Slim chrome drawer pulls are a desirable modern detail.
BELOW: **Marble, wood and ceramic may be traditional materials, but with a sophisticated, Elegant Modern treatment such as this they can be brought right up to date.**

KEY FEATURES

▪ GENEROUSLY SIZED SANITARY WARE IN UNFUSSY SHAPES. AVOID ANYTHING THAT IS PLASTIC OR HAS ORNATE DETAILING. STICK TO WHITE – IT IS SOPHISTICATED AND WILL WORK WITH ANY SCHEME.

▪ CLASSIC MATERIALS, SUCH AS WOOD, STONE, CERAMIC, GLASS AND CHROME, USED IN A PLAIN AND CONTEMPORARY WAY. THINK OF WALLS COVERED IN THIN PANELS OF MARBLE OR BEAUTIFULLY GRAINED WOOD.

▪ EXCELLENT STORAGE, FITTED UNDERNEATH OR AROUND BASINS OR BUILT INTO UNUSED CORNERS. FREE-STANDING STORAGE SHOULD BE CO-ORDINATED WITH THE ROOM.

▪ LARGE MIRRORS, WALL TO WALL IF APPROPRIATE.

▪ A FLEXIBLE LIGHTING SCHEME THAT ADAPTS TO THE WAY YOU USE THE ROOM.

TAKE THE FLOOR STYLE STUDY

The sophisticated simplicity of this style is harder to achieve than it may appear, but in this bathroom the owners have succeeded in creating a space that works efficiently and looks beautiful. Although not a huge room, it has a sense of flowing space, and a gracious harmony that will never go out of fashion.

The starting point for this scheme is a sumptuous floor, luxurious wood tiles with diamond insets, which sets the tone for the entire room. Its two colours are echoed in the dark-painted bath and the paler, matt walls, a monochrome palette that, in its sense of restraint and order, is well suited to the Elegant Modern style.

All the materials here are high quality but used with ultra-simplicity, from glass to chrome to ceramic, while the fittings combine the traditional (a roll-top, claw-foot bath and classic basin taps) with the modern (a wall-hung WC, minimal glass-and-chrome shower, pierced-metal bin and a pair of inset basins) with panache. This is because they are all as simple in design as they could be, with no fussy or ornate detailing, just timelessly attractive features that will never jar the eye. The window treatment, too, is similarly straightforward, a louvred blind that allows privacy but filters light gently. Finally, the storage has been planned for function and appearance, so that everything has a place: matching towels on wooden shelves, toiletries on glass shelves, and less attractive bits and pieces hidden out of sight.

WHY IT WORKS FABULOUS FLOORING ▊ MODERN FEATURES COMBINED WITH CLASSIC PIECES ▊ QUALITY MATERIALS ▊ WELL-PLANNED STORAGE ▊ A UNIFIED COLOUR PALETTE

OPPOSITE ABOVE: **Glass shelves such as these look beautiful, but must be cleaned regularly and kept tidy to maintain the effect.**

OPPOSITE BELOW: **The antique bath dominates the room, a timeless classic that simply enhances its more modern surroundings.**

ABOVE LEFT: **These taps are classic in design, but not overtly 'period', so fit in well with other timeless fittings, even more modern ones.**

CENTRE LEFT: **Double basins make getting ready easier. The large mirrors are not only functional, but increase the sense of space.**

BELOW LEFT: **The elegant, polished wood flooring sets the tone for the whole room.**

ABOVE: **What could be more understated than this barely-there shower unit? Next to it, a set of floor-to-ceiling fitted shelves holds piles of neatly folded spare towels.**

natural

Not everyone wants a bathroom to relax in. For active people, the ideal bathroom offers a slick environment in which to wash, brush up and move on. But it should look beautiful and be a pleasure to use, too. The Natural bathroom offers an ideal compromise. Here are a sophisticated muted palette and classic, enduring finishes, teamed with ultra-efficient fittings and a city-slicker mood.

By necessity, the Natural bathroom looks almost as streamlined as its big sister, the Sleek bathroom. The rougher textures that look so good in Natural-style kitchens or living rooms just aren't an option here. You don't want reclaimed boards under bare feet, and a textural plastered wall needs cocooning fabrics to temper the roughness.

So, instead, use natural, honest surfaces as the decorative starting point, and seek alternatives to white sanitary ware. There are suppliers who will custom-make a stone basin, 'carved' out of a run of worktop, or check out reclamation yards for stone sinks. Think twice about stone baths, which require a strengthened bathroom floor and may be chilly. A Japanese wood soaking tub looks modern, and is a joy to bathe in.

Design the bathroom with uninterrupted stretches of timber, stone or wood panelling, so that the eye is drawn straight to the natural patterns of the surface itself. If storage is built in, use a wood to match the floor for a cohesive finish. If walls are clad in stone, design 'niche' shelving, to give the impression of hand-carved storage. Paint any remaining walls in soft, dull shades from mushroom to parchment, to blend in subtly with the natural surfaces.

KEY FEATURES

■ PICK TIMBER AND STONE FOR MAJOR SURFACES, WITH RICH GRAINS OR VEINING.

■ STAINLESS STEEL MAKES SMART DETAILING FOR HANDLES, TOWEL RAILS AND TAPS.

■ INVEST IN BASINS OR EVEN A BATH CARVED FROM STONE, OR CLAD AN ENTIRE SMALL ROOM WITH STONE FOR AN ORGANICALLY INSPIRED WET-ROOM SHOWER.

■ FLOORING SHOULD BE HARD, IN NATURAL TEXTURES: LIMESTONE, SANDSTONE, WOOD, DECKING, CONCRETE AND MARBLE ARE THE BEST CHOICES.

■ COMBINE TACTILE SURFACES: SMOOTH AND ROUGH, GLOSSY AND MATT.

■ MIRRORED SURFACES, FROM CUPBOARD DOORS TO PANELS, LIFT MUTED TONES.

OPPOSITE LEFT AND RIGHT: **Choose natural flooring with an eye not just for colour and pattern, but for practical texture. Marble and granite are very slippery when wet, whereas limestone or slate offer more reliable grip. Narrow- or broad-planked decking is a good choice for a wet-room shower.**

TOP AND ABOVE LEFT: **There is a satisfying visual purity to a carved stone basin, fed by a single spout tap. Honed stone looks very sleek, whereas a rough concrete sink suits a more urban setting.**

TOP AND ABOVE CENTRE: **Plan streamlined storage with wood-veneer doors and drawer fronts, to blend in with the muted colour palette. Keep handles simple, or dispense with them altogether.**

TOP AND ABOVE RIGHT: **Niche shelving or mirrors break up vast expanses of stone surfaces.**

DAYLIGHT SAVING STYLE STUDY

Fabulously indulgent, this masculine bathroom and dressing room is the ultimate in Natural good looks. With walls, floor, bath, basin and even the loo encased in glossy hardwood panelling, the room itself seems to be hewn out of a single piece of timber. This is a room to be enjoyed in the sombre half-light, all the better to play up its muted, deep tones.

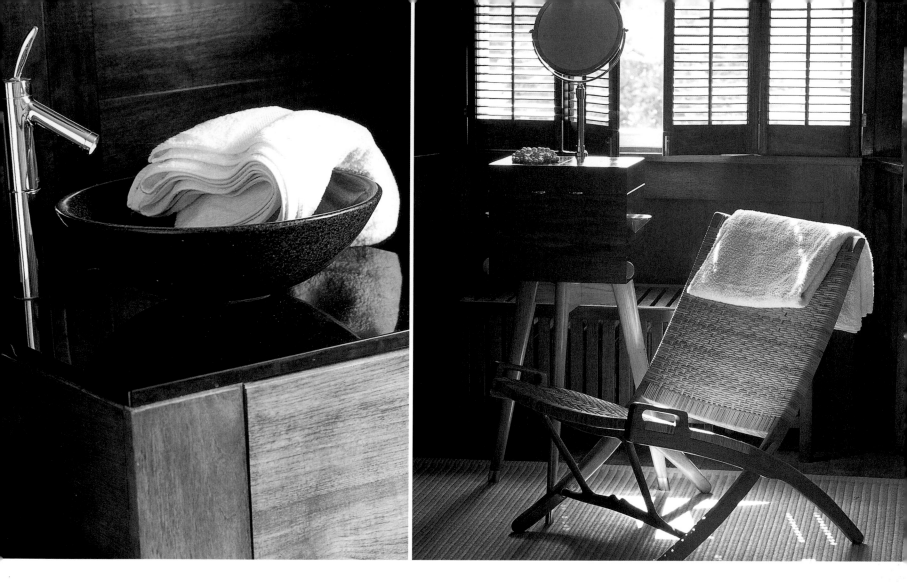

This room is at the sophisticated end of Natural style, luxuriating in dark timber. It derives much of its impact from the play of light and shadow. With wood panelling every surface, it is moody and grown-up. Horizontal surfaces are black granite, as is the stone circular basin. The windows are fitted with timber American-style shutters, which control sunlight, casting dramatic rays to highlight the dark wood and stone.

So that utilitarian details don't detract from the streamlined good looks, panelling conceals built-in cupboards and the radiator. No decorative detail has been left to chance.

The vertical lines on cupboard doors are subtly echoed in the rib of the sisal rug and slats of the blinds, adding contrast to the smooth timbers on walls and floor.

The bathroom looks timelessly classic because it mixes state-of-the-art details such as minimalist taps with original free-standing pieces. A low 20th-century classic chair is teamed with a bespoke dressing stand, bringing modern and traditional styles together. Added to that, accessories are minimal but spot on. The organically shaped soap dish draws on the Natural theme, yet adds a touch of frivolity as well.

OPPOSITE MAIN PICTURE: **This is clearly an expensive treatment, yet the panelling and granite have been used subtly with the minimum of extra detailing. The effect is one of quiet elegance, rather than flashy excess. A utilitarian white loo would have been quite out of place in this bathroom. It therefore made sense to panel it completely: a discreet chrome flush is the only clue to its existence.**
OPPOSITE ABOVE: **The white of the bath, enclosed within its timber panelling, is accented with a few carefully chosen accessories, from the soapstone decorative dishes to fluffy white towels.**
ABOVE LEFT: **Pared down to simple shapes and shiny pleasing textures, the basics for washing become as much a decorative joy as a practical necessity.**
ABOVE RIGHT: **To promote good ambience and a relaxing mood, the bath has been set low against the wall, and the bathroom chair is gently low-slung to match.**

WHY IT WORKS RICHLY TONED WOOD PANELLING ■ BUILT-IN STORAGE ■ GLOSSY BLACK GRANITE ■ ELEGANT FREE-STANDING FURNITURE ■ LIGHT-CONTROLLING WOODEN BLINDS

scandinavian

While clean-lined functionalism is common to all Scandinavian-style bathrooms, that does not mean this room must be a temple to perfection. Warmth and personality are vital, too, and fuss-free practicality is combined with natural materials, good-looking fittings and a sense of understated comfort that makes the room a blissful space in which to indulge yourself.

BELOW: **Wet rooms are wonderfully hedonistic, with plenty of space and just the right pared-down style. This one has abandoned curtains or blinds in favour of a simpler solution – frosted glass.**
OPPOSITE ABOVE LEFT: **What could be more Scandinavian than a sauna? If you have room in your house, consult an expert first for installation advice.**
OPPOSITE ABOVE RIGHT: **Mosaic tiles create a typically graphic pattern here. With such a strong focal**

point, everything else in the room has been kept utterly plain.
OPPOSITE BELOW LEFT: **A beautifully shaped bath and a timber-clad wall are all that is required to make this bathroom look and feel appropriately inviting.**
OPPOSITE BELOW CENTRE: **With its pair of basins, deep wooden shelf and wall-to-wall mirror, this room blends efficiency with luxury.**
OPPOSITE BELOW RIGHT: **Fittings like showerheads can be gorgeous in themselves, as well as functional.**

Space is important in the Scandinavian bathroom – not necessarily the fact that you have a huge space, but more a sense that it is well planned and well used. There are no wasted opportunities for building in extra storage or adding an extra basin, and equally no cramped areas where you jab your elbows on the walls when you try to dry yourself. This is where wall-hung fittings come into their own, as not only do they have the right streamlined, contemporary look, but they make the floor space seem more expansive. You may also want to consider forgoing a bath in favour of a really big, walk-in shower, or sacrificing a shower so you can have a large and luxurious bath.

White ceramic fittings have the right look for this style, though other materials such as glass or metal can work in a more modern context. Keep the outlines smooth and simple, though, and avoid fussy, fake period styles with decorative detailing. Wood, the material that dominates the Scandinavian home, should be used plentifully: on the floor, on the walls, around the bath, as shelving and as cupboard fronts. We're talking pale wood rather than heavy, dark timber, as it is important to avoid making the

KEY FEATURES

▪ A WELL-PLANNED SPACE IN WHICH FUNCTION AND AESTHETICS WORK TOGETHER.

▪ ELEGANTLY SHAPED AND PROPORTIONED FITTINGS, USUALLY IN WHITE CERAMIC, THOUGH GLASS AND METAL WOULD SUIT A MORE MODERN LOOK.

▪ BLOND WOOD USED GENEROUSLY, FOR FLOORS, WALLS, BATH SURROUNDS, SHELVES AND CUPBOARDS.

▪ CLEVER WINDOW TREATMENTS THAT MAXIMIZE LIGHT.

▪ ELEGANT ACCESSORIES THAT CO-ORDINATE WITH THE LOOK, IN PARED-DOWN SHAPES. PICK WOOD, SPONGE, BRISTLE, CERAMIC, METAL AND GLASS.

▪ WHITE CERAMIC TILES ARE SUITABLY SUBTLE, WHILE MOSAIC ADDS INTEREST. KEEP MOSAIC LOW-KEY, IN JUST ONE COLOUR OR A VERY SIMPLE PATTERN.

room feel closed in and claustrophobic. On that note, consider window treatments carefully. Do you really need them, or can you go without? If you do, try to minimize them so that they don't obscure any light when drawn: roller and Roman blinds are ideal, and for certain situations you can find blinds that have holes pierced at regular intervals, that pull up from the bottom rather than downwards, or that are made so that the lower portion is solid while the upper part is sheer, to allow as much light in as possible. Use mirrors, too, to enhance both space and light – wall-to-wall mirroring looks sleek and chic.

If you do not wish to cover the whole expanse of walls with wood, white ceramic tiles are an inexpensive option, while mosaic makes for a still subtle, but more decorative, effect. Choose accessories carefully. Elegance and understatement are what you should keep in mind: avoid plastic (too wacky) and wicker (too rustic), and think of large waffle-textured towels, wood and bristle brushes, ceramic or glass dispensers, natural sponges, loofahs and the like. Put it all together and you have a room where efficiency and hedonism combine in one practical, beautiful and comfortable space.

TOP LEFT: **A whirlpool or hydromassage bath is the last word in luxury. Here, it has been encased in pale wood for a suitably Scandinavian look.**

ABOVE LEFT: **By wall-hanging fixtures you appear to increase the amount of floor area. In this case, the cistern has been concealed, too, adding to the sense of free-flowing, pared-down space.**

ABOVE: **Using mosaic tiles adds interest, but it is best to stick to one colour and combine them with unfussy fittings and accessories.**

21ST-CENTURY SAUNA STYLE STUDY

All the characteristics of traditional Scandinavian style can be seen in this pared-down bathroom, yet it has been brought right into the 21st century with a clever use of good-looking materials and simple fittings.

TOP: **As is common in Finland, this bathroom has its own sauna. Here the clean-lined aesthetic continues; the room is simple as could be.**
ABOVE: **Glass vases bring a decorative element to this plain room, their natural colours and swirling patterns enhancing rather than detracting from its style.**
ABOVE RIGHT: **The room has a bath clad in wenge wood, marble-tiled walls, a glass door and window left bare to let in maximum light.**

This modern bathroom in Finland blends the best of old and new Scandinavian styles. In terms of materials and aesthetic it is traditional: it uses a generous amount of solid wood, teamed with touches of ceramic and glass. Colours are typically subtle, in the natural/neutral range of taupes, stones and deeper browns. And there is, as always, plenty of attention paid to the Scandinavian concerns of space, light and good-looking practicality. Yet this place is contemporary, too, with wenge used to clad the bath rather than blond wood, a frosted-glass screen in place of a door and oversized marble tiles as cladding on the walls. Straightforward though it may look, the detailing is all-important, and the result is a functional simplicity that is not cold or stark but instead elegantly useful, and a warmth and subtle individuality that comes from the room's well-designed, sleek and tactile materials.

WHY IT WORKS BATH CLAD IN CHIC WENGE ■ ULTRA-SIMPLE TAP ■ NEUTRAL WALL TILES

traditional country

This style of bathroom needs a generous space to work well, because the whole point is that it should be furnished like any other room in a Traditional Country home. Think plenty of prints or paintings on the walls, mats on natural floors, plus antique pieces which must include chairs, tables and, if possible, a comfy sofa or armchair.

Because the reality of the countryside is often cold, windy, muddy and dispiriting, Traditional Country style is all about warmth, comfort and relaxation – in the bathroom as much as any other room. This bathroom should be designed so that it encourages you to linger in its generous, old iron bathtub in plenty of hot water and scented steam. In the country, a hot bath is often the quickest way of warming up after a brisk winter walk or summer drenching, so the room should be welcoming, which means it needs comfortable furniture, soft linen and cotton towels and bathmats plus lots going on on the walls. Use oil paintings, old plates, quirky objects such as birdcages or tools, black-and-white prints – anything that will not be damaged by steam. Such bathrooms also give themselves to panelling, whether to cover entire walls or simply as far as a dado rail. Tongued and grooved planks are excellent and can be extended to cover the sides of a less attractive bath. Floors should also be natural, with wonky tiles or bricks or (rather more friendly) smoothed or painted wood planks. A combination of warm neutrals along with plain white – to match your fluffy white towels – works well here.

KEY FEATURES

▪ OLD-FASHIONED IRON TUB BATH WITH CLAW FEET AND ROLLED RIM PLUS LARGE, OLD BASIN AND LAVATORY WITH OVERHEAD CISTERN.

▪ NATURAL FLOOR – TILES, SANDED OR PAINTED WOOD, BRICKS SOFTENED BY OLD RUGS. TILES, WHICH CAN BE PATTERNED, USED FOR SPLASHBACKS TO BATH AND BASIN.

▪ ANTIQUE FURNITURE SUCH AS CANED CHAIRS, OLD TREADLE SEWING MACHINES AS TABLES, PAINTED WHATNOTS AND LOOSE-COVERED EASY CHAIRS.

▪ LOTS OF PICTURES, VICTORIAN PLATES, FOUND OBJECTS AND QUIRKY ANTIQUES HUNG ON THE WALLS TO MAKE A COSY ROOM. ANTIQUE LINENS OR TATTED OR EMBROIDERED HAND TOWELS FOR USE OR DISPLAY.

OPPOSITE LEFT: **The essence of country style, this bathroom has a splendid floor and chunky furniture, with the neat touch of a female nude painting.**

OPPOSITE RIGHT: **The room is a study of neutral, but warmly welcoming, colours. The bath and basin are picked out with black undercarriages.**

THIS PAGE TOP ROW: **The style needs some busy-ness, whether softly striped towels, patterned tiles or walls covered with plates and pictures.**

THIS PAGE BOTTOM ROW: **Wherever possible, antique shapes should be used for baths and basins, furniture or taps. Washed-out pink walls, allied with pink tinted linen, are both warm and welcoming.**

Where an ornate roll-top bath is either too expensive or too big, the Traditional Country effect can be achieved with the no-frills iron bath that superseded it. This can be boxed in with panelled wood, tongued and grooved for the most rural effect. Large washbasins can either be left with their bases and shelves exposed – nothing wrong here with a few painted pipes – or surrounded with their own concealing curtains. With a pair of washbasins, a single curtain will relieve the bulk, but the fabric should be a simple cotton with no more than a stripe or gingham check. Do not,

however, economize on the taps. Old-fashioned brass ones for both bath and basins will make all the difference. They can be found in architectural salvage yards. The rest of the decor is best subordinated to the antiques – whether plumbing equipment or furniture – on display. The ideal is a series of warm, soft creams, from the palest off-white to a Cornish clotted, alleviated by gold-framed pictures to match the taps. Old mirrors are also much more interesting than unframed ones, and it's a neat idea to pick a giant-sized mirror if you are trying to amalgamate a pair of basins.

ABOVE LEFT: **The bulk of a pair of washbasins has been cleverly reduced by curtaining the two undercarriages with a single, softly checked gingham fabric and by effectively making a single unit with the very large mirror placed above both. The mosaic tiles pick up the colours and pattern of the fabric.**
BELOW LEFT: **Where it's not practical to use a roll-top bath, the old-fashioned look is still possible with clever notions such as this chest of drawers at the bath's end.**
ABOVE: **Even if they are not used, pretty Victorian towels are an excellent addition, along with floral curtains and feminine washbags.**

ABOVE: **Objects both decorative and practical are treated equally as decoration in this busy bathroom corner – the toilet-roll holder and antique towels behind the bidet, for example. Glass shelves, with their own curly supports, are added to fit in even more clutter.**

RIGHT: **Brass is the dominant metal, from the splendid set of taps and showerhead, to the plug, soap holder and towel rail. This is picked up in the gilded picture frames, yet the scheme is basically neutral.**

A TOUCH OF BRASS STYLE STUDY

Devotees of this style are inveterate rummagers in antique markets and stalls. The results appear even in bathrooms, which have walls hung with objects and ornate pieces of furniture as tops for yet more antique finds.

While this old-fashioned bathroom seems to be a riot of pattern, ornament, flounces and frills, its basis is actually a series of neutrals. The walls are a warm cream shade, which is given a bit of strength by the addition of tongued and grooved planking up to dado height. This is painted in an earthy eau-de-Nil and effectively holds the disparate elements together. It also serves as a darkish background for the fine roll-top bath, whose ornate feet are picked out in a darker shade of its colour, and for the old-fashioned lavatory with its high-level cistern. The pictures and plates are in soft colours which match, some with toning eau-de-Nil mounts. Brass is the dominant metal, for taps, towel rail, lamp and curly-based table. Much use is made of old hand towels with hand embroidery and tassels – these can be easily picked up for a couple of pounds in flea markets and are still usable.

WHY IT WORKS CONTROLLED COLOURS ■ OLD-FASHIONED EQUIPMENT ■ APPLIED CLUTTER

modern country

Though this style is perfectly fine in urban spaces as much as rural ones, it is similar to Traditional Country in that you need space to get the best effect. This bathroom should ideally be the size of a small bedroom, and feel like a proper room with windows or skylights, but in a small room or large, it is both stylish and easy to compose.

If you look at all these examples of Modern Country style in the bathroom, you will realize that there's not a scrap of pattern anywhere and, for that matter, precious little colour. The whole effect is achieved with monochrome black and white with the unobtrusive addition of natural wood on doors, beams and worktops, mirror and picture frames and with woven baskets which are exactly the same colour. The style, therefore, relies on shape and silhouette to make its mark. For example, the woven baskets tucked into built-in shelves and the dark, louvred screen through which light comes in slats are not much different from abstract paintings. The propped ladders, the anglepoise light above a mirror and the four black pots (complemented in shape by the nude's buttocks alongside) are the equivalent of modern sculptures. Even the easy chair, by being loose-covered in pure white and set against a planked white wall, is there for its shape. Natural light, from above, from deep windows or reflected in mirrors, is used to best effect. These rooms still give the impression of being furnished spaces – some with distressed old chairs and tables – but only just.

KEY FEATURES

▌ A COMBINATION OF OLD-FASHIONED ROLL-TOP IRON BATHS WITH ULTRA-MODERN WASHBASINS OR NEW OR RECONDITIONED BUTLER'S SINKS.

▌ A BLACK AND WHITE PALETTE FOR A MINIMALIST TAKE ON TRADITIONAL MATERIALS.

▌ CAREFULLY CHOSEN LIGHTING, PERHAPS IN UNUSUAL FORMS FOR A BATHROOM – CHANDELIERS, ANGLEPOISES, CANDELABRA.

▌ TREATING THE TUB AS FURNITURE BY PLACING IT IN THE CENTRE OF THE ROOM.

▌ DECORATIVE OBJECTS CHOSEN FOR SHAPE RATHER THAN PATTERN.

OPPOSITE LEFT: While the tub is old-fashioned, the wall-mounted taps are certainly state-of-the-art, as are the small porcelain hand basins. Chunky pots are contrasted with the spindly ladder and table.
OPPOSITE RIGHT: The butler's sink and woven baskets are traditional elements used in a modern way. The taps are wall-mounted, just below a plain mirror.
TOP LEFT: Though the bath and the chandelier in the ceiling's centre are both antique, their use, along with the quirky ladder, is intended ironically.
TOP CENTRE: The dark light and mirror frame contrast with white-on-white walls, linen and shower.
TOP RIGHT: A traditional bathroom – beamed, wood-floored and tubbed – becomes modern in white.
BOTTOM ROW, FROM LEFT TO RIGHT: A slatted screen, treated as an abstract, divides bed and bathroom. A gentler, top-lit, room has a cosy, white armchair by a white tub. White-painted tongue-and-groove is a key element of the Modern Country bathroom.

ABOVE LEFT: **The use of slubby linen fabric intended for tea towels characterizes the modern idea of changing uses. It also reproduces the pattern of the glazing bars.**

ABOVE RIGHT: **A distressed set of wirework lockers has been transformed into a useful storage space for towels, soap and even an old mirror. The glass chemist's bottles and florist's bucket with its cow parsley show how to rework old finds. Such pieces are plentiful in antique markets and car boot sales; the eye for them is rarer.**

OPPOSITE: **An undistinguished Victorian dresser base has been transformed into a generous worktop by adding a small, modern basin, which has wall-mounted taps. The greige paint is the perfect complement to the soft terracotta floor tiles.**

The gap between Traditional and Modern styles is not about the objects used but the way that they are treated. A traditionalist will use the object – ladder, sideboard, glass vase – in the way it was intended. The modernist likes to find variations on the theme, to search the shops and markets for old pieces which are beautiful in their shape and distress, and then to display them almost as works of art. But practical works of art. An example of this treatment is the use of a set of old wire lockers (presumably that was their original purpose), not only as useful storage for white towels,

pebble-shaped soaps and handy brushes, but also for the silhouette of the mesh. This is set beside a worn florist's bucket, picked up and made elegant. The modernist look takes undistinguished pieces of Victorian furniture and paints them to bring out an unsuspected charm. Even the dullest chairs, limed white, distressed and waxed, can be things of beauty, as are such natural *objets trouvés* as stems of white coral, sea-washed pebbles, loofahs and sponges. In this style of decor, each addition, each object, is carefully chosen and sited. Too many, and the whole look will vanish.

CRAFTED IN THE COUNTRY STYLE STUDY

Faced with a cottagey, beamed interior, this bathroom has been transformed by treating it in an Arts and Crafts manner, which means glorifying the beauty of wood and craftsmanship. The large, heavily panelled doors are essential here and are the only decoration. The plain but clearly well-designed dressing table beside the basin could have come from Ernest Gimson's workshop.

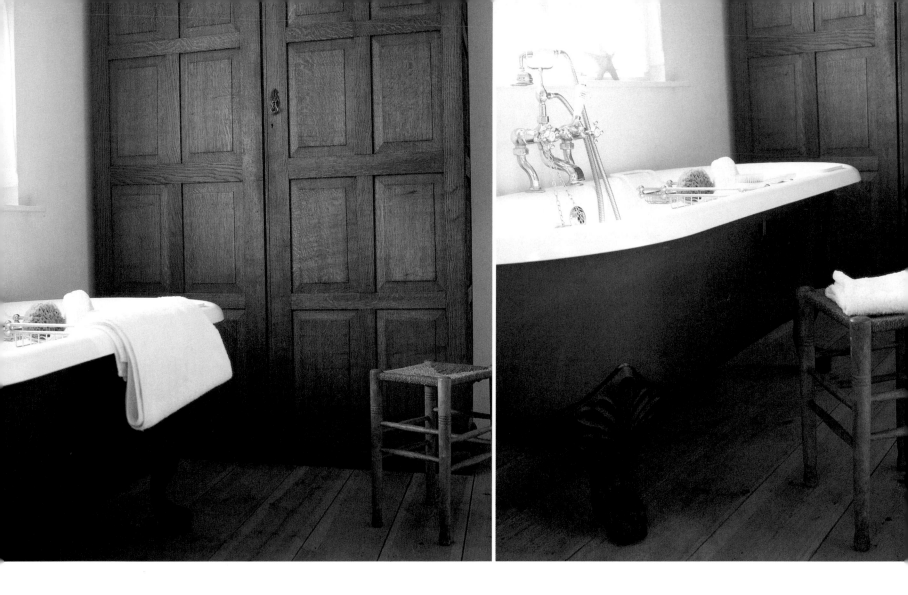

The influence of such important British 19th- and 20th-century designers as Ambrose Heal, Ernest Gimson and William Morris is very evident in this stylish but extremely practical bathroom. The space is not over-generous for such a treatment, but that problem has been solved by concealing all evidence of clutter behind the traditionally panelled oak doors at one end. The clever dressing table (if that's how to describe it) is in the same tradition of carefully considered craftsmanship. It combines worktop with a towel rail at one side. It also, through its solidity and bulk,

takes attention away from the over-rural beams. The basin and roll-top bath, which is placed to seem free-standing, are both traditional, yet the use of chrome taps marks the difference between Traditional and Modern styles. So, indeed, does the unremitting black of the bath's underbelly, which reduces, rather than emphasizes, the effect of the ornate feet. The only furniture consists of two rush-seated stools, again in a neutral wood to match the floor beneath. These are clearly 19th century in style, but their simplicity, allied to good, practical design, gives them a modest distinction.

OPPOSITE MAIN PICTURE: **Even a room in a beamed 17th-century cottage, as this clearly is, can be given the modern treatment. This has been done with a lack of colour and clutter and the employment of the simplest furniture, such as the dressing table and useful stool.**

OPPOSITE ABOVE: **A traditional decor would have used brass for the taps but, in a Modern Country setting, chrome is the answer, as is the neutral glass shelf above. The mirror has been cut so the structural beams make its frame.**

ABOVE LEFT: **The main, and beautiful, feature of this bathroom is the pair of heavily panelled oak doors, which are all about the simplicity and dignity of unadorned wood. Church-like in style, the neat drop handle is all that is needed.**

ABOVE RIGHT: **More chrome is used for taps on this old bath – and its base is unrelieved black.**

WHY IT WORKS GREAT MIX OF WARM OAK AND WHITE WALLS ■ BATH'S UNDERBELLY IN IMPOSING BLACK ■ BEAMS ARE SUBORDINATE ■ DOOR PANELS SIMPLE BUT BOLD

KEY FEATURES

▌ LUXURY IN EVERYTHING: THINK MARBLE, MAHOGANY, PILES OF THE FLUFFIEST WHITE TOWELS, FILM-STAR LIGHTING.

▌ IT COULD BE A GRAND HOTEL. INSPIRATIONS INCLUDE ART DECO, MODERNE AND ARTS AND CRAFTS STYLES.

▌ A BIG TUB IS ESSENTIAL, AND DEFINITELY SOMETHING TO WALLOW IN. EQUALLY, BIG TAPS SHOULD GUSH GALLONS OF HOT WATER.

▌ MIRRORS COVER THE WALLS, ARCHED, CURVED AND CARVED. IT'S NO GOOD BEING SHY.

classic period style

We've all seen bathrooms in this category, but usually in a gasp-session visiting a grand hotel. The very stuff of luxury, Classic Period style demands marble on the floor, around the basin, up the wall. Baths are Roman in their size, taps veritable geysers and the showerheads as large as dinner plates. Materials include white tubs, chrome square taps and flattering lighting.

This is no style for the faint-hearted. The ideal is this: a space big enough for a dining room; marble tiles (which may need the ceiling joists below to be strengthened), a small run of marble worktop, or mosaics in classical patterns; and the biggest and best bath you can find, along with the sort of taps and showerheads typical of the Savoy or Claridges. You are aiming to recreate an interior where the quality of everything is unrestrained. Luckily, this allows followers of the style to be disciplined about the cheaper things of life, such as what colour to use on the walls or the bath sheets: the answer is

none. The colours should be luxurious neutrals – though the tones do not need to be especially warm, since the central heating will be near tropical. Limit ornament to several huge mirrors, either wall-hung with chrome screw heads or in silver- or gold-leaf, modern frames. They can be lit with film-star bars of light bulbs or with the most flattering ceiling lights. A chandelier is more for show than help with the make-up. There's no need to bother about decor, given the beauty of the wood and marble you've used – a Twenties stool for the piles of white towels will do the trick.

OPPOSITE ABOVE LEFT: **A pile of towels on an antique Chinese stool stands ready beside the Moderne twin washbasins, each with its own mirror.**

OPPOSITE ABOVE RIGHT: **Classical moulding decorates built-in cupboards, which are surrounded by built-in mirrors on three sides. A Regency colza lamp hangs from a central boss.**

OPPOSITE BELOW LEFT: **Old-fashioned bath, basin and lavatory are in the essential white porcelain. The floor is a softly polished wood.**

OPPOSITE BELOW RIGHT: **Plenty of mirrors with careful lighting are a typical feature of Classic Period style, as are the craftsman-built fitted cupboards.**

ABOVE LEFT: **Arched mirrors over a huge bath make this into a temple to hygiene, as do the mosaic floor and vaguely classical stool.**

ABOVE CENTRE: **An old arched mirror is posed above a massive pair of twin washbasins, with taps to scale.**

ABOVE RIGHT: **An oriental rug covers the floor beside a Roman-style bath.**

TEMPLE TO BATHING STYLE STUDY

Make no mistake: this bathroom considers cleanliness as near to godliness as it gets. At the centre is a huge, free-standing bath, an altar to the virtue of a good scrub. Every element breathes luxury and power – the atmosphere is not so much welcoming as reverent.

This opulent bathroom has been designed to make a grand impression (although it may not be part of a very grand property). It's a good example of how clever use of accessories and finishes can elevate standard white sanitary ware to designer status. The huge, free-standing bath – in its luxury panelling – is placed so the lucky bather can look out over green trees, and its generous rim supports a helpful array of lotions. The taps are big enough to fill the whole bath in minutes, even though it holds gallons, and the showerhead is traditional in style. In keeping with the country-house atmosphere, the curtains are lavish, heavy and have ornamental tie-backs, and the bath panels are 18th-century copies, as is the candle wall-light. All the impedimenta – toothbrush holder and even plain toothpaste and brushes, chrome ring for the waffle towel, and the matching mirrors above the twin basins – have been bought to reinforce the theme. Even the classy, antique Chinese chest, its multiple drawers so useful for cosmetics and soaps, has been teamed with a modern Chinese work of art. Indeed, this whole room is a work of art in itself.

WHY IT WORKS ENORMOUS TWIN WASHBASINS ▮ HUGE, PANELLED FREE-STANDING TUB ▮ 18TH-CENTURY CURTAIN DETAIL ▮ CHROME FITTINGS ▮ ANTIQUE FURNITURE

OPPOSITE LEFT: **A multiple-drawered Chinese pharmacist's chest is both decorative and useful to hide oils and unguents. Above it is a Chinese painting.**
OPPOSITE RIGHT: **This style needs complete attention to detail. The waffle towel in a chrome ring has just the right mix of textures.**

ABOVE LEFT: **A huge bathtub needs taps to scale. The chrome mixer tap and showerhead is a classic.**
CENTRE LEFT: **Perfectionists need to control even the colour and shape of the toothpaste tube and matching toothbrushes.**
BELOW LEFT: **Each of the pair of large basins is topped by heavy**

circular mirrors. Even the waste bin is classical in inspiration.
ABOVE: **A gigantic altar to the goddess hygiene, the bath takes centre stage in a large room and has a fine view of outside greenery. The curtains, tie-backs and bath's panelling are all 18th century in inspiration.**

KEY FEATURES

▮ A ROLL-TOP BATH IS AN IDEAL FOCAL POINT, DEEP AND LUXURIOUS AS WELL AS CLASSICALLY GOOD-LOOKING. CAST-IRON VERSIONS ARE HEAVY – CHECK THAT YOUR JOISTS CAN SUPPORT THE WEIGHT. MODERN ACRYLIC IS MORE CONVENIENT AND LIGHTER, THOUGH CHEAPER VERSIONS CAN LOOK PLASTIC-LIKE; PRESSED STEEL IS A GOOD COMPROMISE.

▮ CHUNKY STYLING ON BASINS AND TOILETS – SQUARE SHAPES WITH ZIGGURAT DETAILING ARE JUST RIGHT.

▮ CROSS-HEAD TAPS AND 'TELEPHONE' BATH MIXERS, PLUS LARGE, DRENCHING SHOWERHEADS.

▮ WHITE CERAMIC TILES, SQUARE OR BRICK-SHAPED, OR TONGUE-AND-GROOVE ON THE WALLS.

▮ VINYL, LINOLEUM OR RUSH MATTING ON THE FLOOR.

vintage & retro

A comfortable bath in which you can lounge for hours, taps that feel nicely heavy in the hand, big basins with room to splash and a large showerhead that really drenches you – these are just some of the ingredients that might make up the Vintage and Retro bathroom. It just goes to show that practical good looks never go out of date.

There's something reassuringly solid about a Vintage and Retro bathroom – even reproduction pieces come in pleasingly square lines and large sizes, and the overall look is generous and relaxing. A one-off item such as a roll-top, claw-foot bath can transform a room. It could be a cast-iron reclamation-yard find, or a contemporary example in acrylic or pressed steel – with sides painted to match your colour scheme and a telephone-style shower attachment. Or you could go the whole hog and install an Art Deco-style suite with chunky outlines or (for the daring) a retro suite in typically sugary pastel colours. Other special pieces might include a huge shower rose, a set of chrome-and-ceramic cross-head taps or a giltwood mirror – this is a style that relies on classic, but not overly imposing or ornate, fittings. Some interesting storage could fit the bill, too: perhaps an old trunk, a wire basket or some wooden seed trays. Combine these eye-catching things with a plain background. White ceramic tiles or tongue-and-groove painted in a pale colour are ideal for walls, while rush matting, linoleum or vinyl in a black-and-white check would suit the floor – literally – down to the ground.

BUILT TO LAST STYLE STUDY

This style is as much about tough practicality as it is about good looks, as is demonstrated by this striking bathroom, where the authentically retro fittings and accessories look as impressively durable, hard-wearing and easy to care for as they are characterful and attractive.

Taking the problem features of a room and turning them into highlights are the mark of an excellent designer, and the owners of this Vintage and Retro bathroom have done a brilliant job at transforming a small, dark room into a practical, cosy space. The lack of natural light has been compensated for by keeping the colours monochromatic, the furniture layout straightforward and the artificial lighting authentic in style as well as useful. The floor plan is well thought out, making the most of every inch, with details such as a recessed soap tray, wall-mounted bath taps and a long, slim glass shelf.

As for the fittings themselves, they make a dramatic style statement: chunky and generously sized, possessing a distinctive period feel without being overtly 'antique'. Taps and levers make distinctive features, while the solid, rectangular mirror and retro table are great accessories, as well as being usefully functional. Brick-shaped white ceramic tiles, and a black-and-white checked mosaic floor, have a certain utilitarian chic and, overall, everything is solid, heavy and well made – you feel it has already lasted several lifetimes and will keep going for many more.

WHY IT WORKS AUTHENTIC FITTINGS ■ GOOD-LOOKING ACCESSORIES ■ EVERYTHING IS FUNCTIONAL AND TOUGH ■ WELL-PLANNED LAYOUT ■ MONOCHROMATIC SCHEME

OPPOSITE LEFT: **The square lines, solid form and ziggurat detailing of this basin make it wonderfully authentic and eye-catching.**
OPPOSITE RIGHT: **Glass and silver storage pots have a retro feel that suits the room perfectly.**
ABOVE LEFT: **A recessed soap tray is a space-saving touch.**

CENTRE LEFT: **Wall-mounted bath controls free up space, and in themselves are an attractive accessory that helps define the Vintage and Retro style.**
BELOW LEFT: **Details make all the difference in creating a look, and this chrome-plated WC lever and plumbing make a fabulous feature.**

ABOVE: **Ceramic tiles on the walls and a black-and-white-checked floor are simple and fitting in this small room. The light over the basin mirror has an interesting – and authentically retro – shape; overall, the soft lighting makes this room, which lacks natural light, feel cosy and comfortable.**

bedrooms

Once bedroom style was divided into masculine and feminine. No longer. The ideal decor is a combination of softly natural textures generously displayed (the feminine side) and a lack of pattern, flounce and strong colour (the masculine bit). The result is a calm space that encourages lounging and lingering. Generally, all storage is hidden behind closed doors.

KEY FEATURES

▌ THE BED IS THE FOCAL POINT, DRESSED WITH TAILORED COVERS AND AN UPHOLSTERED HEADBOARD OF EXAGGERATED RECTANGULAR PROPORTIONS.

▌ KEY COLOURS ARE WHITE, TAUPE, EAU-DE-NIL, SAND AND PALEST GREY, WITH BEDLINEN IN WHITE OR NEUTRAL SHADES.

▌ VERY SIMPLE BEDSIDE TABLES SHOULD BE CUBIC, OR BUILT IN. THERE SHOULD BE ABSOLUTELY NO CLUTTER OTHER THAN SIDE LAMPS OR WALL-MOUNTED READING LIGHTS.

▌ STORAGE MUST LOOK SEAMLESS, PREFERABLY CONTAINED IN A SINGLE WALL-TO-WALL BUILT-IN UNIT, WITH FLUSH CUPBOARD DOORS, OR A TALL, SLIM CHEST OF DRAWERS.

▌ SLEEK YET TACTILE FLOORING INCLUDES WOOD BOARDS OR STONE, WITH A SOFT 100 PER CENT WOOL RUG, OR FITTED PALE CARPET THROUGHOUT.

OPPOSITE TOP LEFT: **Use a single fabric type, in one or two complementary shades, to pull the room together. In this bedroom, cream linen has been used for the curtains, and a matching oatmeal to upholster headboard and footstool.**

OPPOSITE RIGHT: **Streamlined fitted cupboards should be equipped with ample hanging space, as well as open shelves and drawers, so there's no excuse for leaving clothes lying around.**

OPPOSITE CENTRE LEFT: **Take the vogue for high upholstered headboards to the extreme, and panel a wall in quilted satin.**

OPPOSITE CENTRE RIGHT: **The bed must look sleek, yet luxurious. Cushions and bedcovers must be fitted, but choose silks or taffeta for subtle sheen.**

OPPOSITE BELOW AND THIS PAGE BELOW RIGHT: **If there's a beautiful view, simple window treatments will maximize it: plain gathered curtains or tailored blinds look best.**

BELOW LEFT: **Built-in bedside tables look smart, and can be designed as an integral part of a wooden headboard.**

sleek

With design's obsession for pared-down spaces has come a new mood for bedrooms: Zen-like oases of purity and calm. Stripped to the minimum, yet with comfort still paramount, these night-time retreats offer a haven for busy people who need to switch off and chill out. Essentials are a generous bed, mood lighting and pale colours, while a great view and birdsong are optional extras.

Few of us wished to mimic the white box decor of the minimalist's bedroom, but more of us embraced a softer version, popularized by chic hotels and the notion of a glamorous room with ambient lighting and a huge bed. Yet this is not a look to undertake lightly: beware those who drop clothes on the floor or collect piles of books.

To create a tranquil space, with unadorned walls and natural lighting, plan your layout early. Sort clothes storage first. This is no place for a lumpy wardrobe: either locate cupboards in an adjacent bedroom, or devote one wall to a seamless run of cupboards. Kit them out with ample shelf space as well as hanging rails, and you can dispense with a chest of drawers. Cupboard doors should be flush, painted to match walls, or wood-veneered for a slick finish.

Select textures to create a pampering mood. Consider curtain and upholstery fabrics in crisp linen, sheeny silks or faux suede, and sheets in Egyptian cotton, linen or even satin. Stick to plains, as patterns will detract from the tranquil ambience. For that reason, plain-painted walls are best. Try to site the bed close to a window, so that you wake to a soothing view outside, as well as in.

SOMBRE SERENITY STYLE STUDY

At once moody and tranquil, this positively monastic bedroom is a masterful mix of tonal shifts and good space planning. Set into the corner of a much larger city loft, it maintains an intimate and serene atmosphere, with all storage hidden from view. Surfaces are hard and urban, yet the inclusion of natural, ethnic textures softens the look.

In this cool and pure bedroom, the space has been expertly planned to direct all the attention onto the bed. Dressed in crisp white bedding, and appearing to float from the wall on a Japanese-style sleeping platform, there's no question that this is the place for relaxing and chilling out. Although the bed zone is within a much larger open-plan loft space, it has been cleverly enclosed within a series of partition walls. The giant pillar acts as a full stop at the end of the active living area, signalling the start of tranquillity.

Storage has been neatly hidden behind the bedhead wall, and in here there are floor-to-ceiling cupboards with ample shelves. Such

seamless storage is important, because within the sleeping area itself there is no free-standing furniture to distract the eye. A long, lean rattan bench is the only exception: this can usefully hold clothes in transit before they are carefully stored from view.

The sombre colour scheme is a brave choice for a bedroom, yet ultimately it's successful. The dark timber wall defines the space and adds a dramatic contrast to the white bed. Elsewhere, there's a mix of pure white, and steel partition walls, which draw together the muted tones of the stone floor and the timber finish. Adaptable day and night lighting is the final finishing touch.

OPPOSITE LEFT: **The bed is surrounded by partition walls mixed with floor-to-ceiling sliding panels, which can be left open or slid across for privacy. Sliding panels are also useful when controlling natural light.**

OPPOSITE RIGHT: **With no bedside tables or reading lamps, this is a bed designed to have zero distractions.**

ABOVE: **Although the space has lofty proportions, it was important to enclose the bed zone within a confined space, to make it seem intimate and warm. The bed and bench are set low, to enhance a feeling of relaxation.**

RIGHT AND FAR RIGHT: **In a monochromatic room such as this, the inclusion of bright accent colours would have created too brash a contrast. Instead, the muted natural textures of wood and rattan bring just enough warmth to the scheme.**

WHY IT WORKS HONEY-TONED RATTAN AND WOOD ▪ MONOCHROMATIC COLOUR PALETTE ▪ CRISP WHITE HIGHLIGHTS ▪ SEAMLESS, HIDDEN STORAGE ▪ ATMOSPHERIC LIGHTING

mellow modern

We all wish for a cosy, comfortable bedroom. The best versions offer an energizing start to the day – with storage to hand and lots of natural sunlight – and an ambient mood at night, with subdued lighting and cocooning blankets and covers. Properly planned, the Mellow Modern bedroom delivers both, as well as looking streamlined, modern and chic.

OPPOSITE ABOVE LEFT: **For a neat look, sandwich drawer units between two floor-to-ceiling wardrobes, rather than breaking up the wall with a free-standing piece. A long, thin unit no higher than the bed keeps things streamlined.**
OPPOSITE ABOVE RIGHT: **In summer, swap a puffy duvet for flat sheets and a blanket, which provides a tailored outline on the bed.**
OPPOSITE BELOW LEFT: **Mellow Modern style looks best kept tidy, but there's nothing wrong with a**
casually tossed throw, or a bedroom chair to take a few clothes. Have a daily tidy-up to ensure neatness.
OPPOSITE BELOW CENTRE AND RIGHT: **With a dark or mid-toned headboard and white sheets, there's lots of potential for a blend of decorative looks on the bed. Add a silk eiderdown in winter, and a lighter blanket in summer.**
BELOW: **Hotel-style wall-mounted side lights look slick and free up space on the bedside table for books and a glass of water.**

A decade ago, the definition of a cosy bedroom might have included a mountain of scatter cushions, interlined curtains, and bedside tables piled with books. Thankfully, that look is long gone. Now, those in search of a comfortable bedroom can welcome in streamlined style, which melds the best of modern Sleek (a tailored bed, built-in storage) with the indulgence of soft, relaxed textures. In place of scatter cushions, there's a deeply upholstered headboard, and curtains are frequently unlined and simple. And the bedside table has cleaned up, with a single drawer for clutter and enough room for a few selected titles.

You want to create a creamy, neutral shell, so start by picking major surfaces like flooring and walls. Although glossy timber floorboards are acceptably warm underfoot, many of us still prefer the comforting texture of wool, so either get a large plain wool rug to cover boards, or go for wall-to-wall carpeting. Avoid sisal or coir, as they are too scratchy. You can't lose with a neutral or grey carpet, as it looks good with a cream- or white-based scheme, yet teams easily with darker colours, too. Keep to plain painted walls in off-whites or cream, or choose a fine-textured

KEY FEATURES

■ THE BED MUST LOOK INVITING; EITHER A SIMPLE DIVAN OR WITH A RECTANGULAR UPHOLSTERED HEADBOARD.

■ BIG WINDOWS, WITH LOTS OF SUN AND PREFERABLY A GREAT VIEW, ADD TO THE NATURAL, RELAXED MOOD.

■ WARM WOOD BOARDS OR FITTED CARPET IN NEUTRAL TONES ARE BEST UNDERFOOT.

■ CRISP WHITE BEDDING TEAMED WITH A NEATLY FOLDED QUILTED SATIN OR WOOL/CASHMERE THROW.

■ A MUTED COLOUR PALETTE, COMBINING FRESH WHITE OR PALE DOVE GREY WITH TAUPE, LICHEN OR SLATE.

■ TEXTURES ARE EASY AND SOFT, USED AS SIMPLE GATHERED CURTAINS, LOOSE COVERS, OR ON TAILORED VALANCES AND CUSHION COVERS.

wallpaper. A bedroom should promote tranquillity, so don't put distracting pattern on the walls.

It's a good idea to plan a mix of built-in furniture, to store most clothes, as well as a few free-standing pieces. There are now many contemporary-looking wooden chests of drawers. These are still the best way to store smaller clothing, like knickers and T-shirts, and the top provides much-needed display space for a special family photo, the TV, or simply flowers. A run of fitted cupboards may be panelled in a mellow wood veneer, to add warmth to the scheme, or with simply panelled MDF doors, painted in a shade to match the walls.

Pay attention to the bed, as it is the true focus of the room. For this look, you want a plain divan with a tall, rectangular upholstered headboard. A bedroom chair or sofa might be upholstered to match. Great touchy-feely textures for the headboard are linen, wool, faux suede and velvet, though if you pick a light colour it's a good idea to fit the headboard with a loose cover, to prevent marks. Never before has there been such a choice of fashionable bedding accessories. With your white bedlinen, you can mix a cashmere throw, a faux fur blanket, satin eiderdown or wool blanket, or layer several at the end of the bed.

ABOVE LEFT: **Take care to achieve balance and symmetry: look for matching bedside tables and identical lamps, and arrange cushions in a neat line.**

BELOW LEFT: **For a particularly energizing take on the style, adopt a fresh all-white palette – especially effective if the room has a leafy view.**

ABOVE: **Pick unlined, loose-weave curtains and/or blinds to add privacy, and to filter sunlight prettily. This guarantees a gentle, welcoming mood by day, while side lights and overhead illumination on a dimmer take care of good lighting at night.**

CHIAROSCURO CHIC STYLE STUDY

Glamorous and indulgent, with its satin curtains and faux fur throw, this bedroom is the ultimate boudoir. There's a strong textural story, from dense to smooth, crunchy to shiny, and colours from a grown-up palette.

TOP: **While the finish is glamorous, the bedroom introduces quirky, offbeat details to add drama, such as the organically shaped ceramic lamp bases, and the African-inspired pillowcases.**
ABOVE: **An elegant French antique chair enhances the boudoir image.**
ABOVE RIGHT: **A burst of pattern would disturb the soothing plains and textures, but there's a subtler element at work. The vertical folds on the silk curtains are echoed in the deep-pile stripes on the throw.**

This chic room proves that you don't need a huge bedroom to achieve film-star style. Wonderful textures draw the eye to the bed and the window, and away from tiny proportions. If anything, the enveloping walls heighten the cocooning mood.

The colours are carefully layered, to create a sophisticated chiaroscuro. Instead of stark all-white on the bed, dark tribal-weave pillowcases interleave the sheets and top pillows, and the faux fur throw

visually links the bed with the bronze silk curtains. In a similar vein, white side lamps sit on top of glossy dark-wood bedside tables. To heighten the light/dark theme, there are slatted wooden blinds.

Textures have been picked to provide maximum glamour to the eye, yet perfect comfort in bed. The linen bedding, crunchy white bedspreads and a linen padded headboard provide cool, natural surfaces to promote a good night's sleep.

WHY IT WORKS CHOCOLATE/BRONZE PALETTE ■ LUXURIOUS TEXTURES ■ WHITE HIGHLIGHTS

KEY FEATURES

■ GREAT STORAGE, FITTED OR FREE-STANDING (THE LATTER MUST BE WELL CO-ORDINATED). AS WELL AS WARDROBES AND CHESTS OF DRAWERS, TRY BOXES THAT ROLL UNDER THE BED, CHESTS THAT DOUBLE AS SEATS, OR CUPBOARDS BUILT INTO A DEEP HEADBOARD.

■ COOL, CALM NEUTRAL/NATURAL COLOURS – OFF-WHITE, TAUPE AND STONE, CHOCOLATE AND MOCHA, OR PALE GREY AND CHARCOAL. PATTERNS SHOULD BE MINIMAL.

■ WELL-PLACED, GOOD-LOOKING LAMPS FOR READING AND PUTTING ON MAKE-UP; GENERAL LIGHTING THAT CAN ADJUST TO BE BRIGHT, OR SOFT AND SUBTLE.

■ SOFT FLOORING IN A PLAIN COLOUR THAT CO-ORDINATES WITH YOUR SCHEME.

elegant modern

In the bedroom, atmosphere and ambience are as important as visual style, and in the ideal Elegant Modern bedroom the aim is to create a private world of rest and relaxation, a haven that feels far away from the bustle of everyday life. Here, laid-back good looks go hand in hand with a scheme that does everything possible to promote serenity and calm.

Storage is undoubtedly the key to creating this style – it is impossible to be elegant in an environment filled with clutter, and bedrooms can amass all sorts of bits and pieces surprisingly quickly. Fitted storage tends to look sleeker, as well as making excellent use of space, though unfitted pieces that are well co-ordinated may be more beautiful.

Lighting is another important element. As well as lamps by the bed and at the dressing table, you'll need general illumination, preferably on a dimmer for a warm and intimate atmosphere. It is important that colours are harmonious – neutrals

and naturals are best – and that both furniture and window treatments are really simple in style. Plain, gathered curtains or a Roman blind are ideal, while beds, tables and chairs should be clean-lined and unfussy; timeless chic is the aim. Underfoot, the best option is a plain-coloured, soft, woollen carpet. Overall, it is best to avoid too much pattern and decoration, though you should not pare the room down so much that it feels stark and minimal. To pull the look together, add some luxurious accessories such as a velvet throw, some plump cushions, a vase of flowers or a beautiful picture.

OPPOSITE ABOVE LEFT: **A classic four-poster bed has been brought up to date by a unified colour palette of white and ivory. The Roman blinds at the windows are wonderfully simple.**

OPPOSITE ABOVE RIGHT: **The use of pattern here is minimal – just enough to add interest without being overpowering.**

OPPOSITE BELOW: **Useful storage at the foot of the bed doubles as a comfortable seat; this scheme is businesslike in function but still comfortable and attractive.**

ABOVE LEFT: **A bedside table needs just enough space for a lamp, a book and perhaps one or two trinkets. This decorative lamp base co-ordinates with the warm wood used for the fashionable headboard/wall.**

ABOVE CENTRE: **A choice of boldly shaped, yet plain and simple, furniture gives this room a calm, contemporary feel.**

ABOVE RIGHT: **Textural contrasts add a sense of luxury to a scheme where colours are very restrained.**

EFFORTLESS APPEAL STYLE STUDY

When classic combines with contemporary in a way that is subtle and harmonious, the result is Elegant Modern. Yes, you can use antique furnishings and still create a look that is up to date - as this bedroom, which mixes old and new with calm colour and quiet detailing, so ably demonstrates.

Sometimes getting a look right is all about not trying too hard, and in this room the feel is definitely laid-back rather than overdone. Like all the best schemes, it seems to have come together effortlessly. Whether you have eclectic taste or have inherited a few antique pieces, you can emulate this style easily. The antique chair, for example, has simply been re-covered with unbleached cotton, its plain looks offsetting the detailed carvings of the frame. And the period chest-cum-desk has been slotted in between a pair of built-in wardrobes to provide attractive storage for all sorts of items. These old pieces work well with the dark-stained, polished floorboards, a timeless classic. To co-ordinate, the owners chose pared-down modern furniture: a bed and side tables that are straight, boxy and fuss-free. The colours on the walls are soft, matt and muted, given extra interest by the choice of different tones for above and below the dado; the bedlinen complements these shades perfectly. Clutter has been banned, and just a few accessories add finesse. In all, the effect is chic but comfortable, with an ambience of relaxed order.

OPPOSITE ABOVE: **Neat piles of cushions and pillows appear very modern, though in style these are rather classic. Either way, the look is chic and comfortable.**

OPPOSITE BELOW: **Bedlinen in soft shades co-ordinates with the overall colour scheme. The informal mismatch of the bedside lamps works well because both are simple but pretty in style. The bed and bedside table are modern and rather minimal; their understated look balances the more decorative features of the antique pieces in the room.**

ABOVE LEFT: **An antique chair has been updated with some new, plain upholstery.**

ABOVE RIGHT: **The Empire-style chest has its own niche, tucked between a pair of built-in wardrobes, which allow all clutter to be hidden away. The use of antiques means the wardrobes don't dominate the room.**

WHY IT WORKS CAREFUL MIX OF ANTIQUE AND NEW FURNITURE ■ SOFT, PALE COLOURS ■ FITTED AND UNFITTED STORAGE ■ WELL-ARRANGED FURNITURE CREATES A SENSE OF SPACE

KEY FEATURES

▌ AGED TIMBER BEAMS MAY BE USED AS A DECORATIVE STARTING POINT, OR ADD NEW WOOD PANELLING FOR A WARM, COMFORTING SHELL.

▌ THE BED SHOULD RETAIN A MODERN, SPARE OUTLINE, WITH A WOOD OR METAL BED FRAME, OR PANELLED WOOD HEADBOARD.

▌ TEXTURES ARE KEY, WITH WOOLS, CRUNCHY LINEN, COTTON AND HESSIAN HIGH ON THE LIST.

▌ WINDOW TREATMENTS SHOULD GIVE AN UNSTRUCTURED OUTLINE, FROM GATHERED LINEN OR CALICO CURTAINS TO EASY, PULL-UP BLINDS.

▌ KEY SURFACES ARE TIMBER, FROM RECLAIMED FLOORING TO NEW HARDWOOD BOARDS, LEATHER AND STEEL.

OPPOSITE TOP LEFT AND CENTRE: **For the most contemporary take on Natural, cover the whole of one wall or panel cupboards in timber. If wood panelling is to be used in place of a headboard, choose a sleek, well-finished veneer.**

OPPOSITE TOP RIGHT: **A wall-hung textile banner – most effective in stiff linen or hessian – makes a dramatic alternative to a wooden headboard.**

OPPOSITE CENTRE LEFT: **The warm timbers in this attic bedroom were the inspiration for a leather rug and a leather chest of drawers.**

OPPOSITE CENTRE: **For a truly casual look, swap a bed for a wooden Japanese-style sleeping platform, with a mattress or a roll-up futon.**

OPPOSITE CENTRE RIGHT: **Timber-framed windows should be adorned with very simple fabrics like hessian or calico.**

OPPOSITE BELOW: **At the rough end of Natural, use textural woods, from reclaimed timber to driftwood, for unusual furniture options.**

THIS PAGE: **For a sophisticated take on Natural, choose wall panelling in a richly grained timber.**

natural

The bedroom is the place we feel at our most relaxed, with time to appreciate beautiful surroundings. For those who like to be enveloped with unusual surfaces, subtle pattern and a warm, muted colour scheme, the Natural look is ideal. As a style, it may be interpreted as casual, with tossed blankets and bare boards, or pared down and urban: either way, it's a joy.

Not everyone wants to wake up to pristine walls and pared-down accessories. For some of us, a soothing bedroom means good things to feel and look at. To gain inspiration, look first to the fabric of the building. If the property is old, there may be exposed beams or existing wall panelling to start you off. If converting an attic into a bedroom, it may be possible to expose the rafters.

Team wood-panelled or plain-painted walls with a hard floor, from sanded boards to more luxurious options like leather. If you want a casual look, pick materials from the shabby-chic end of the style, in which case you want your leather scuffed and floorboards reclaimed. It's a good idea to layer textures, so hard floors may be teamed with a faux animal skin, cotton runner or leather rug.

Modern Natural style is less about symmetry and more about unstructured, relaxed living. So choose bedding that looks good when a little crumpled (try linen/cotton mixes or seersucker), and pick occasional chairs or mismatched bedside tables, to add variety. If you want a cosier look, opt for antique pieces: for the urban finish, choose modern furniture with distressed metal detailing.

TIMBER AND TEXTURE STYLE STUDY

Highly contemporary, yet skilfully mixing urban and exotic design influences, this is a bedroom to spend time in, as well as for sleeping. Although the shell is very ordinary, with its hardwood floor and whitewashed brick walls, the bedroom has been planned just as carefully as one might a sitting room. Accessories, art and furniture are as crucial here as the bed itself.

Here is a modern Natural bedroom with a twist. Streamlined and contemporary it may be, but it is full of character, too. While decorative accessories have been picked according to a strict colour palette (note the similar muted tones of the modern art and cylindrical wood containers), they also lend a quirky, personal tone, adding a sense of history to a self-consciously modern room.

Instead of inspiring a decorative theme, the major surfaces – brick walls and timber floor – play second fiddle to a selection of newer surfaces. These define the space. High wood panelling wraps around the bed to create intimacy, imparting subtle patterns with its warm grain and even warmer tones. A tall mirror gives the impression of another room beyond. And on the floor, a nubbly water hyacinth rug adds new depth to the timber boards, at the same time echoing the stripes in the modern art.

Despite the exotic influences, the room looks very modern. There's hi-tech lighting and crisp white bedding, for a start. Added to that, the furniture is a mix of streamlined contemporary pieces and a 20th-century classic chair, all in tempting timber and leather to confirm the Natural theme.

OPPOSITE ABOVE: **The power of Natural style lies in sticking to a very muted colour palette, so bright fresh flowers could tip the balance. Dried grasses, twigs and seed pods are a more interesting, and subtler, alternative.**
OPPOSITE BELOW: **Every texture in the room has been carefully thought out. The white cotton bedspread has a similar nubbly weave to the natural-fibre rug.**
ABOVE LEFT: **There's a satisfying contrast between the super-modern lighting and the organic, ever-changing grain of the wood panelling just behind. When introducing a new wood, like these macassar ebony tables, go for contrast rather than trying to match. It's more dramatic to pick varied tones and grains, so that pale and dark appear in decorative layers.**
ABOVE RIGHT: **With its dark woods and crisp white bedding, the bedroom has an almost masculine mood. Yet the textural rugs and mellow timber grain soften it to a gently tailored finish.**

WHY IT WORKS EXOTIC GRAINED WOODS ▮ URBAN BRICKS ▮ SUBTLE TEXTURAL STRIPES ▮ MODERN FURNITURE SHAPES ▮ ETHNIC ART AND ACCESSORIES ▮ LIGHT-AND-DARK PALETTE

scandinavian

The appreciation of space and light is no less dominant in the Scandinavian-style bedroom than in any other room, though here it is combined rather more with an appreciation of warmth, comfort and relaxation. This is a relatively straightforward look to put together, and one that is supremely satisfying to live with.

OPPOSITE ABOVE LEFT: **This room has a well-balanced mix of plain with pattern, pale with dark. The furry throw is a luxurious touch, adding warmth and opulence in an otherwise clean-lined room.**

OPPOSITE ABOVE RIGHT: **For those who prefer a more minimal approach, wardrobes and other storage can be built in, fronted with beautiful solid-wood doors to tone with the floorboards. A simple bed, a plain rug and sheer curtains to filter light are the only other requirements.**

OPPOSITE BELOW, FROM LEFT TO RIGHT: **Plain white bedlinen is all that's needed to give a Scandinavian bedroom a clean, crisp look. If there are no privacy issues, you can avoid window treatments altogether if you wish; in this case, the square window then becomes a graphic element in the room. All in neutral tones, the textures of wood, wool and paper blend together for a tactile mix.**

BELOW: **A stove is sometimes a key feature in a Scandinavian-style bedroom.**

When comfort counts, what you take out can be just as important as what you put in. And the Scandinavian bedroom is a great example of how this theory works. Instead of piling on the colour, the pattern, the textiles and the furniture, rooms of this style are lessons in knowing when to stop. They are certainly not minimal but, instead, they demonstrate a careful sense of restraint that ensures a look and feel that is quietly restful and calmly satisfying.

Colour, for a start, falls very much into the neutral/natural range – white or off-white, with taupe, stone, cream and chocolate, teamed with the golden glow of blond wood, which may be used for floors, furniture and wardrobe doors. Keeping the room as pale as possible all over enhances the sense of light and space, but mixing in a touch of a darker shade brings a sense of warmth and, importantly, decorative balance. Pattern is minimal, restricted to the subtleties of the grain of wood, the weave of a natural wool rug or the variegation of handmade paper, although a graphic element can be introduced with a bold geometric print as a strong

KEY FEATURES

▌ BLOND WOOD, IN THE FORM OF FLOORS, FURNITURE OR WARDROBE AND CUPBOARD DOORS. ITS PALE GLOW PERMEATES THE ROOM.

▌ PLAIN, PALE COLOURS, POSSIBLY COUNTERPOINTED WITH DARKER SHADES FOR BALANCE. CHOCOLATE WORKS VERY WELL WITH IVORY, CREAM AND TAUPE.

▌ A MIX OF LUSCIOUS TEXTURES TO GIVE THE ROOM WARMTH AND INDIVIDUALITY, WHETHER FAKE FUR, NATURAL MATTING, WOOD OR GLASS.

▌ A SIMPLE BED WITH PLAIN LINEN, TOPPED BY A GOOD-LOOKING THROW.

▌ FUNCTIONAL LIGHTING, BOTH GENERAL AND SPECIFIC, THAT IS ATTRACTIVE BUT DOES NOT DRAW TOO MUCH ATTENTION TO ITSELF.

counterpoint. Textures, on the other hand, are luscious and luxurious, though not over the top, from soft fake fur to crisp cotton, nubbly sisal to polished parquet.

Beds and bedlinen in this style of bedroom are utterly simple. A clean-lined divan, for example, is ideal – no frills or fancies to distract the eye. Then add white cotton or linen sheets and duvet covers, layered with a sophisticated bedcover or throw in a suitably laid-back colour and pattern. Wardrobes and chests of drawers may be similarly understated in style, or even built in for efficiency and convenience. Any additional furniture should be

kept to a minimum – just a useful bedside table and a good-looking chair or stool, for example. Finally, lighting shares the same grown-up, good-looking, functional aesthetic. Though fittings are attractive in themselves, they are relatively plain; what is more important is the quality of the light that they cast – in the form of directional spotlights for reading in bed and maybe at a dressing table, and dimmable overhead light for general illumination. These are the building blocks, all equally easygoing and appealing; putting them together should be, as long as you employ a little control and order, child's play.

TOP LEFT: **Neutral walls and bedlinen ensure a calm, soothing atmosphere. Even the chest of drawers is simple in style, though the pleated paper lamp adds understated visual interest.**

BOTTOM LEFT: **In this ultra-simple room, the curtain and bedlinen complement each other perfectly. Their woven texture contrasts nicely with that of the smooth, polished-wood floor.**

ABOVE: **A row of coloured bottles provides decorative contrast in an otherwise pared-down bedroom.**

CRUX OF THE MATTER STYLE STUDY

This Stockholm bedroom features modern furnishings, but pays respect to the traditional features of Scandinavian design. Its limited use of colours and pattern is combined with a sense of calming order and restraint.

TOP: **Above the bedroom cabinets is hung a series of photographs – carefully co-ordinating with the room scheme, of course.**
ABOVE: **Sweden has a strong tradition of innovative and beautiful studio glass. On the left is a Soap Bubble vase; on the right, an experiment with colours, both by Ann Wåhlström.**
ABOVE RIGHT: **A strong style statement, this throw is now an icon of modern Swedish design.**

While plain white walls are the backdrop for this bedroom, it is far from being stark and minimal. The warmth of wood and of wool is combined with the bold graphic design of the bed throw and the cabinets to create a room that has great personality, yet still feels pleasantly restful. As is usual in most Scandinavian homes, the floor is made of polished wood, a glowing gold in colour which matches that of the picture frames, carefully

hung in a neat row. White Snow cabinets, by Thomas Sandell and Jonas Bohlin, provide useful storage and – thanks to their smiley, cut-out handles – a sense of witty spontaneity. Carefully chosen accessories include glassware by Ann Wåhlström for the Swedish company Kosta Boda. Perhaps the most dominant feature, however, is the Crux felt throw by Pia Wallén, which has become an icon of modern Swedish design.

WHY IT WORKS PLAIN WALLS AS A BACKDROP ■ A GRAPHIC PATTERN AS A FOCAL POINT

KEY FEATURES

▌ OLD-FASHIONED BEDS, FROM CURLY
IRON AND BRASS BEDHEADS TO FRENCH
AND SWEDISH BOAT BEDS AND, OF
COURSE, FOUR-POSTERS.

▌ CONTROLLED COLOUR SCHEME,
GENERALLY FEATURING SHADES OF WHITE
ALONG WITH A SINGLE SOFT PRIMARY,
SKY BLUE, SOFT ROSE OR FADED LILAC.

▌ PATTERNED COTTONS PROVIDE VARIETY
AND COLOUR. THESE SHOULD BE EITHER
TRADITIONALLY FADED, FLOWERY OR A
SIMPLE GINGHAM CHECK.

▌ FLOORS UNCARPETED WITH BEDSIDE
RUGS SUCH AS RAG RUGS, PLAITED
CIRCLES OR ELDERLY ORIENTALS.

▌ FURNITURE, OF TRADITIONAL SHAPES,
PAINTED TO FADE INTO THE BACKGROUND.

traditional country

Though not by any means flouncy, the old-fashioned country look is fabric-led and involves plenty of pretty patterns. The fabrics provide the main interest by making various types of traditional bed the main object of interest in the room. Paint colour is also important here, in that walls, ceiling, some beams, the furniture and, quite often, the bed itself are all painted the same colour.

Country style is all about compensating for what is happening outside the house. The country is often wet, muddy, howling with gales, cold and bleak. A house in the country therefore needs to be warm, comfortable, cosy and welcoming. It needs to shut out what is happening beyond the windows or, since slanting rain and gales can be very noisy, especially at night, to make you feel enjoyably protected from the weather. Though country bedrooms may have open fires – and little is more comforting than glowing coals on a winter's night – most do not. It is therefore up to the decor of

the room to provide the comfort. This should be done by choosing warm colours – not violent reds or oranges, for that is not the country way, but whites on the verge of creaminess, blues that recall warm Mediterranean seas and the whole range of rose, soft pink and faded lilac. Think of sugared almonds when designing a Traditional Country bedroom. Most of the colour in what should be a disciplined scheme is best kept to the many fabrics that will feature. Use traditional patterns such as Victorian chintz flowers, tiny Regency bouquets originally designed as curtain linings, and woven

OPPOSITE ABOVE LEFT: **A traditional French-style boat bed, painted a soft green, is eased into the space under a sloping ceiling. Though the window is placed unconventionally, it really works.**

OPPOSITE BELOW LEFT: **Though fabrics are very much in evidence in this charming corner, they don't really flounce because the colours are so disciplined. The blind and main cushion on the bed match each other, while the faded florals are all soft pink.**

OPPOSITE ABOVE RIGHT: **The prettiest white lacy linen has been chosen here to add welcome to the curly iron bedstead. Old towels are easily found in antique markets. The only colour is the pale pink wall, consciously emphasized by the pink pyjamas and newspaper.**

ABOVE LEFT AND RIGHT: **The symmetrical placing of the wall lamps and double set of cushions on the bed transforms a small room into a formal scheme. Colour is only provided by the toile de Jouy cushions.**

geometrics such as ticking and gingham. Flowers can also be mixed with checks and stripes, as long as the colours are similar. The fabrics should appear not only as generous curtains but draped over the bed. Try for piles of cushions to welcome an early-morning read, for old flowery quilts as counterpanes along with plenty of throws. Another good idea is to search out old French linen sheets, with colourful monograms if possible, and make them into cushion covers, curtains and bedspreads. Wooden chairs need soft cushions and, of course, the bed itself can be given added importance with fabric draped from a central corona.

Traditional Country bedrooms also need to welcome the summer, when the weather is warm or even sultry and all the flowers are blooming. By choosing a single colour backed with a warm white or cream, you will find the bedroom makes the transition easily and, if you have decided on translucent fabrics around the bed, these will be perfectly in keeping with the look. Of course, a country bedroom can be given a slightly different, lighter look in warm weather. This is easily achieved by changing the curtains for blinds and removing the woollier cushions around the place.

TOP LEFT: **A centrally placed, gilded corona turns an antique iron bed into a near four-poster. Note how blue is the only colour here.**
ABOVE LEFT: **The iron bedstead here has been painted white to give more importance to the pretty chest of drawers and antique mirror.**
ABOVE: **There are at least four differently patterned fabrics in this comfortable bedroom but, because each is the same pink and white, they complement each other.**
OPPOSITE: **This room has seven different patterns, from the oversized gingham pelmet to tiny floral lampshades. Again, it's the colour that makes it work.**

IN THE PINK STYLE STUDY

A range of soft, faded pinks are the only colours allowed in this charming
bedroom, but the shade is perfectly chosen to give a welcome warmth on
cold nights as well as to make the whole seem relaxing in balmy summer
weather. The wall of beams is very much Traditional Country style but,
happily, not too many have been left exposed to make the whole over-fussy.

This bedroom has clearly been influenced by 18th-century styles in
Sweden and France. The curly painted chairs with their cabriole
legs are distinctly Swedish, as is their matt white colour. The
bedhead, coloured a shade darker than the chalky walls and thus
a soft, French grey, is decorated with simply carved swags and
flowers, very much in the provincial style. Its carvings are almost
covered, however, by two large square pillows (another Continental
touch), which are covered in a quilted, faded pink flowery cotton.
The pretty quilt with its scalloped edges matches. Yet more interest
is added with two different gingham checks in the same pink. An
even bigger gingham, still in the same pink, covers the comfortable
armchair. Its seat has toile de Jouy cushions, while the window seat
has pink ticking. Yet another pink floral fabric ties back the plain
curtains. Perhaps the strongest colour in the whole room comes
from the intricate oriental rug at the end of the bed. This is central
to the decor in that it complements the whole range of pinks, the
soft greys of the furniture and the walls, while the geometric
pattern adds a sense of structure, as do the wonky beams in the
window wall. The only ornament in the room is a formal birdcage,
which complements the grille of beams.

OPPOSITE AND ABOVE: The wall of beams attracts immediate attention in a bedroom full of soft curves and colours. Beams in Traditional Country rooms should not be over-emphasized by darkening them; natural wood or softly limed is best. The chairs' elegant shapes are silhouetted against the window.

ABOVE RIGHT: Because all three fabrics – check, stripe and toile – in this pretty corner are soft pink and white, they work together.

RIGHT: Another amalgam of mixed patterns makes a bed less formal. The scatter of flowers on the pillows is echoed in the scalloped quilt, while the large check underneath is balanced with a tiny check on the back.

FAR RIGHT: Ties do not need to be over-formal. A simple strip of fabric can be knotted to keep the curtains pulled back for maximum light.

WHY IT WORKS MONOCHROME COLOUR SCHEME ■ FADED FABRICS ■ COUNTRIFIED ROUGH BEAMS ■ ALL FURNITURE PAINTED TO MATCH ■ CAREFULLY CHOSEN PATTERNS

KEY FEATURES

▮ SUBTLY UPDATED TRADITIONAL COUNTRY LOOKS. FABRIC PATTERNS, FOR INSTANCE, ARE CHANGED IN SCALE.

▮ LIGHTING IS LOW-KEY, OR MODERNIST LAMPS TAKE THE PLACE OF TABLE LAMPS.

▮ OBJECTS CHOSEN FOR DECORATION ARE QUIRKY; OFTEN TRADITIONAL EQUIPMENT GIVEN A DIFFERENT ROLE.

▮ STRONG COLOURS ARE UNIMPORTANT, AS IS PATTERN. THE EFFECTS ARE ACHIEVED BY SILHOUETTED FURNITURE, HEAVY TEXTURES AND LINES FROM PANELLING AND FLOORBOARDS.

modern country

There is a fine line between Traditional and Modern Country styles, but the main difference is that Modern Country could equally be modern urban. This is a look which is ideal for city attics as much as for rooms under the thatch, because it is spartan and controlled. Its warmth and welcome must come from real warmth – and that means central heating.

There is absolutely no element of flounce or pattern in this composed look. Some of the rooms shown are only country in feeling because they have that Toblerone attic shape – a difficult one to deal with, because walls can be too low either for beds or furniture. Often these spaces under the roof also have interesting structural effects such as ceiling beams and floor-to-ceiling braces. But these are found equally in old town-house attics, in industrial spaces and lofts. Because these types of rooms are extremely fashionable at present, there are plenty of objects to suit them, from the

washed-out range of paint colours in the string, bone and stone range to the variety of natural floor coverings such as sisal, seagrass, kilims and oriental rugs. While the style mostly uses old-fashioned furniture such as Victorian iron bedsteads, rustic bedside cupboards and rush-seated chairs, it veers to the modern in the choice of fabrics. Here again, there is lots of choice, though not in patterns. The fabrics used in Modern Country bedrooms should be neutral in colour and devoid of any but a geometric pattern. Where you can make choices is with texture: waffle blankets, geometric-scaled

OPPOSITE ABOVE LEFT: **The geometric lines in this room, whether the wall and ceiling beams or the horizontally planked walls, are so strong that nothing other than a forceful painting is needed.**

OPPOSITE BELOW LEFT: **Structural beams and struts have been toned down with paint and their colour echoed in the colours and geometric patterns of the throws and cushions on the bed. The toy sheep adds humour.**

OPPOSITE ABOVE RIGHT: **Modern Country schemes still rely on antique furniture, but this curvy, painted chair has an overscaled gingham seat cover. The fabric's background off-white matches the paintwork.**

ABOVE LEFT: **The iron bedstead is traditional, but it is plainly dressed in a modern colour. It is placed so that the knobs and bars are silhouetted against the window, thus providing, with the room's sharp angles, the only pattern.**

ABOVE RIGHT: **Texture is important in this style. The bed is covered with a waffle throw and a pile of neutral rugs sits on an old trunk.**

throws, houndstooth tweeds, smooth and matt leather and even faux
furs such as wolf and mink (though not ocelot). In general, the walls
will be in shades of stone, and the various fabrics should be somewhat
darker, though still in the beige, tan, brown spectrum. Natural wood
also plays a part here, from the grids of beams and struts in the room
to the natural wood floors and occasional piece of traditional furniture.
And don't forget a single, quirky touch such as the toy sheep or old
trunk shown here. Any paintings or pictures – and there should be no
more than a couple – are definitely modern. Look for strong oils or
watercolours of 20th-century landscapes or classic black-and-white
photographs, either hung on walls or propped on furniture. Then just
add a bunch of country flowers and you've got a very successful look.

ABOVE: **All evidence of clothes, shoes and bedroom impedimenta has been concealed in this cool, calm bedroom. Simple panelling and angular louvred shutters are, rightly, left unadorned.**

ABOVE RIGHT: **Because it's not possible to have a high bed under an attic's eaves, this bedhead and foot have been carved into a curvy pattern to make them important.**

CENTRE RIGHT: **A classic modern light and old iron café table with clean lines are characteristic of Modern Country style. Clever stylists will match a posy with some element of the room – here the striped cushions.**

BELOW RIGHT: **Pictures in Modern Country rooms are as frequently propped on tables and shelves as they are hung on the walls.**

FLOWER POWER STYLE STUDY

What makes this pretty bedroom modern in feeling? It must be the emphasis on clean lines, from the planked walls to the built-in cupboards. Even busy curtains fail to overturn the strong sense of control found here.

TOP: **The vigorously floral curtains which flow onto the floor frame a traditional iron radiator. The green carpet picks up the colour of the curtains' leaves.**
ABOVE: **The built-in cupboards are designed to blend with the walls, with similar vertical planking.**
ABOVE RIGHT: **The strong bars of the bed echo the white planks on the walls. The floral theme of the painting pulls together the bunch of pink flowers and the colourful blooms on the curtains.**

Before central heating, panelling was often used to provide warmth and insulation. This bedroom is given a period feeling by the use of vertical planks on the walls, but it could as easily be a town-house room as a cottage one. The owners here have gone for an Arts and Crafts inspiration, especially with the wooden bed, which is a 20th-century take on the traditional 19th-century version. Its wide, upright bars fit very neatly into the verticals of the wall behind, which is emphasized by a wide and shallow splashy modern painting. The curtains, however, are entirely traditional, a large-scale floral cotton generously sized so the fabric flows onto the floor. These curtains will protect sleepers from a draughty window. Yet they look quite at home with the plain modern white lamp that sits on a plain, modern white cupboard. Only the bunch of flowers and artwork refer back to the fabric.

WHY IT WORKS NEUTRAL COLOURS ■ HIDDEN STORAGE ■ FLORAL FABRIC USED WITH IRONY

KEY FEATURES

▮ GRAND AND IMPOSING BEDS – CURTAINED FOUR-POSTERS; CARVED AND SWAGGED BEDHEADS; EMBROIDERED AND PAINTED BEDHEADS.

▮ GENEROUS AMOUNTS OF CURTAINS WITH ANTIQUE PELMETS FRAMING LARGE, 18TH-CENTURY WINDOWS. CURTAINS MAY BE IN TWO LAYERS – ONE TRANSLUCENT FOR DAY, THE OTHER FULLY LINED FOR NIGHT.

▮ ANTIQUE MIRRORS ON THE WALLS, BOTH FOR PRACTICAL REASONS AND IN PLACE OF PICTURES. THESE HAVE ELEGANT AND SHOWY FRAMES.

▮ ARCHITECTURAL DETAILS SUCH AS SKIRTINGS, CORNICES AND CEILING ROSES, WHICH CAN BE REAPPLIED IF THEY HAVE GONE MISSING.

▮ AT LEAST ONE GOOD PIECE OF ANTIQUE FURNITURE, CHOSEN TO BE IN THE GENERAL STYLE OF THE ROOM AND THE BED.

OPPOSITE TOP LEFT AND CENTRE: This room suggests the airy space of an Italian villa, with its washed terracotta walls and formally upholstered large bed in shades just deeper than the walls.

OPPOSITE TOP RIGHT: **Elegant pelmets frame the generously proportioned windows and equally generous curtains. Note the symmetrical display on the central chest.**

OPPOSITE CENTRE AND CENTRE LEFT: **More symmetry on the cabriole-legged dressing table, with its large mirror and Chinese lamps. The bedhead is upholstered in an 18th-century-style fabric.**

OPPOSITE CENTRE RIGHT: **A four-poster, here an 18th-century design, always needs a Classic Period room for its best looks.**

OPPOSITE BELOW: **Architectural swags and panelling have been added to the wall behind this bed, probably to conceal a cupboard at its back.**

RIGHT: **The soft pink of this French-inspired scheme has been carefully chosen not to be over-sugary. The mirrored table at the base of the bed is designed to catch the light.**

classic period style

This is the style of the English country house, Parisian family home or New York apartment. It needs an imposing room, preferably with wide windows letting in plenty of light. It is also an amalgam of good-quality antiques and fabrics with a certain grand coolness. The 'period' feeling – generally the 18th century – is only hinted at, so several different styles can be mixed.

These bedrooms are grand without being imposing. That is, everything is of high quality, from the bed itself to the fabrics from the best designers, but the whole is informed with elegance and simplicity. There's nothing over the top about this style, but it rather evokes the idea of a family home that has been lived in for generations. The bedroom will be a mixture of furniture and objects bought over long periods, yet with a similar taste and eye. Since the inhabitants have always been confident of their own style, nothing is showy or designed to impress. It is designed to be easy

on the eye, a room which at base is comfortable and practical but one that is a pleasure to be in. As the best linen is almost invariably white and plain, the room starts from there, adding soft and gentle colours and restrained patterns to complement the bedding and towels. In tune with the country-house theme, charming vases of flowers are common ornaments and table lights are pretty rather than plain. As in all classical rooms, symmetry is important, with matching bedside tables and lights and comfortable armchairs. Mirrors, beautifully framed, are used to increase the light and space.

CLASSIC CHINOISERIE STYLE STUDY

The cool grey tone which the owners have used throughout this room is a perfect backdrop for the charming and elegant chinoiserie fabric with its asymmetric, rococo pattern. The spare design of the rest of the room means the frankly ornate treatment of the bed is just this side of tasteful. The dark crimson, picked up from the fabric's pattern, is used as edging and a form of control.

This frivolous bedroom is definitely not confined to a single period; it roams around the 18th century and its various enthusiasms for chinoiserie, for random patterns and ornament. It could be nothing but French in its elegance and charm. Along with the strength of the fabric, the owners have a love of gilding and lustre, as seen in the golden table lamp, the black lacquered wall clock above the bed, the metal wall lamps and even decorated keys. The notion of placing the bed against the length of a wall, rather than standing out from it, is also very French. It allows the bed to be treated as a piece of furniture – a generous sofa, maybe – rather than an imposing central lump. Added to that, the bed's position means that it is possible to create a large, upholstered corona the whole width above it. This treatment is at least as grand as a four-poster would be. The same rococo fabric is used for the counterpane, the curtains above the bed and blinds at the windows, and for the large cushions piled at the bedhead. But the inclusion of a single purple cushion along with purple cushion edging and the crimson edging of the corona fabric gives the scheme its bones.

WHY IT WORKS ONE ELEGANT FABRIC THROUGHOUT ▮ NEUTRAL PAINTWORK ▮ CHAIRS AND CHEST ARRANGED SYMMETRICALLY ▮ ORIENTAL INSPIRATION HANDLED LIGHTLY

OPPOSITE ABOVE: **Symmetry is employed in the central carving above the mirror and the placing of the lamps on the chest.**

OPPOSITE BELOW LEFT: **The Chinese-style lidded vase on the desk is decorated with decalcomania, a 19th-century technique.**

OPPOSITE BELOW CENTRE: **No expense was spared when choosing this charming fabric.**

OPPOSITE BELOW RIGHT: **An 18th-century French chest of drawers fits neatly between two large windows. Another decalcomania vase takes centre stage.**

ABOVE: **The French grey used for the walls and panelling and the paintwork of the bed makes the ideal neutral background for the exuberant rococo fabric on the bed. The fabric is the focal point around which this room is designed. Its background is white, which helps to bring it forward.**

KEY FEATURES

■ A BEAUTIFUL BED, PERHAPS CURLY METAL (VICTORIAN OR REPRODUCTION), A WOODEN FOUR-POSTER, AN IMPRESSIVE SLEIGH BED OR A SIMPLE MODERN DIVAN WITH A PRETTY HEADBOARD.

■ GORGEOUS TEXTILES, IN PILES OF PILLOWS, CUSHIONS, THROWS, QUILTS AND EIDERDOWNS. THEY MIGHT BE PLAIN, STRIPED, CHECKED OR FLORAL-PATTERNED – A HARMONIOUS MIX IS IDEAL.

■ FREE AND EASY STORAGE. AVOID MESSY CLUTTER, BUT HAVING THINGS ON SHOW IS IMPORTANT, SO DON'T TRY FOR FLOOR-TO-CEILING PERFECTION.

■ FREE-STANDING FURNITURE THAT YOU HAVE FOUND IN JUNK SHOPS, AUCTIONS OR JUMBLE SALES – THEY DON'T HAVE TO MATCH PERFECTLY, BUT SHOULD SHARE A SIMILAR DESIGN AESTHETIC.

vintage & retro

If you have ever lusted after a romantic bedroom filled with pretty pattern and gentle colour, then this is the ideal look for you. With a gorgeous bed as the focal point, you can fill the space with beautiful textiles and attractively mismatching furniture, creating a very personal and individual haven of tranquillity, peace and harmony.

The Vintage and Retro bedroom is relaxed and homely, a very private and personal space in which you can flop onto the bed, eat chocolates and read a romantic novel without feeling that you have to be too smart or tidy. Here, hand-me-down pieces might be put together with revamped junk, plus a few simple modern things – an eclectic combination with character and easygoing good looks.

The centrepiece of this room is almost always a beautiful bed, whether it is curly metal, a wooden four-poster or a simple divan with an attractive headboard. It might, perhaps, be draped with

sheer curtains, and it will almost certainly be layered with old linens, quilts, throws and cushions in a lovely mix of plains, stripes and florals. Antique chintz eiderdowns are lovely, too, as are Provençal *boutis* or American patchwork quilts.

With this look, the idea is to have pretty things on show rather than hidden away, so storage can be free and easy rather than floor-to-ceiling sleek. You could use a free-standing wardrobe or French armoire, a pine blanket chest or an old school locker, perhaps combined with some built-in pieces for convenience, while your bedside table could be

OPPOSITE ABOVE LEFT: **A simple platform bed has been layered with pretty pink fabrics. The rather randomly displayed books are all part of the decorative effect.**

OPPOSITE ABOVE RIGHT: **Draping a bed – even a relatively plain one – with panels of sheer fabric is a great way to achieve this look quickly and easily.**

OPPOSITE BELOW: **Mixing plains, stripes and florals in layers of textiles creates a sense of homely comfort with character and charm.**

ABOVE LEFT: **A casual mix of retro pieces makes for a highly personal and comfortable room.**

ABOVE CENTRE: **Fitted wardrobes may look too sleek and studied for this style. Here, patterned fabric curtains cover a set of clothes rails. The effect is casual and pretty.**

ABOVE RIGHT: **A beautiful bed and an elegant armoire are the focal points for this Vintage decorating scheme.**

ABOVE LEFT: **Rich pink textiles and the gorgeous grain of polished wood create a luscious, luxurious feel here. The other furnishings, however, are kept relatively simple, ensuring that the room is not too overpowering.**

ABOVE RIGHT: **If you've got it, flaunt it: vintage dresses are as good as any type of painting, hung around the walls of this white-painted room as if in an art gallery.**

BELOW: **Antique floral fabrics are ideal for this look, and create a cosy, romantic feel. It is best to combine them carefully, ensuring that scale and colours work together. Here, the pretty pinks and reds are offset by cooler, plain blues.**

OPPOSITE: **This wonderfully ornate bed has been teamed with gorgeous gilt furniture. To provide the perfect backdrop, the walls and floor are really plain and simple.**

a carved Victorian antique or a more down-to-earth painted kitchen chair with a flat seat – whatever takes your fancy and works with the overall style.

When the furniture is relatively plain, you could cover the floor with a decoratively patterned carpet; if you prefer a more restrained look, however, natural matting or wooden boards and a rug would be ideal. Allow in plenty of natural light, and keep window treatments simple: panels of plain or patterned voile, a blind with a pretty edge trim, or a gathered curtain in chintz, linen, wool or felt, hung from a wooden or metal pole. Plain walls offset this look best, perhaps just simply painted with a matt emulsion in cream or a very pale pastel, or wallpapered with stripes or a subtle pattern. As a decorative flourish, they could be covered with rows of pictures or photographs, a collection of handbags or even vintage dresses hung from pretty hangers. In general, soft colours work best as a background, given a dash of interest with touches of a bolder shade such as fuchsia pink, cornflower blue or saffron yellow. The aim is to surround yourself with things you love, whether new, antique or just plain old, so that the look is warm and inviting, informal and unstudied.

PALE AND INTERESTING STYLE STUDY

It can take courage to go for the less-is-more approach, but this is a great example of just how well that sort of leap of faith can work. The white background is a blank canvas for carefully chosen delicate florals and vintage pieces. The result is fresh and feminine, an easy-to-live-in room with a simple, laid-back vibe.

The owners of this pale and interesting room have taken a theme of whites and florals as a starting point, with the aim of creating a scheme that is fresh and airy, unpretentious, calm and relaxing. Despite its all-white walls and floor and plain white blind, this is far from being a bland and uninspiring room. It has a good structure in the form of the Edwardian fireplace, cast-iron column radiator and clean-lined wooden bed, and its casual mix of furniture and accessories promotes the effect of romantic serenity. Old and new are juxtaposed everywhere, from the modern bed with vintage covers to the fireplace, on which are displayed some simple pictures and ornaments. An inexpensive wardrobe with a roll-up canvas front means that patterned dresses can contribute to the decorative scheme, while woven baskets in various shapes and sizes hide bits and pieces neatly away. Though the room is full of light during the day, a carefully positioned wall lamp – a Thirties design classic – placed over the bed is useful for night-time reading. And, finally, a floral fabric handbag hung on the door knob is just the right type of delicate accessory to complete the look.

WHY IT WORKS A UNIFIED WHITE BACKGROUND ■ DELICATE FLORALS ADD COLOUR AND CHARACTER ■ MIX OF OLD AND NEW PIECES ■ WARDROBE IS A PICTURE FRAME FOR CLOTHES

OPPOSITE ABOVE: **A simple fabric bag is the ideal accessory, hung casually from the door knob.**

OPPOSITE BELOW: **The Edwardian fireplace, given the whitewash treatment, becomes almost ghost-like, but is a pretty, characterful part of the room's structure.**

TOP LEFT: **Pale floral fabrics layer the bed, their softness and delicacy contrasting with the clean and simple lines of its modern wood frame.**

CENTRE LEFT: **The canvas-fronted wardrobe acts like a picture frame for the colourful clothes inside.**

BOTTOM LEFT: **Woven storage baskets are an inexpensive way to store bits and pieces out of sight.**

ABOVE: **A plain white blind ensures that nothing stops the daylight that floods in through the window. At night, a Thirties-design wall lamp is great for reading in bed.**

DIRECTORY

STORAGE, PLUS GENERAL AND DEPARTMENT STORES

Many of these also do mail order and online shopping.

Aram
110 Drury Lane
London WC2B 5SG
020 7557 7557
www.aram.co.uk
Four floors of modern furniture and lighting.

Baileys Home & Garden
The Engine Shed
Station Approach
Ross-on-Wye
Herefordshire HR9 7BW
01989 561931
www.baileyshomeandgarden.com
Wide range of home accessories by mail order.

Bhs
252–258 Oxford Street
London W1N 9DC
020 7629 2011
www.bhs.co.uk
Good-value lighting and bathroom accessories.

California Closets
Unit 8
Staples Corner Business Park
1000 North Circular Road
London NW2 7JP
020 8208 4544
www.calclosets.co.uk
Bespoke wardrobe systems, plus storage solutions for every room.

The Chair Company
60 Eden Street
Kingston upon Thames
Surrey KT1 1EE
020 8547 2211
www.thechair.co.uk
Chair specialists.

The Conran Shop
Michelin House
81 Fulham Road
London SW3 6RD
020 7589 7401
www.conran.co.uk
One-stop shopping for tasteful modern furniture and accessories.

Lloyd Davies
14 John Dalton Street
Manchester M2 6JR
0161 832 3700
www.lloyddavies.co.uk
Contemporary pieces.

General Trading Company
2 Symons Street
Sloane Square
London SW3 2TJ
020 7730 0411
www.generaltradingcompany.co.uk
Good range of tasteful accessories from tapestry cushions to Venetian-style mirrors.

Graham & Green
4 & 10 Elgin Crescent
London W11 2JA
020 7727 4594
www.grahamandgreen.co.uk
Glamorous furniture and accessories.

Habitat
196 Tottenham Court Road
London W1T 7LG
020 7631 3880
www.habitat.net
Stylish contemporary home furniture and accessories.

Heal's
196 Tottenham Court Road
London W1T 7LQ
020 7636 1666
www.heals.co.uk
Storage and accessories.

Hitch Mylius
020 8443 2616
www.hitchmylius.com
Upholstered furniture.

The Holding Company
241–245 King's Road
London SW3 5EL
020 7352 1600
www.theholdingcompany.co.uk
Endless ideas for storage.

House of Fraser
Metro Centre
Gateshead
Tyne & Wear NE11 9YE
0870 160 7242
www.houseoffraser.co.uk
Homeware.

IKEA
2 Drury Way
255 North Circular Road
London NW10 0TH
0845 355 1141
www.ikea.com
Good-value self-assembly furniture for every room.

InHouse
28 Howe Street
Edinburgh EH3 6TG
0131 225 2888
and at

24–26 Wilson Street
Glasgow G1 1SS
0141 552 5902
www.inhousenet.co.uk
Wide-ranging contemporary design.

Lakeland Limited
Alexandra Buildings
Windermere LA23 1BQ
01539 488100
www.lakelandlimited.com
Great storage solutions.

John Lewis
278–306 Oxford Street
London W1A 1EX
020 7629 7711
www.johnlewis.com
Classic and modern style.

MacCulloch & Wallis
25 Dering Street
London W1R 0BH
020 7629 0311
www.macculloch-wallis.co.uk
Great range of fabrics and trimmings.

Ian Mankin
109 Regent's Park Road
London NW1 8UR
020 7722 0997
Utility fabrics, ticking, checks and stripes. Also gingham, plain cotton and linen.

Marks and Spencer
458 Oxford Street
London W1C 1AP
020 7935 7954
www.marksandspencer.com
Good-value modern classics.

Momentum
31 Charles Street
Cardiff CF10 2GA
029 2023 6266
www.momentumcardiff.com
Four floors of European-designed furniture.

Monsoon Home
48 Brompton Road
London SW3 1DP
020 7581 1408
www.monsoon.co.uk
Decorative accessories for the home.

Muji
6–17 Tottenham Court Road
London W1 9DP
020 7436 1779
www.muji.co.uk
Practical and stylish items from Japan. Good for basic storage needs, small and large.

Oka
0870 160 6002
www.okadirect.com
Mail-order furniture, including a painted range.

Osborne & Little
304 King's Road
London SW3 5UH
020 7352 1456
www.osborneandlittle.com
Fabrics and trimmings to suit all styles of interior.

The Pier
200 Tottenham Court Road
London W1T 7PL
020 7637 7001
www.pier.co.uk
Inexpensive furniture and accessories.

Purves & Purves
220–224 Tottenham Court Road
London W1T 7QE
020 7580 8223
www.purves.co.uk
Modern furniture, lighting and accessories.

Selfridges
400 Oxford Street
London W1A 1AB
0870 837 7377
www.selfridges.com
Fashionable home design. Also in Manchester and Birmingham.

KITCHENS

Aga Rayburn
0845 712 5207
www.agarayburn.co.uk
Classic cast-iron heat storage cookers, essential for the country kitchen.

Alno
Unit 10, Hampton Farm Industrial Estate
Hampton Road West
Hanworth
Middlesex TW13 6DB
020 8898 4781
www.alno.co.uk
Stylish modern kitchens.

Alternative Plans
9 Hester Road
London SW11 4AN
020 7228 6460
www.alternative-plans.co.uk
Kitchen systems by makers such as Boffi.

Bulthaup
37 Wigmore Street
London W1H 9LD
020 7495 3663
www.bulthaup.com
*Contemporary and hi-tech kitchens,
high-quality and clever design.*

Buyers and Sellers
120 Ladbroke Grove
London W10 5NE
020 7243 5400
www.buyersandsellersonline.co.uk
*American-style refrigerators; stainless-
steel and coloured appliances.*

Divertimenti
33–34 Marylebone High Street
London W1U 4PT
020 7935 0689
www.divertimenti.co.uk
Cooking equipment and accessories.

DuPont Corian
0800 962116
www.corian.com
*Stain- and heat-resistant worktops
and surfaces.*

Franke
0161 436 6280
www.franke.co.uk
*Stainless-steel and ceramic sinks
and taps.*

David Mellor
4 Sloane Square
London SW1W 8EE
020 7730 4259
www.davidmellordesign.co.uk
*Specialists in cutlery and fine
kitchenware.*

Miele UK
01235 554455
www.miele.co.uk
Smart kitchens and appliances.

Plain English Kitchen Design
Stowupland Hall
Stowupland
Stowmarket
Suffolk IP14 4BE
01449 774028
www.plainenglishdesign.co.uk
*Well-designed, simple wooden kitchens
suitable for traditional and period
interiors.*

Poggenpohl
01604 763482
www.poggenpohl.co.uk
Contemporary German design.

Smallbone of Devizes
The Hopton Workshop
Devizes
Wiltshire SN10 2EU
01380 729090
www.smallbone.co.uk
*Wide range of kitchen designs
from country and traditional
to contemporary.*

SMEG
0870 990 9907
www.smeguk.com
*Stainless-steel kitchen appliances and
retro-style fridges in a range of colours.*

LIVING ROOMS
B & B Italia
250 Brompton Road
London SW3 2AS
020 7591 8111
www.bebitalia.it
*Contemporary Italian furniture
and homeware.*

Chesney's
194 Battersea Park Road
London SW11 4ND
020 7627 1410
www.chesneys.co.uk
*Huge range of modern and
antique fireplaces.*

Designers Guild
267 & 277 King's Road
London SW3 5EN
020 7351 5775
www.designersguild.com
*Fabrics and bedlinen, wallpaper
and furniture.*

Geoffrey Drayton
85 Hampstead Road
London NW1 2PL
020 7387 5840
www.geoffrey-drayton.co.uk
Modern furniture.

Grand Illusions
41 Crown Road
St Margarets
Middlesex TW1 3EJ
020 8607 9446
www.grandillusions.co.uk
Pretty furniture.

Interiors Bis
60 Sloane Avenue
London SW3 3DD
020 7838 1104
www.interiorsbis.com
Modern furniture and accessories.

Knoll
020 7236 6655
www.knoll.com
*Design classics by Florence Knoll, Mies
van der Rohe, Saarinen, Breuer and
Frank Gehry.*

Christian Liaigre
68–70 Fulham Road
London SW3 6HH
020 7584 5848
Fashionable furniture with clean lines.

Loft
24–28 Dock Street
Leeds LS10 1JF
0113 305 1515
www.loftonline.net
Modern designer furniture.

Ochre
0870 787 9242
www.ochre.net
Furniture and lighting.

Sofa Workshop
01798 343400
www.sofaworkshop.co.uk
Classic and modern sofas.

Viaduct
1–10 Summer's Street
London EC1R 5BD
020 7278 8456
www.viaduct.co.uk
*Contemporary European furniture
and lighting.*

Vitra Ltd
30 Clerkenwell Road
London EC1M 5PQ
020 7608 6200
www.vitra.com
Classic modern designs.

BATHROOMS
Aston Matthews
141–147a Essex Road
London N1 2SN
020 7226 7220
www.astonmatthews.co.uk
*Traditional and modern fixtures
and fittings.*

Bathroom City
Tyseley Industrial Estate
Birmingham B25 8ET
0121 753 0700
www.bathroomcity.co.uk
Bathroom superstore.

Bathstore.com
410–414 Upper Richmond Road West
London SW14 7JX
020 8878 2727
www.bathstore.com
Everything for the bathroom.

Catchpole & Rye
Saracens Dairy
Pluckley
Kent TN24 0SA
01233 840840
www.crye.co.uk
Antique and reproduction sanitary ware.

Colourwash
165 Chamberlayne Road
London NW10 3NU
020 8459 8918
www.colourwash.co.uk
*Contemporary bathroom fittings
and accessories.*

C.P. Hart
Newnham Terrace
Hercules Road
London SE1 7DR
020 7902 1000
www.cphart.co.uk
*Inspiring showrooms for kitchens as
well as bathrooms. Wide range of
sanitary ware.*

Czech & Speake
39c Jermyn Street
London SW1Y 6DN
020 7439 0216
www.czechspeake.com
Traditional-style fittings.

Samuel Heath & Sons
Leopold Street
Birmingham B12 0UJ
0121 772 2303
www.samuel-heath.com
*High-quality taps and bathroom
accessories.*

Ideal Standard and Sottini
The Bathroom Works
National Avenue
Hull HU5 4HS
01482 346461
www.ideal-standard.co.uk
*Plain and functional baths and other
bathroom fixtures.*

Majestic Shower Company
1 North Place
Edinburgh Way
Harlow
Essex CM20 2SL
01279 443644
www.majesticshowers.com
*Glass tiles and frameless shower
enclosures.*

Old Fashioned Bathrooms
The Foresters Hall
52 High Street
Debenham
Suffolk IP14 6QW
01728 860926
www.oldfashionedbathrooms.co.uk
*Victorian, Edwardian and reproduction
fixtures.*

Sitting Pretty
122 Dawes Road
London SW6 7EG
020 7381 0049
www.sittingprettybathrooms.co.uk
*Classical bathroom suites, accessories
and a large range of wooden loo seats.*

Stiffkey Bathrooms
89 Upper St Giles Street
Norwich NR2 1AB
01603 627850
www.stiffkeybathrooms.com
*Antique sanitary ware and their
own range of period and bespoke
bathroom accessories.*

Villeroy & Boch
267 Merton Road
London SW18 5JS
020 8871 4028
www.villeroy-boch.com
Stylish fittings and furniture.

Vola
Unit 12
Ampthill Business Park
Station Road, Ampthill
Bedfordshire MK45 2QW
01525 841155
www.vola.co.uk
*Sleek modern designs, including taps
and fittings by Arne Jacobsen.*

Water Monopoly
16–18 Lonsdale Road
London NW6 6RD
020 7624 2636
www.watermonopoly.co.uk
*Restored antique and reproduction
French and English sanitary ware.*

BEDROOMS
Amazing Emporium
347–349 King's Road
London SW3 5ES
020 7351 0511
www.amazingemporium.com
*Beds including boat beds, daybeds and
Art Deco styles.*

Laura Ashley
0870 562 2116
www.lauraashley.com
*Chintzes and other traditional designs;
also reproduction metal bedsteads and
bedroom furniture.*

And So To Bed
0808 144 4343
www.andsotobed.co.uk
*Comprehensive range of beds and
bedlinen.*

Couverture
310 King's Road
London SW3 5UH
020 7795 1200
www.couverture.co.uk
Pretty bedlinen.

The Iron Bed Company
83 Tottenham Court Road
London W1T 4SZ
020 7436 7707
www.ironbed.com
*Wrought-iron beds and bedroom
furniture.*

McKinney & Co
71 Warriner Gardens
London SW11 4XW
020 7627 5077
*Curtain poles, finials, poles, pelmets
and coronas for beds.*

Melin Tregwynt
28–30 Royal Arcade
Cardiff CF10 1AE
02920 224997
01348 891644 for mail order
www.melintregwynt.co.uk
*Pure wool blankets and throws in
checks, plains and pinstripes.*

The White Company
8 Symons Street
London SW3 2TJ
020 7823 5322
0870 900 9555 for mail order
www.thewhiteco.com
Bedlinen, throws and accessories.

LIGHTING
Anglepoise
02392 250934
www.anglepoise.com
The classic Thirties lamps.

Artemide
106 Great Russell Street
London WC1B 3NB
020 7631 5200
www.artemide.com
*Acclaimed Italian lighting design
company, responsible for many modern
lighting classics.*

Atrium
22–24 St Giles High Street
London WC2H 8TA
020 7379 7288
*Lighting from renowned contemporary
designers, as well as modern classics.*

Beaumont & Fletcher
261 Fulham Road
London SW3 6HY
020 7352 5594
www.beaumontandfletcher.co.uk
*Decorative wall lights based on Regency
and Georgian originals.*

Best & Lloyd
0121 558 1191
www.bestlite.co.uk
*Thirties floor, wall-mounted and table
'Bestlite', still in production.*

Candela Limited
47 IMEX Business Centre
Ingate Place
London SW8 3NS
020 7720 4480
www.candela.ltd.uk
*English manufacturer specializing in
low-voltage downlighters.*

John Cullen Lighting
585 King's Road
London SW6 2EH
020 7371 5400
www.johncullenlighting.co.uk
*Extensive range of light fittings and
a lighting design service.*

London Lighting Company
135 Fulham Road
London SW3 6RT
020 7589 3612
www.londonlighting.co.uk
The cream of modern design.

McCloud Lighting
01373 813600
www.mccloud.co.uk
*Decorative wall lights, chandeliers and
contemporary lighting.*

Mr Light
275 Fulham Road
London SW10 9PZ
020 7352 7525
www.mrlight.co.uk
Contemporary and traditional fittings.

Ryness Electrical
45 Old Compton Street
London W1V 5PN
020 7437 8833
www.ryness.co.uk
Lighting essentials.

Christopher Wray Lighting
8–10 Headingley Lane
Leeds LS6 2AS
0113 278 2653
020 7751 8701 for branches
www.christopherwray.co.uk
Vast range of lighting.

FLOORING
The Alternative Flooring Company
01264 335111
www.alternative-flooring.co.uk
*Flooring products made of 100 per cent
natural fibres from renewable sources:
seagrass, coir, sisal, jute and wool.*

Crucial Trading
79 Westbourne Park Road
London W2 5QH
020 7221 9000
www.crucial-trading.com
All types of natural floorings.

Dalsouple
01278 727733
www.dalsouple.com
*Textured and smooth rubber floor tiles
in a wide range of colours.*

Delabole Slate
Pengelly
Delabole
Cornwall PL33 9AZ
01840 212242
www.delaboleslate.co.uk
*Riven slate or slate slabs suitable for
work surfaces, fireplaces and flooring.*

The Flokati Rug Company
Unit 12, The Osiers Estate
Enterprise Way
London SW18 1EJ
020 8337 3005
www.flokatirugco.co.uk
*Widest range in UK of 100 per cent
pure wool flokati rugs. Also Greek kilims.*

Junckers
01376 534700
www.junckers.co.uk
Solid hardwood flooring.

Limestone Gallery
Arch 47, South Lambeth Road
London SW8 1SS
020 7735 8555
www.limestonegallery.co.uk
*Limestone flooring, also handmade
French ceramic tiles and terracotta tiles.*

Marmoleum
01592 643777
www.marmoleum.co.uk
Linoleum flooring.

Roger Oates Design
The Long Barn
Eastnor
Herefordshire HR8 1EL
01531 631611
www.rogeroates.co.uk
*All kinds of natural floorings, plus
flatweave rugs and felt matting.*

Siesta Cork Tile Co.
020 8683 4055
www.siestacorktiles.co.uk
*Suppliers of matt, satin or colour-tinted
cork tiles.*

Solid Floor
53 Pembridge Road
London W11 3HG
020 7221 8977
www.solidfloor.co.uk
Solid wood flooring.

ANTIQUES & SALVAGE
Damask
Broxholme House
New King's Road
London SW6 4AA
020 7731 3553
www.damask.co.uk
*Painted furniture, classic linens
and accessories.*

Judy Greenwood Antiques
659 Fulham Road
London SW6 5PY
020 7736 6037
*French antique beds, mirrors and
chandeliers are a speciality.*

LASSCO House & Garden
St Michael's Church
Mark Street (off Paul Street)
London EC2A 4ER
020 7749 9944
www.lassco.co.uk
*Huge stock of everything from
fireplaces to floors to stained glass,
panelling and staircases, plus a very
authentic range of replicas.*

The Old French Mirror Company
0118 948 2444
www.oldfrenchmirrors.com

Pimpernel & Partners
596 King's Road
London SW6 2DX
020 7731 2448
*Antique and vintage furniture
and home accessories.*

Josephine Ryan Antiques
63 Abbeville Road
London SW4 9JW
020 8675 3900
www.josephineryanantiques.co.uk
*Antique armoires, wirework and
painted furniture.*

Solopark
Station Road
near Pampisford
Cambridgeshire CB2 4HB
01223 834663
www.solopark.co.uk
Vast range on a six-acre site.

**Andy Thornton Architectural
Antiques**
Victoria Mills
Stainland Road
Greetland
Halifax
West Yorkshire HX4 8AD
01422 377314
www.andythornton.com
*Warehouse of architectural antiques
including fireplaces, doors and
panelled rooms.*

Walcot Reclamation
108 Walcot Street
Bath BA1 5BG
01225 444404
www.walcot.com
*Extensive stock including architectural
antiques.*

COUNTRY
An Angel at My Table
116a Fortress Road
London NW5 2HL
020 7424 9777
*French-style furniture including tables,
desks, chairs and beds.*

Baer & Ingram
01373 813800
www.baer-ingram.com
Toiles sold online and by mail order.

Bennison Fabrics
16 Holbein Place
London SW1W 8NL
020 7730 8076
*Tea-stained chintzes for a look of
faded grandeur.*

Colefax and Fowler
39 Brook Street
London W1K 4JE
020 7493 2231
www.colefaxantiques.com
*Quintessentially English fabrics
and wallpapers.*

English Country Living
The Chapel
Chapel Lane
Caythorpe
near Grantham
Lincolnshire NG32 3EG
01400 273632
*Antiques, painted furniture, sofas,
chairs, mirrors, lighting, fabric and
accessories.*

Nordic Style
109 Lots Road
London SW10 0RN
020 7351 1755
www.nordicstyle.com
*Furniture, accessories and fabrics
inspired by Swedish Gustavian originals.
Painted country furniture.*

Scumble Goosie
Lewiston Mill
Toadsmoor Road
Brimscombe
Stroud
Gloucestershire GL5 2TB
01453 731305
www.scumblegoosie.com
*French and Gustavian-style furniture in
MDF, ready to be painted.*

Shaker
72–73 Marylebone High Street
London W1U 5JW
020 7935 9461
www.shaker.co.uk
*Shaker-style accessories and furniture,
traditionally made.*

George Smith
587–589 King's Road
London SW6 2EH
020 7384 1004
www.georgesmith.co.uk
*Capacious traditional sofas and
armchairs.*

SCANDINAVIAN
Coexistence
288 Upper Street
London N1 2TZ
020 7354 8817
www.coexistence.co.uk
*Furniture by Alvar Aalto, David Design,
Arne Jacobsen, Poul Kjærholm and
other Scandinavian designers.*

Flin Flon
138 St John Street
London EC1V 4UA
020 7253 8849
www.flinflon.co.uk
*Furniture by Hans Wegner, Børge
Mogensen, Alvar Aalto and more, as
well as textiles, ceramics and glassware.*

Marimekko
16–17 St Christopher's Place
London W1U 1NZ
020 7486 6454
www.marimekko.co.uk
*Bright, dramatically patterned fabrics
and accessories.*

SCP
135–139 Curtain Road
London EC2A 3BX
020 7739 1869
www.scp.co.uk
*Alvar Aalto and Arne Jacobsen furniture
and Poul Henningsen and Verner Panton
lighting. Some Scandinavian accessories.*

Skandium
86 Marylebone High Street
London W1U 4QS
020 7935 2077
www.skandium.com
*The largest retailer of original
Scandinavian design in the UK.*

VINTAGE & RETRO
After Noah
121 Upper Street
London N1 1QP
020 7359 4281
www.afternoah.com
*An eclectic range of vintage furniture
and home accessories.*

Boom!
115–117 Regent's Park Road
London NW1 8UR
020 7722 9222
*Retro plastic furniture and lighting as
well as original glass and textiles.*

Century
68 Marylebone High Street
London W1U 5JH
020 7487 5100
Original and reissued American classics.

Flying Duck Enterprises
320–322 Creek Road
London SE10 9SW
020 8858 1964
*Designs from the Fifties to the
Seventies.*

Focus on the Past
25 Waterloo Street
Bristol BS8 4BT
0117 973 8080
Sixties- and Seventies-style pieces.

Cath Kidston
8 Clarendon Cross
London W11 4AP
020 7221 4000
www.cathkidston.co.uk
*Fifties-style furniture and retro-style
home accessories.*

Twentytwentyone
274 Upper Street
London N1 2UA
020 7288 1996
www.twentytwentyone.co.uk
*A wide range of designer furniture,
both original pieces and contemporary
reproductions.*

Valerie Wade
108 Fulham Road
London SW3 6HS
020 7225 1414
www.valeriewade.com
*Art Deco pieces, together with new
chrome lighting and silver bedroom
furniture.*

picture credits

Key: ph=photographer, a=above, b=below, r=right, l=left, c=centre.

Page **1** ph Chris Everard/apartment of Amy Harte Hossfeld and Martin Hossfeld; **2** ph Chris Everard/architect Jonathan Clark's home in London; **3** ph Christopher Drake/designed by McLean Quinlan Architects; **4** ph Andrew Wood/Freddie Daniells' loft in London designed by Brookes Stacey Randall Architects, chair courtesy of SCP; **5** ph Jan Baldwin/Claire Haithwaite and Dean Maryon's home in Amsterdam; **6–7** ph Chris Everard/architect Jonathan Clark's home in London; **8** ph Chris Everard/Central Park West Residence, New York City designed by Bruce Bierman Design, Inc.; **10l** ph Debi Treloar; **10c** ph Andrew Wood/Jo Shane, John Cooper and family, apartment in New York; **10r** ph Chris Everard; **11al** ph Alan Williams/Donata Sartorio's apartment in Milan; **11bl** ph Chris Everard/Lulu Guinness' house in London; **11r** ph Alan Williams/Lisa Fine's apartment in Paris; **12l** ph Debi Treloar/Nicky Phillips' apartment in London; **12c** ph Polly Wreford/Sawmills Studios; **12–13** ph Jan Baldwin/Alfredo Paredes and Brad Goldfarb's loft in Tribeca, New York designed by Michael Neumann Architecture; **13** ph Debi Treloar/Ian Hogarth's family home; **14al** ph Chris Everard/Nadav Kander and Nicole Verity's house; **14ar** ph Andrew Wood/a house in Stockholm, Sweden; **14bl** ph Jan Baldwin/interior architect Joseph Dirand's apartment in Paris; **14br** ph Polly Wreford/Robert Merrett and Luis Peral's apartment in London; **15al** ph Jan Baldwin/Emma Wilson's house in London; **15ar** ph Jan Baldwin/Peter and Nicole Dawes' apartment designed by Mullman Seidman Architects; **15 inset** ph Andrew Wood/Isoceles Land Pte Ltd's house in Singapore designed by Chan Soo Khian of SCDA Architects; **15b** ph Jan Baldwin/a family home in Parsons Green, London. Architecture by Nicholas Helm and Yasuyuki Fukuda (architectural assistant) of Helm Architects. Interior design and all material finishes supplied by Maria Speake of Retrouvius Reclamation & Design; **16l** ph Chris Everard/designed by Mullman Seidman Architects; **16r** ph Chris Everard/Michael Nathenson's house in London; **17al** ph Christopher Drake/a house in Salisbury designed by Helen Ellery of The Plot London; **17ar** ph Catherine Gratwicke/designer Caroline Zoob's home in East Sussex; **17bl** ph Chris Everard/a house in London designed by Helen Ellery of The Plot London, paintings by Robert Clarke; **17bc** ph Chris Everard/Nadav Kander and Nicole Verity's house; **17br** ph James Merrell/Douglas and Dorothy Hamilton's apartment in New York; **18** ph Jan Baldwin/the owner of Tessuti, Catherine Vindevogel-Debal's house in Kortrijk, Belgium; **20al** ph Chris Everard/Ian Chee of VX design & architecture; **20bl** ph James Morris/Upper East Side town house in New York City designed by Ogawa/Depardon Architects; **20–21** ph Chris Everard/Michael Nathenson's house in London; **21** ph Jan Baldwin/the owner of Tessuti, Catherine Vindevogel-Debal's house in Kortrijk, Belgium; **22l & c** ph Christopher Drake/Florence Lim's house in London – architecture by Voon Wong Architects, interior design by Florence Lim Design; **22–23a** ph Chris Everard/a London apartment designed by architect Gavin Jackson; **22–23b** ph Chris Everard/an actor's London home designed by Site Specific; **23** ph Chris Everard/an apartment in Milan designed by Tito Canella of Canella & Achilli Architects; **24** ph Jan Baldwin/the Meiré family home designed by Marc Meiré; **25al** ph Jan Baldwin/Sophie Eadie's family home in London; **25ar** ph Christopher Drake/a house in London, architectural design and procurement by Tyler London Ltd, interior design by William W. Stubbs, IIDA; **25b** ph Chris Everard/Ben Atfield's house in London; **26 both** ph Debi Treloar/Nicky Phillips' apartment in London; **27** ph Andrew Wood/media executive's house in Los Angeles, Architect: Stephen Slan, Builder: Ken Duran, Furnishings: Russell Simpson, Original Architect: Carl Maston c. 1945; **28a** ph Jan Baldwin/Wendy Jansen and Chris Van Eldik, owners of J.O.B. Interieur's house in Wijk bij Duurstede, The Netherlands; **28bl** ph David Montgomery/the House of Crypton living laboratory apartment showroom in New York City designed by CR Studio Architects, PC; **28br** ph Chris Everard/Jonathan Wilson's apartment in London; **28–29a & 29b** ph Jan Baldwin/

Wendy Jansen and Chris Van Eldik, owners of J.O.B. Interieur's house in Wijk bij Duurstede, The Netherlands; **30a** ph Andrew Wood/an apartment in London designed by James Gorst; **30b, 31 & 32a both** ph Christopher Drake/William Yeoward and Colin Orchard's home in London; **32b** ph Chris Everard/an apartment in Milan designed by Daniela Micol Wajskol, interior designer; **33** ph Jan Baldwin/interior designer Didier Gomez's apartment in Paris; **34** ph James Merrell/Michèle Rédélé, interior designer; **35 both** ph Andrew Wood/Roger and Suzy Black's apartment in London designed by Johnson Naylor; **36a** ph Chris Everard/Yuen-Wei Chew's apartment in London designed by Paul Daly Design Studio Ltd; **36b** ph Jan Baldwin/interior architect Joseph Dirand's apartment in Paris; **37l** ph Chris Everard/architect Jonathan Clark's home in London; **37ar** ph Andrew Wood/a house at Jalan Berjaya, Singapore designed by Chan Soo Khian of SCDA Architects; **37br** ph Jan Baldwin/Emma Wilson's house in London; **38** ph Andrew Wood/the Mogensen family's home in Gentofte, Denmark; **38–39** ph Andrew Wood/Century, 020 7487 5100; **40al & bl** ph Andrew Wood/a house in Stockholm, Sweden; **40r** ph Andrew Wood/Mikko Puotila's apartment in Espoo, Finland. Interior design by Ulla Koskinen; **41a** ph Andrew Wood/Michael Asplund's apartment in Stockholm, Sweden; **41b** ph Andrew Wood/Matti and Pirjo Sanaksenaho's house in Espoo designed by Matti and Pirjo Sanaksenaho, Sanaksenaho Architects; **42** ph Christopher Drake/owners of La Cour Beaudeval Antiquities, Mireille and Jean Claude Lothon's house in Faverolles; **44–45** ph James Merrell; **45** ph Christopher Drake/Annie-Camille Kuentzmann-Levet's house in the Yvelines; **46a** ph Sandra Lane/Harriet Scott of R.K. Alliston's apartment in London; **46b** ph Caroline Arber; **47l** ph Christopher Drake/Vivien Lawrence, an interior designer in London (020 8209 0562); **47ar** ph Chris Everard/Mark Kirkley and Harumi Kaijima's house in Sussex; **47br** ph Christopher Drake/Melanie Thornton's former home in Gloucestershire; **48** ph Chris Everard/a house in London designed by Helen Ellery of The Plot London; **49a** ph Polly Wreford/Mary Foley's house in Connecticut; **49b** ph Sandra Lane; **50l** ph Andrew Wood/Fay and Roger Oates' house in Ledbury; **50r** ph Debi Treloar/Kristiina Ratia and Jeff Gocke's family home in Norwalk, Connecticut; **51** ph Jan Baldwin/Mark Smith's home in the Cotswolds; **52a & br** ph Debi Treloar/Paul Balland and Jane Wadham of jwflowers.com's family home in London; **52bl** ph Debi Treloar/Kristiina Ratia and Jeff Gocke's family home in Norwalk, Connecticut; **52–53a** ph Chris Tubbs/Mike and Deborah Geary's beach house in Dorset; **53b** ph Ray Main/Marina and Peter Hill's barn in West Sussex designed by Marina Hill, Peter James Construction Management, Chichester, The West Sussex Antique Timber Company, Wisborough Green, and Joanna Jefferson Architects; **54** ph Andrew Wood/Charlotte Crosland's house in London; **56** ph Polly Eltes/Emily Todhunter's house in London designed by Todhunter Earle Interiors; **57al** ph Polly Eltes/Debby and Jeremy Amias' house in London designed by Carden Cunietti; **57ar** ph Jan Baldwin/Christopher Leach's apartment in London; **57b** ph Alan Williams/Katie Bassford King's house in London designed by Touch Interior Design; **58 both** ph Christopher Drake/a house in Salisbury designed by Helen Ellery of The Plot London; **59al** ph Polly Wreford; **59ar** ph Christopher Drake/a house in Salisbury designed by Helen Ellery of The Plot London; **59b** ph Chris Everard/Emma and Neil's house in London, walls painted by Garth Carter; **60l** ph Debi Treloar/a London apartment designed by James Soane and Christopher Ash of Project Orange; **60r** ph Jan Baldwin/Olivia Douglas and David DiDomenico's apartment in New York designed by CR Studio Architects, PC; **61al** ph Andrew Wood/Guido Palau's house in north London designed by Azman Owens Architects; **61bl** ph Jan Baldwin/Mona Nerenberg and Lisa Bynon's house in Sag Harbor; **61r** ph James Morris/a house in London designed by Alan Power; **62al** ph Catherine Gratwicke/Lucy and Marc Salem's London home; **62bl** ph Debi Treloar/Annelie Bruijn's home in Amsterdam; **62r** ph Alan Williams/Margot Feldman's house in New York designed by Patricia Seidman of Mullman Seidman Architects; **63a** ph Andrew Wood/an apartment in The San Remo on the Upper West Side of Manhattan designed by John L. Stewart and Michael D'Arcy of SIT; **63b** ph Debi Treloar/Mark and Sally of Baileys Home & Garden's house in Herefordshire; **64** ph Jan Baldwin/the Meiré family home designed by Marc Meiré; **66** ph Jan Baldwin/Christopher Leach's apartment in London; **68al** ph Jan Baldwin/the owner of Tessuti, Catherine Vindevogel-Debal's house in Kortrijk, Belgium; **68ar** ph Chris Everard/Ian Chee of VX design & architecture; **68b all** ph Chris Everard/Suze Orman's apartment in New York designed by Patricia Seidman of Mullman Seidman Architects; **69** ph Chris Everard/Michael Nathenson's house in London; **70al** ph Chris Everard/a London apartment designed by architect Gavin Jackson; **70ar, bl & br** ph Chris Everard/John Barman's Park Avenue apartment; **70–71a, 71ar & bl** ph Chris Everard/Vicson Guevara's apartment in New York designed by Yves-Claude Design; **71bc & br** ph Chris Everard/Michael Nathenson's house in London; **72–73** ph Chris Everard/Hudson Street Loft designed by Moneo Brock Studio; **74al** ph Chris Everard/Charles Bateson's house in London; **74ac** ph Debi Treloar/Susan Cropper's family home in London – www.63hlg.com; **74ar & br** ph Christopher Drake/a house in London, architectural design and procurement by Tyler London Ltd, interior design by William W. Stubbs, IIDA; **74c** ph Jan Baldwin/a family home in Parsons Green, London. Architecture by Nicholas Helm and Yasuyuki Fukuda (architectural assistant) of Helm Architects. Interior design and all material finishes supplied by Maria Speake of Retrouvius Reclamation & Design; **74cr** ph Debi Treloar/Nicky Phillips' apartment in London; **74bl** ph Jan Baldwin/the Fitzwilliam-Lay's family home. Architecture by Totem Design, interior design by Henri Fitzwilliam-Lay and Totem Design; **75 all** ph Jan Baldwin/Sophie Eadie's family home in London; **76–77** Chris Everard/Kampfner's house in London designed by Ash Sakula Architects; **78l** ph Christopher Drake/William Yeoward and Colin Orchard's home in London; **78r** ph Polly Eltes/a house in London designed by Charlotte Crosland Interiors; **79al** ph Alan Williams/interior designer and Managing Director of the Société Yves Halard, Michelle Halard's own apartment in Paris; **79ac** ph Chris Everard/an apartment in Milan designed by Daniela Micol Wajskol, interior designer; **79ar** ph Chris Everard/interior designer Ann Boyd's own apartment in London; **79bl** ph Polly Eltes/Emily Todhunter's house in London designed by Todhunter Earle Interiors; **79bc & br** ph Christopher Drake/Valentina Albini's home in Milan; **80–81** ph Chris Everard/designed by Mullman Seidman Architects; **82a both** ph Andrew Wood/Roger and Suzy Black's apartment in London designed by Johnson Naylor; **82c both** ph Andrew Wood/a house in London designed by Bowles and Linares; **82b** ph Chris Everard/Central Park West residence, New York City designed by Bruce Bierman Design, Inc.; **83l** ph Chris Everard/Yuen-Wei Chew's apartment in London designed by Paul Daly Design Studio Ltd; **83c** ph Andrew Wood/an apartment in London designed by James Gorst; **83r** ph Chris Everard/an actor's London home designed by Site Specific; **84–85** ph Chris Everard/Arlene Hirst's New York kitchen designed by Steven Sclaroff; **86al** ph Andrew Wood/Andrew Duncanson's (owner of Modernity) apartment in Stockholm, Sweden; **86ac & ar** ph Andrew Wood/Michael Asplund's apartment in Stockholm, Sweden; **86cr** ph Andrew Wood/Ristomatti Ratia's apartment in Helsinki, Finland; **86cl** ph Andrew Wood/Eero Aarnio's house in Veikkola, Finland; **86c** ph Andrew Wood/Antti Nurmesniemi's house in Helsinki, Finland; **86b** ph Andrew Wood/Norma Holland's house in London; **87** ph Andrew Wood/the Kjærholms' family home in Rungsted, Denmark; **88–89** ph Andrew Wood/architect Grethe Meyer's house, Hørsholm, Denmark. Built by architects Moldenhawer, Hammer and Frederiksen, 1963; **90al** ph James Merrell; **90ar** ph Henry Bourne; **90c both** ph Christopher Drake/refurbishment and interior design by Chichi Meroni Fassio, Parnassus; **90b** ph Christopher Drake/Vivien Lawrence, an interior designer in London (020 8209 0562); **91l** ph Catherine Gratwicke/interior designer Sue West's house in Gloucestershire; **91c** ph Caroline Arber; **91r** ph Catherine Gratwicke/owner of Adamczewski, Hélène Adamczewski's house in Lewes – antique patchwork quilt from Grace & Favour; **92–93** ph Christopher Drake/a house in Salisbury designed by Helen Ellery of The Plot London; **94l** ph Christopher Drake/a house designed by artist Angela A'Court, extension and alteration to rear of property by S.I. Robertson at 23 Architecture;

94r ph Jan Baldwin/Constanze von Unruh's house in London; **95al** ph Andrew Wood/the Pasadena, California, home of Susan D'Avignon; **95ac** ph Henry Bourne; **95ar** ph Christopher Drake/a house designed by artist Angela A'Court, extension and alteration to rear of property by S.I. Robertson at 23 Architecture; **95bl** ph Jan Baldwin/Mona Nerenberg and Lisa Bynon's house in Sag Harbor; **95bc & br** ph Chris Everard/a house in London designed by Helen Ellery of The Plot London, paintings by Robert Clarke; **96l & br** ph Andrew Wood/the home of Gwen Aldridge and Bruce McLucas; **96ar** ph Chris Everard/an apartment in Milan designed by Daniela Micol Wajskol, interior designer; **97al** ph Debi Treloar/Kristiina Ratia and Jeff Gocke's family home in Norwalk, Connecticut; **97ar & bl** ph Jan Baldwin/Mark Smith's home in the Cotswolds; **97cr** ph Jan Baldwin/Constanze von Unruh's house in London; **97br** ph Chris Everard/an apartment in Milan designed by Daniela Micol Wajskol, interior designer; **98–99** ph Christopher Drake/Nordic Style kitchen; **100al & b both** ph Andrew Wood/Curtice Booth's house in Pasadena, California; **100r** ph David Montgomery/Annabel Astor's house in London is full of furniture and accessories designed exclusively for her OKA Direct mail-order catalogue; **101l** ph Christopher Drake/Jane Churchill's house in London; **101c** ph Christopher Drake/Lincoln Cato's house in Brighton; **101r** ph Jan Baldwin/Clare Mosley's house in London; **102–103** ph James Merrell/Douglas and Dorothy Hamilton's apartment in New York; **104l** ph Debi Treloar/Anna Massee of Het Grote Avontuur (The Great Adventure)'s home in Amsterdam; **104r** ph Thomas Stewart; **105al** ph Debi Treloar; **105ac & r** ph Tom Leighton; **105bl** ph Catherine Gratwicke/Rose Hammick's home in London; **105bc** ph Jan Baldwin/Emma Wilson's house in London; **105br** ph Jan Baldwin/Jan Hashey and Yasuo Minagawa; **106al** ph Andrew Wood/Charlotte Crosland's house in London; **106ar** ph Andrew Wood/Neil Bingham's house in Blackheath, London; **106c** ph Chris Everard/an apartment in London designed by Jo Hagan of Use Architects; **106bl** ph Catherine Gratwicke/Lucy and Marc Salem's London home; **106bc** ph Christopher Drake/Marisa Cavalli's home in Milan; **106br** ph Catherine Gratwicke/Claudia Bryant's house in London; **107al** ph Chris Tubbs/Mike and Deborah Geary's beach house in Dorset; **107ar** ph Thomas Stewart/Ron Wigham and Rachel Harding's apartment in London; **107bl & br** ph Andrew Wood/Nanna Ditzel's home in Copenhagen; **107bc** ph Tom Leighton; **108–109** ph James Merrell/Etienne and Mary Millner's house in London; **110** ph Christopher Drake/Florence Lim's house in London – architecture by Voon Wong Architects, interior design by Florence Lim Design; **112al** ph Chris Everard/Ian Chee of VX design & architecture; **112ar** ph Jan Baldwin/Peter and Nicole Dawes' apartment designed by Mullman Seidman Architects; **112cl** ph Chris Everard/Ben Atfield's house in London; **112cr** ph Chris Everard/designed by Mullman Seidman Architects; **112b** ph Chris Everard/a London apartment designed by architect Gavin Jackson; **113l & r** ph Christopher Drake/designed by McLean Quinlan Architects; **113c** ph Chris Everard/Hudson Street Loft designed by Moneo Brock Studio; **114–115** ph Christopher Drake/Florence Lim's house in London – architecture by Voon Wong Architects, interior design by Florence Lim Design; **116al** ph Debi Treloar/Nicky Phillips' apartment in London; **116ac** ph Chris Everard/Charles Bateson's house in London; **116ar** ph Jan Baldwin/the Meiré family home designed by Marc Meiré; **116c** ph Tom Leighton; **116cr** ph Debi Treloar/Susan Cropper's family home in London – www.63hlg.com; **116bl** ph Jan Baldwin/Jan Hashey and Yasuo Minagawa; **116br** ph David Montgomery/the House of Crypton living laboratory apartment showroom in New York City designed by CR Studio Architects, PC; **117l & c** ph Jan Baldwin/the Fitzwilliam-Lay's family home. Architecture by Totem Design, interior design by Henri Fitzwilliam-Lay and Totem Design; **117r** ph Jan Baldwin/Alfredo Paredes and Brad Goldfarb's loft in Tribeca, New York designed by Michael Neumann Architecture; **118al & 119** ph Jan Baldwin/Wendy Jansen and Chris Van Eldik, owners of J.O.B. Interieur's house in Wijk bij Duurstede, The Netherlands; **118ar** ph Alan Williams/Alannah Weston's house in London designed by Stickland Coombe Architecture; **118b** ph Andrew Wood; **120–121** ph Jan Baldwin/a family home in Parsons Green, London. Architecture by Nicholas Helm and Yasuyuki Fukuda (architectural assistant) of

Helm Architects. Interior design and all material finishes supplied by Maria Speake of Retrouvius Reclamation & Design; **122 both** ph Tom Leighton/Keith Varty and Alan Cleaver's apartment in London designed by Jonathan Reed; **123al** ph Chris Everard/designed by Mullman Seidman Architects; **123ac & bc** ph Andrew Wood/Charlotte Crosland's house in London; **123ar** ph Jan Baldwin/art dealer Gul Coskun's apartment in London; **123bl** ph Chris Everard/an apartment in Milan designed by Daniela Micol Wajskol, interior designer; **123br** ph Alan Williams/Margot Feldman's house in New York designed by Patricia Seidman of Mullman Seidman Architects; **124–125** ph Christopher Drake/William Yeoward and Colin Orchard's home in London; **126al** ph Jan Baldwin/Emma Wilson's house in London; **126ar** ph Chris Everard/Nadav Kander and Nicole Verity's house; **126cl** ph Andrew Wood/a house in London designed by Bowles and Linares; **126cr** ph Andrew Wood/Philip and Barbara Silver's house in Idaho designed by Mark Pynn A.I.A. of McMillen Pynn Architecture L.L.P.; **126b** ph Tom Leighton/Caroline and Michael Breet's house in Emst; **127l** ph Andrew Wood/a house in London designed by Bowles and Linares; **127c** ph James Merrell/Michèle Rédélé, interior designer; **127r** ph Andrew Wood/Philip and Barbara Silver's house in Idaho designed by Mark Pynn A.I.A. of McMillen Pynn Architecture L.L.P.; **128–129** ph James Merrell; **130** ph Andrew Wood/a house in Stockholm, Sweden; **131l** ph Andrew Wood/Eero Aarnio's house in Veikkola, Finland; **131ar** ph Andrew Wood/Peter Holmblad's apartment in Klampenborg, Denmark, designed by architect Arne Jacobsen in 1958; **131cr** ph Andrew Wood/architect Grethe Meyer's house, Hørsholm, Denmark. Built by architects Moldenhawer, Hammer and Frederiksen, 1963; **131br** ph Andrew Wood/Century, 020 7487 5100; **132l & 133** ph Andrew Wood/Christer Wallensteen's apartment in Stockholm, Sweden. Lighting: Konkret Architects/Gerhard Rehm; **132r** ph Andrew Wood/Matti and Pirjo Sanaksenaho's house in Espoo designed by Matti and Pirjo Sanaksenaho, Sanaksenaho Architects; **134–135** ph Andrew Wood/the Kjærholms' family home in Rungsted, Denmark; **136al** ph Christopher Drake/Nelly Guyot's house in Ramatuelle, France, styled by Nelly Guyot; **136r** ph Catherine Gratwicke/interior designer Sue West's house in Gloucestershire; **136b** ph David Montgomery/Sasha Waddell's house in London; **137l** ph Christopher Drake/Clara Baillie's house on the Isle of Wight; **137c & r** ph Henry Bourne; **138–139** ph Christopher Drake/Vivien Lawrence, an interior designer in London (020 8209 0562); **140l** ph Jan Baldwin/the owner of Tessuti, Catherine Vindevogel-Debal's house in Kortrijk, Belgium; **140r** ph Jan Baldwin/Mark Smith's home in the Cotswolds; **141al** ph Christopher Drake/Lee Freund's summerhouse in Southampton, New York; **141ac** ph Polly Wreford/Mary Foley's house in Connecticut; **141ar & br** ph Chris Everard/a house in London designed by Helen Ellery of The Plot London, paintings by Robert Clarke; **141bl** ph Tom Leighton; **141bc** ph Debi Treloar/Paul Balland and Jane Wadham of jwflowers.com's family home in London; **142–143** ph Polly Wreford/Mary Foley's house in Connecticut; **144al** ph Christopher Drake/Valentina Albini's home in Milan; **144ar & br** ph Alan Williams/owner of Gloss, Pascale Bredillet's own apartment in London; **144bl** ph Jan Baldwin/Clare Mosley's house in London; **144bc** ph Jan Baldwin/Christopher Leach's apartment in London; **145** ph Christopher Drake/Vivien Lawrence, an interior designer in London (020 8209 0562); **146–147** ph Alan Williams/Lisa Fine's apartment in Paris; **148al** ph Jan Baldwin/Mona Nerenberg and Lisa Bynon's house in Sag Harbor; **148ar** ph Debi Treloar/Anna Massee of Het Grote Avontuur (The Great Adventure)'s home in Amsterdam; **148bl** ph Chris Everard/apartment of Amy Harte Hossfeld and Martin Hossfeld; **148bc** ph Debi Treloar/Mark and Sally of Baileys Home & Garden's house in Herefordshire; **148br** ph Andrew Wood/Norma Holland's house in London; **149** ph Chris Everard/photographer Guy Hills' house in London designed by Joanna Rippon and Maria Speake of Retrouvius; **150al** ph Debi Treloar/artist David Hopkins' house in east London designed by Yen-Yen Teh of Emulsion; **150ar** ph Debi Treloar/Mark and Sally of Baileys Home & Garden's house in Herefordshire; **150bl** ph Jan Baldwin/Jan Hashey and Yasuo Minagawa; **150br & 150–151a** ph Andrew Wood/an apartment in The San Remo on the Upper West Side of Manhattan designed by John L. Stewart and Michael D'Arcy of SIT; **151ar** ph Thomas Stewart/Neil Bingham's house in Blackheath, London;

151bl ph Debi Treloar/artist David Hopkins' house in east London designed by Yen-Yen Teh of Emulsion; **151bc** ph Andrew Wood/Nanna Ditzel's home in Copenhagen; **151br** ph Chris Everard/a New York apartment designed by Shamir Shah. Paintings, artist Malcolm Hill; **152–153** ph Polly Wreford/Clare Nash's former home in London; **154** ph Christopher Drake/a family home near Aix-en-Provence with interior design by Daisy Simon; **156 both** ph Chris Everard/a house in Hampstead, London designed by Orefelt Associates; **157al** ph Chris Everard/Simon Brignall and Christina Rosetti's loft apartment in London designed by David Mikhail Architects; **157bc** ph Chris Everard/One New Inn Square, a private dining room and home of chef David Vanderhook, all enquiries 020 7729 3645; **157ac** ph Chris Everard/the Sugarman–Behun house on Long Island; **157ar** ph Chris Everard/Ian Chee of VX design & architecture; **157bl** ph Chris Everard/architect Jonathan Clark's home in London; **157br** ph Chris Everard/Freddie Daniells' apartment in London designed by Brookes Stacey Randall; **158al** ph Jan Baldwin/interior designer Didier Gomez's apartment in Paris; **158bl & br** ph Chris Everard/Freddie Daniells' apartment in London designed by Brookes Stacey Randall; **158ar, 158–159a & 159ar** ph Chris Everard/Calvin Tsao and Zack McKown's apartment in New York designed by Tsao and McKown; **159bl** ph Chris Everard/an apartment in New York designed by Mullman Seidman Architects; **159br** ph Debi Treloar/new build house in Notting Hill designed by Seth Stein Architects; **160–161** ph Christopher Drake/designed by McLean Quinlan Architects; **162al & r** ph Chris Everard/Suze Orman's apartment in New York designed by Patricia Seidman of Mullman Seidman Architects; **162bl** ph Debi Treloar/Susan Cropper's family home in London – www.63hlg.com; **163l** ph Chris Everard/Richard Oyarzarbal's apartment in London designed by Jeff Kirby of Urban Research Laboratory; **163c & r** ph Chris Everard/Paul Brazier and Diane Lever's house in London designed by Carden & Cunietti; **164al** ph David Montgomery/Laura Bohn's apartment in New York designed by Laura Bohn Design Associates; **164ac** ph Jan Baldwin/Olivia Douglas and David DiDomenico's apartment in New York designed by CR Studio Architects, PC; **164ar** ph Chris Everard/Charles Bateson's house in London; **164bl** ph Alan Williams/Gail and Barry Stephens' house in London; **164br** ph Jan Baldwin/Sophie Eadie's family home in London; **165** ph Alan Williams/Katie Bassford King's house in London designed by Touch Interior Design; **166–167** ph Christopher Drake/a house designed by artist Angela A'Court, extension and alteration to rear of property by S.I. Robertson at 23 Architecture; **168al & r** ph Chris Everard/a house in Highbury, London designed by Dale Loth Architects; **168bl** ph Christopher Drake/an apartment in Milan designed by Daniela Micol Wajskol, interior designer; **168bc & br** ph Chris Everard/an apartment in New York designed by Mullman Seidman Architects; **169** ph Jan Baldwin/Peter and Nicole Dawes' apartment designed by Mullman Seidman Architects; **170–171** ph Chris Everard/John Minshaw's house in London designed by John Minshaw; **172 both** ph Chris Everard/Simon Brignall and Christina Rosetti's loft apartment in London designed by David Mikhail Architects; **173al** ph Andrew Wood/Isosceles Land Pte Ltd's house in Singapore designed by Chan Soo Khian of SCDA Architects; **173ac & ar** Andrew Wood/'Melwani House' designed by Bedmar & Shi Designers in Singapore; **173br** ph Chris Everard/a house in London designed by Carden & Cunietti; **173bl** ph Chris Everard/Heidi Wish and Philip Wish's apartment in London designed by Moutarde and Heidi Wish; **173bc** ph Chris Everard/a house in Paris designed by Bruno Tanquerel; **174–175** ph Jan Baldwin/designer Chester Jones' house in London; **176** ph Chris Everard/Heidi Wish and Philip Wish's apartment in London designed by Moutarde and Heidi Wish; **177al** ph Chris Everard/a house in Hampstead, London designed by Orefelt Associates; **177ar** ph Debi Treloar/Ian Hogarth's family home; **177bl** ph Andrew Wood/Roger and Suzy Black's apartment in London designed by Johnson Naylor; **177bc** ph Chris Everard/Simon Crookall's apartment in London designed by Urban Salon Ltd; **177br** ph Chris Everard/One New Inn Square, a private dining room and home of chef David Vanderhook, all enquiries 020 7729 3645; **178al & bl** ph Chris Everard/Richard Hopkin's apartment in London designed by HM2; **178r** ph Andrew Wood/Christer Wallensteen's apartment in Stockholm, Sweden; **179 all** ph Andrew

Wood/Mikko Puotila's apartment in Espoo, Finland. Interior design by Ulla Koskinen; **180l** ph Tom Leighton/Caroline and Michael Breet's house in Emst; **180r & 181l** ph Christopher Drake/Eva Johnson's house in Suffolk, interiors designed by Eva Johnson; **181c both, r both** ph Christopher Drake/Enrica Stabile's house in Le Thor, Provence; **181bl** ph Henry Bourne; **182l both** ph Christopher Drake/Vivien Lawrence, an interior designer in London (020 8209 0562); **182r** ph Catherine Gratwicke/designer Caroline Zoob's home in East Sussex, **183 both** ph Christopher Drake/Enrica Stabile's house in Milan; **184l** ph Jan Baldwin/Angela and David Coxon's family home in Kent; **184r** ph Jan Baldwin/Claire Haithwaite and Dean Maryon's home in Amsterdam; **185al** ph Christopher Drake/interior designer Carole Oulhen; **185ac** ph Henry Bourne; **185ar** ph Christopher Drake/Monique Davidson's family home in Normandy; **185bl** ph Christopher Drake/Alain and Catherine Brunel's hotel, La Maison Douce, Saint-Martin-de-Ré; **185bc** ph Debi Treloar/Kristiina Ratia and Jeff Gocke's family home in Norwalk, Connecticut; **185br** ph Henry Bourne; **186l** ph James Merrell; **186r** ph Henry Bourne; **187** ph Christopher Drake/interior designer Carole Oulhen; **188–189** ph Chris Everard/Mark Kirkley and Harumi Kaijima's house in Sussex; **190al** ph Chris Everard/an apartment in Paris designed by architect Paul Collier; **190bl** ph Andrew Wood/the Caroline Deforest House in Pasadena, California, home of Michael Murray and Kelly Jones; **190br** ph Andrew Wood/the Shell House, California, home of Chuck and Evelyn Plemons; **190ar & 191al** ph Chris Everard/an apartment in New York designed by Nasser Nakib, architect and Bunny Williams Inc., decorator; **191c** ph Christopher Drake/a house in Salisbury designed by Helen Ellery of The Plot London; **191r** ph Tom Leighton; **192–193** ph Chris Everard/Philippa Rose's house in London designed by Caroline Paterson/Victoria Fairfax of Paterson Gornall Interiors, together with Clive Butcher Designs; **194al** ph Chris Everard/Gentucca Bini's apartment in Milan; **194ar** ph Tom Leighton; **194c both & 194b** ph Chris Everard/Eric De Queker's apartment in Antwerp; **195l** ph Debi Treloar/Debi Treloar's family home in north-west London; **195c** ph Debi Treloar/Morag Myerscough's house in Clerkenwell, London – her house/gallery/shop; **195r** ph Chris Everard/Lulu Guinness' house in London; **196–197** ph Chris Everard/New York City apartment designed by Marino + Giolito; **198** ph Andrew Wood/Charlotte Crosland's house in London; **200al** ph Christopher Drake/Florence Lim's house in London – architecture by Voon Wong Architects, interior design by Florence Lim Design; **200ar** ph Chris Everard/designed by Mullman Seidman Architects; **200bc** ph David Montgomery/the House of Crypton living laboratory apartment showroom in New York City designed by CR Studio Architects, PC; **200cr** ph David Montgomery/the Montevetro apartment in London designed by David Collins, photographed courtesy of Taylor Woodrow Capital Developments Ltd; **200b** ph Christopher Drake/designed by McLean Quinlan Architects; **201l** ph Chris Everard/designed by Mullman Seidman Architects; **201r** ph Ray Main/a house in London designed by Mark Guard Architects; **202–203** ph Chris Everard/an apartment in New York designed by Gabellini Associates; **204al** ph Chris Everard/Central Park West residence, New York City designed by Bruce Bierman Design, Inc.; **204ar** ph Jan Baldwin/interior designer Didier Gomez's apartment in Paris; **204bl** ph Alan Williams/Alannah Weston's house in London designed by Stickland Coombe Architecture; **204bc** ph Jan Baldwin/Wendy Jansen and Chris Van Eldik, owners of J.O.B. Interieur's house in Wijk bij Duurstede, The Netherlands; **204br** ph Jan Baldwin/the Campbell family's apartment in London, architecture by Voon Wong Architects; **205** ph Tom Leighton/Keith Varty and Alan Cleaver's apartment in London designed by Jonathan Reed; **206al** ph Chris Everard/Mark Weinstein's apartment in New York designed by Lloyd Schwan; **206bl** ph Jan Baldwin/the Meiré family home designed by Marc Meiré; **206r** ph Jan Baldwin/Claire Haithwaite and Dean Maryon's home in Amsterdam; **207** ph Jan Baldwin/art dealer Gul Coskun's apartment in London; **208al** ph Polly Eltes/a house in London designed by Charlotte Crosland Interiors; **208bl** ph David Montgomery/Carlton Gardens apartment in London designed by Claire Nelson at Nelson Design; **208ar & 209l** ph Christopher Drake/William Yeoward and Colin Orchard's home in London; **209c** ph David Montgomery/Laura Bohn's apartment in New York designed by Laura Bohn Design Associates; **209r** ph David Montgomery/a house in south London designed by Todhunter Earle Interiors; **210–211** ph Christopher Drake/an apartment in Milan designed by Daniela Micol Wajskol, interior designer; **212al** ph Andrew Wood/Roger and Suzy Black's apartment in London designed by Johnson Naylor; **212ac** ph Chris Everard/Yuen-Wei Chew's apartment in London designed by Paul Daly Design Studio Ltd; **212ar** ph David Montgomery/Sheila Scholes' house near Cambridge; **212cl** ph Jan Baldwin/Michael D'Souza of Mufti; **212c** ph Andrew Wood/Johanne Riss' house in Brussels; **212cr** ph Debi Treloar/Wim and Josephine's apartment in Amsterdam; **212b** ph Polly Wreford/Jo Plismy, Gong; **213** ph Andrew Wood/an apartment in London designed by James Gorst; **214–215** ph Catherine Gratwicke/Kimball Mayer and Meghan Hughes' apartment in New York designed by L.A. Morgan; **216al** ph Andrew Wood/Century, 020 7487 5100; **216ar** ph Andrew Wood/gallery owner Mikael Andersen's studio house in Denmark designed by Henning Larsen; **216bl** ph Andrew Wood/Richard and Sue Hare's house in Idaho designed by Mark Pynn A.I.A. of McMillen Pynn Architecture L.L.P.; **216bc** ph Chris Tubbs/Nickerson–Wakefield House in upstate New York/anderson architects; **216br** ph Andrew Wood/Andrew Duncanson's (owner of Modernity) apartment in Stockholm, Sweden; **217** ph Chris Tubbs/Jonathan Adler's and Simon Doonan's house on Shelter Island near New York designed by Schefer Design; **218al** ph Chris Everard/Christina Wilson's house in London; **218bl** ph Andrew Wood/a house in Stockholm, Sweden; **218r** ph Andrew Wood/Ristomatti Ratia's apartment in Helsinki, Finland; **219 all** ph Andrew Wood/Michael Asplund's apartment in Stockholm, Sweden; **220al** ph Simon Upton; **220bl** ph David Montgomery/Sasha Waddell's house in London; **220ar** ph Polly Wreford/Linda Garman's home in London; **221 both** ph Christopher Drake/Florence and Pierre Pallardy, Domaine de la Baronnie, St-Martin-de-Ré; **222al** ph Christopher Drake/Enrica Stabile's house in Brunello; **222bl** ph Christopher Drake/owners of French Country Living, the Hill family's home on the Cote d'Azur; **222r & 223** ph Christopher Drake/Enrica Stabile's house in Le Thor, Provence; **224–225** ph Christopher Drake/owners of La Cour Beaudeval Antiquities, Mireille and Jean Claude Lothon's house in Faverolles; **226al** ph Ray Main/Marina and Peter Hill's barn in West Sussex designed by Marina Hill, Peter James Construction Management, Chichester, The West Sussex Antique Timber Company, Wisborough Green, and Joanna Jefferson Architects; **226bl** ph Jan Baldwin/Mark Smith's home in the Cotswolds; **226ar & 227l** ph Debi Treloar/The Swedish Chair – Lena Renkel Eriksson; **227r** ph Andrew Wood/Fay and Roger Oates' house in Ledbury; **228l** ph Jan Baldwin/Sophie Eadie's family home in London; **228ar** ph Alan Williams/the Arbuthnott family's house near Cirencester designed by Nicholas Arbuthnott, fabrics designed by Vanessa Arbuthnott; **228cr** ph Polly Wreford; **228br** ph Alan Williams/Warner Johnson's apartment in New York designed by Edward Cabot of Cabot Design Ltd.; **229 all** ph Chris Everard/a house in London designed by Helen Ellery of The Plot London, paintings by Robert Clarke; **230al & ac** ph Alan Williams/Donata Sartorio's apartment in Milan; **230ar** ph Polly Eltes/Emily Todhunter's house in London designed by Todhunter Earle Interiors; **230cl & c** ph Christopher Drake/Nordic Style bedroom; **230cr** ph Sandra Lane; **230b** ph Chris Everard/an apartment in Paris designed by architect Paul Collier; **231** ph Alan Williams/Lisa Fine's apartment in Paris; **232–233** ph Christopher Drake/Clare Mosley's house in London; **234al** ph Debi Treloar/Cristine Tholstrup Hermansen and Helge Drenck's house in Copenhagen; **234bl** ph Sandra Lane/Sophie Eadie's family home in London; **234ar** ph Debi Treloar/Annelie Bruijn's home in Amsterdam; **235l** ph Andrew Wood/Century, 020 7487 5100; **235c & r** ph Chris Everard/fashion designer Carla Saibene's home in Milan; **236al** ph Alan Williams/owner of Gloss, Pascale Bredillet's own apartment in London; **236ar** Debi Treloar/Morag Myerscough's house in Clerkenwell, London – her house/gallery/shop; **236bl** ph Debi Treloar; **237l** ph Polly Wreford/Ros Fairman's house in London; **238–239** ph Debi Treloar/Susan Cropper's family home in London – www.63hlg.com.

architects & designers whose work is featured in this book

23 Architecture
S.I. Robertson
318 Kensal Road
London W10 5BZ
020 8962 8666
stuart@23arc.com
www.23arc.com
Pages 94l, 95ar, 166–167

27.12 Design Ltd.
333 Hudson Street, 10th Floor
New York, NY 10014
USA
+1 212 727 8169
www.2712design.com
Pages 1, 148bl

Eero Aarnio
fax +35 89 25 68 547
www.eero-aarnio.com
Pages 86cl, 131l

Angela A'Court
Artist
orangedawe@hotmail.com
Pages 94l, 95ar, 166–167

Adamczewski
Fine houseware
88 High Street
Lewes
East Sussex BN7 1XN
01273 470105
adamczewski@onetel.net.uk
Page 91r

Jonathan Adler
Pottery, lighting and textiles
available through
465 Broome Street
New York, NY 10013
USA
+1 212 941 8950
Page 217

anderson architects
555 West 25th Street
New York, NY 10001
USA
+1 212 620 0996
info@andersonarch.com
www.andersonarch.com
Page 216bc

Vanessa Arbuthnott
Vanessa Arbuthnott Fabrics
The Tallet
Calmsden
Cirencester GL7 5ET
www.vanessaarbuthnott.co.uk
Holiday lets: www.thetallet.co.uk
Page 228ar

Ash Sakula Architects
24 Rosebery Avenue
London EC1R 4SX
020 7837 9735
info@ashsak.com
www.ashsak.com
Pages 76–77

Asplund
Showroom and shop
Sibyllegatan 31
114 42 Stockholm
Sweden
+46 8 662 52 84
Pages 41a, 86ac, 86ar, 219 all

Azman Owens Architects
18 Charlotte Road
London EC2A 3PB
020 7739 8191
www.azmanowens.com
Page 61al

Baileys Home & Garden
The Engine Shed
Station Approach
Ross-on-Wye
Herefordshire HR9 7BW
01989 563015
sales@baileys-home-garden.co.uk
www.baileyshomeandgarden.com
Pages 63b, 148bc, 150ar

John Barman Inc.
Interior design and decoration
500 Park Avenue
New York, NY 10022
USA
+1 212 838 9443
john@barman.com
www.johnbarman.com
Pages 70ar, 70bl, 70br

JoAnn Barwick Interiors
P.O. Box 982
Boca Grande, FL 33921
USA
Page 220al

Charles Bateson Design Consultants
Interior design
18 Kings Road
St Margarets
Twickenham
Middlesex TW1 2QS
020 8892 3141
charles.bateson@btinternet.com
Pages 74al, 116ac, 164ar

Bedmar & Shi Designers Pte Ltd
12a Keong Saik Road
Singapore 089119
+65 22 77117
fax +65 22 77695
Pages 173ac, 173ar

behun/ziff design
153 East 53rd Street, 43rd Floor
New York, NY 10022
USA
+1 212 292 6233
fax +1 212 292 6790
Page 157ac

Bowles and Linares
32 Hereford Road
London W2 5AJ
020 7229 9886
Pages 82c both, 126cl, 127l

Ann Boyd Design Ltd
33 Elystan Street
London SW3 3NT
020 7591 0202
Page 79ar

Brookes Stacey Randall Architects
16 Winchester Walk
London SE1 9AQ
020 7403 0707
info@bsr-architects.com
www.bsr-architects.com
Pages 4, 157br, 158bl, 158br

Bruce Bierman Design, Inc.
29 West 15th Street
New York, NY 10011
USA
+1 212 243 1935
www.biermandesign.com
Pages 8, 82b, 204al

Annelie Bruijn
+31 653 702869
annelie_bruijn@email.com
Pages 62bl, 234ar

Claudia Bryant
020 7602 2852
Page 106br

Clive Butcher Designs
The Granary
The Quay, Wivenhoe
Essex CO7 9BU
01206 827708
Pages 192–193

Lisa Bynon Garden Design
P.O. Box 897, Sag Harbor, NY 11963
USA
+1 631 725 4680.
Pages 61bl, 95bl, 148al

Cabot Design Ltd
Interior design
1925 Seventh Avenue, Suite 71
New York, NY 10026
USA
+1 212 222 9488
eocabot@aol.com
Page 228br

Tito Canella
Canella & Achilli Architects
Via Revere # 7/9
20123 Milano
Italy
+39 02 46 95 222
fax +39 02 48 13 704
ac@planet.it
www.canella-achilli.com
Page 23

Carden Cunietti
83 Westbourne Park Road
London W2 5QH
020 7229 8630
www.carden-cunietti.com
Pages 57al, 163c, 163r, 173br

Caroline's Antiek & Brocante
Nieuwweg 35a
1251 LH Laren
The Netherlands
Pages 126b, 180l

Garth Carter
07958 412953
Page 59b

Lincoln Cato
01273 325334
Page 101c

Century
68 Marylebone High Street
London W1U 5JH
020 7487 5100
shop@centurydesign.f9.co.uk
Pages 38–39, 131b, 216al, 235l

Jane Churchill Interiors Limited
81 Pimlico Road
London SW1W 8PH
020 7730 8564
janechurchill@jcildircon.co.uk
Page 101l

Jonathan Clark Architects
020 7286 5676
jonathan@jonathanclark
   architects.co.uk
Pages 2, 6–7, 37l, 157bl

Paul Collier, Architect
209 Rue St Maur
75010 Paris
France
+33 1 53 72 49 32
paul.collier@architecte.net
Pages 190al, 230b

David Collins
Architecture and design
Units 6 & 7 Chelsea Wharf
Lots Road
London SW10 0QJ
020 7349 5900
Page 200cr

Coskun Fine Art London
93 Walton Street
London SW3 2HP
020 7581 9056
info@coskunfineart.com
www.coskunfineart.com
Pages 123ar, 207 all

Susan Cropper
www.63hlg.com
Pages 74ac, 116cr, 162bl, 238–239

Charlotte Crosland Interiors
62 St Mark's Road
London W10 6NN
020 8960 9442
mail@charlottecosland.com
www.charlottecrosland.com
Pages 54, 78r, 106al, 123ac, 123bc, 198, 208al

CR Studio Architects, PC
6 West 18th Street, 9th Floor
New York, NY 10011
USA
+1 212 989 8187
fax +1 212 924 4282
victoria@crstudio.com
www.crstudio.com
Pages 28bl, 60r, 116br, 164ac, 200bc

Paul Daly Design Studio Ltd
11 Hoxton Square
London N1 6NU
020 7613 4855
studio@pauldaly.com
www.pauldaly.com
Pages 36a, 83l, 212ac

J&M Davidson
Gallery:
97 Golborne Road
London W10 5NL
Shop:
42 Ledbury Road
London W11 2SE
Page 185ar

Dirand Joseph Architecture
338 Rue des Pyrenees
75020 Paris
France
+33 01 47 97 78 57
JOSEPH.dirand@wanadoo.fr
Pages 14bl, 36b

Nanna Ditzel MDD FCSD
Industrial designer specializing in furniture, textiles, jewellery and exhibitions
Nanna Ditzel Design
Klareboderne 4
DK-1115 Copenhagen K
Denmark
www.nanna.ditzel.design.dk
Pages 107bl, 107br, 151bc

Eric De Queker
DQ–Design In Motion
Koninklijkelaan 44
2600 Bercham
Belgium
Pages 194c both, 194b

Domaine de la Baronnie
21 Rue Baron de Chantal
17410 Saint-Martin-de-Ré
France
+33 5 46 09 21 29
info@domainedelabaronnie.com
www.domainedelabaronnie.com
Page 221 both

Helen Ellery
The Plot London
77 Compton Street
London EC1V 0BN
020 7251 8116
helen@theplotlondon.com
www.theplotlondon.com
Pages 17al, 17bl, 48, 58 both, 59ar,
92–93, 95bc, 95br, 141ar, 141br,
191c, 229 all

Agnes Emery
Moroccan tiles, concrete floor tiles,
selected paints
Emery & Cie
+32 2 513 58 92
fax +32 5 513 3970
Pages 15b, 74c, 120–121

Emulsion
172 Foundling Court
Brunswick Centre
London WC1N 1QE
020 7833 4533
contact@emulsionarchitecture.com
www.emulsionarchitecture.com
Pages 150al, 151bl

Henri Fitzwilliam-Lay
Interior design
Hfitz@hotmail.com
Pages 74bl, 117l, 117c

French Country Living
Antiques and decoration
21 Rue de l'Eglise
06250 Mougins
France
+33 4 93 75 53 03
f.c.l.com@wanadoo.fr
Page 222bl

Gabellini Associates
665 Broadway, Suite 706
New York, NY 10012
USA
+1 212 388 1700
www.gabelliniassociates.com
Pages 202–203

Galerie Mikael Andersen
Bredgade 63
DK-1260 Copenhagen
Denmark
+45 33 33 05 12
www.gma.dk
Page 216ar

Gloss Ltd
Designers of home accessories
274 Portobello Road
London W10 5TE
020 8960 4146
pascale@glossltd.u-net.com
Pages 144ar, 144br, 236al

Gong
joplismy@hotmail.com
Page 212b

James Gorst Architects
House of Detention
Clerkenwell Close
London EC1R 0AS
020 7336 7140
fax 020 7336 7150
Pages 30a, 83c, 213

Mark Guard Architects
161 Whitfield Street
London W1P 5RY
020 7380 1199
Page 201r

Lulu Guinness
3 Ellis Street
London SW1X 9AL
020 7823 4828
www.luluguinness.com
Pages 11bl,195br

Nelly Guyot
Interior designer and
photographic stylist
12, Rue Marthe Edouard
92190 Meudon
France
Page 136al

Yves Halard
Interior decoration
27 Quai de la Tournelle
75005 Paris
France
+33 1 44 07 14 00
fax +33 1 44 07 10 30
Page 79al

Helm Architects
2 Montagu Row
London W1U 6DX
020 7224 1884
nh@helmarchitects.com
Pages 15b, 74c, 120–121

her house
30d Great Sutton Street
London EC1V ODS
020 7689 0606/0808
morag@herhouse.uk.com
www.herhouse.uk.com
Pages 195c, 236ar

Guy Hills
Photographer
020 7916 2610/07831 548 068
guyhills@hotmail.com
Page 149

HM2 Architects
Architects and designers
33–37 Charterhouse Square
London EC1M 6EA
020 7600 5151
andrew.hanson@
 harper-mackay.co.uk
Pages 178al, 178bl

The Housemade
Sue West
Interior and product design
01453 757771
sue.west@btopenworld.com
www.avaweb.co.uk/
 coachhouse.html
Pages 91l, 136r

Gavin Jackson Architects
07050 097561
Pages 22–23a, 70al, 112b

Joanna Jefferson Architects
222 Oving Road
Chichester
West Sussex PO19 4EJ
01243 532 398
jjeffearch@aol.com
Pages 53b, 226al

J.O.B. Interieur
Dijkstraat 5
3961 AA Wijk bij Duurstede
The Netherlands
+31 343 578818
JOBINT@xs4all.nl
Pages 28a, 28–29a, 29b, 118al &
119, 204bc

Eva Johnson
Interior designer and distributor
of TRIP TRAP wood floor
treatment products
01638 731362
www.evajohnson.com
Pages 180r, 181al

Johnson Naylor
13 Britton Street
London EC1M 5SX
020 7490 8885
brian.johnson@johnsonnaylor.co.uk
www.johnsonnaylor.co.uk
Pages 35 both, 82a both, 177bl,
212al

Chester Jones Ltd
Interior designers
240 Battersea Park Road
London SW11 4NG
020 7498 2717
chester.jones@virgin.net
Pages 174–175

jwflowers.com
Units E8 & 9
1–45 Durham Street
London SE11 5JH
020 7735 7771
jane@jwflowers.com
www.jwflowers.com
Pages 52a, 52br, 141bc

Mark Kirkley
Designer and manufacturer of
interior metalwork
01424 812613
Page 47ar, 188–189

Kjærholm's
Rungstedvej 86
DK-2960 Rungsted Kyst
Denmark
+45 45 76 56 56
info@kjaerholms.dk
www.kjaerholms.dk
Pages 87, 134–135

**Annie-Camille Kuentzmann-
Levet Décoration**
3 Ter, Rue Mathieu le Coz
La Noue
78980 Mondreville
France
+33 1 30 42 53 59
Page 45

L.B.D.A.
Laura Bohn Design Associates, Inc.
30 West 26th Street
New York, NY 10010
USA
+1 212 645 3636
fax +1 212 645 3639
Pages 164al, 209c

La Maison Douce
25 Rue Mérindot
17410 Saint-Martin-de-Ré
France
+33 546 09 20 20
www.lamaisondouce.com
Page 185bl

Vivien Lawrence Interior Design
Interior designer of private homes
London
020 8209 0058/020 8209 0562
vl-interiordesign@cwcom.net
Pages 47l, 90b, 138–139, 145, 182l
both

Christopher Leach Design Ltd
Interior designer
07765 255566
mail@christopherleach.com
Pages 57ar, 66, 144bc

Littman Goddard Hogarth
12 Chelsea Wharf
15 Lots Road
London SW10 9AS
020 7351 7871
info@lgh-architects.co.uk
www.lgh-architects.co.uk
Pages 13, 177ar

Dale Loth Architects
1 Cliff Road
London NW1 9AJ
020 7485 4003
mail@daleotharchitects.ltd.uk
www.dalelotharchitects.ltd.uk
Page 168a both

Mireille and Jean Claude Lothon
La Cour Beaudeval Antiquities
4 Rue des Fontaines
28210 Faverolles
France
+33 2 37 51 47 67
Pages 42, 224–225

McLean Quinlan Architects
2a Bellevue Parade
London SW17 7EQ
020 8767 1633
info@mcleanquinlan.com
www.mcleanquinlan.com
Pages 3, 113l, 113r, 160–161, 200b

Josephine Macrander
Interior designer
+31 299 402804
Page 212cr

Marino + Giolito
Architecture/Interior design
161 West 16th Street
New York, NY 10011
USA
+1 212 675 5737
marino.giolito@rcn.com
Pages 196–197

Anna Massee
Het Grote Avontuur
Haarlemmerstraat 25
1013 EJ Amsterdam
The Netherlands
+31 20 62 68 596
www.hetgroteavontuur.nl
Pages 104l, 148ar

Arne Maynard Garden Design
71 New King's Road
London SW6 4SQ
Page 191r

Marc Meiré
meirefamily@aol.com
Pages 24, 64, 116ar, 206bl

Grethe Meyer
Designer and architect MAA
Royal Scandinavia A/S
Smallegade 45
2000 Frederiksberg
Denmark
+45 38 14 48 48
Pages 88–89, 131c

David Mikhail Architects
Unit 29
1–13 Adler Street
London E1 1EE
020 7377 8424
info@davidmikhail.com
Pages 157al, 172 both

John Minshaw Designs Ltd
17 Upper Wimpole Street
London W1H 6LU
020 7258 5777
enquiries@johnminshaw
   designs.com
Pages 170–171

Modernity
Köpmangatan 3
111 31 Stockholm
Sweden
+46 8 20 80 25
www.modernity.se
Pages 86al, 216br

Belen Moneo & Jeff Brock
Moneo Brock Studio
Francisco de Asis Mendez
Casariego, 7 – bajo
28002 Madrid
Spain
+34 661 340 280
contact@moneobrock.com
www.moneobrock.com
Pages 72–73, 113c

L.A. Morgan
Interior designer
P.O. Box 39
Hadlyme, CT 06439
USA
+1 860 434 0304
fax +1 860 434 3013
Pages 214–215

Clare Mosley
Gilding, eglomisé panels and
mirrors, lampbases, finials and
curtain accessories
020 7708 3123
Pages 101r, 144bl, 232–233

Mufti
789 Fulham Road
London SW6 5HA
020 7610 9123
www.mufti.co.uk
Pages 212cl

Mullman Seidman Architects
Architecture and interior design
443 Greenwich Street # 2A
New York, NY10013
USA
+1 212 431 0770
msa@mullmanseidman.com
www.mullmanseidman.com
Pages 15ar, 16l, 62r, 68b all, 80–81,
112ar, 112cr, 123al, 123br, 159bl,
162al, 162ar, 168bc, 168br, 169,
200ar, 201l

**Nasser Nakib, architect and
Bunny Williams Inc., decorator**
306 61st Street, 5th Floor
New York, NY 10021
USA
Pages 190ar, 191al

Clare Nash
House stylist
020 8742 9991
Pages 152–153

Michael Nathenson
Unique Environments
Design and Architecture
33 Florence Street
London N1 2FW
020 7431 6978
mbn@compuserve.com
www.unique-environments.co.uk
Pages 16r, 20–21, 69, 71bc, 71br

Claire Nelson
Nelson Design
169 St John's Hill
London SW11 1TQ
020 7924 4542
Page 208b

Mona Nerenberg
Home and garden products
and antiques
Bloom
43 Madison Street
Sag Harbor, NY 11963
USA
+1 631 725 4680
Pages 61bl, 95bl, 148al

Michael Neumann Architecture
Principal: Michael Neumann
Project Manager: Jairo Camelo
Design Team: Talin Rudy
Also involved in this project:
Design Consultant: John Heist
Woodwork: Daniel DeMarco
Kitchen: Metal Master
Metal walls: Face Design
11 East 88th Street
New York, NY 10128
USA
+1 212 828 0407
www.mnarch.com
Pages 12–13, 117r

Nordic Style
Classic Swedish interiors
109 Lots Road
London SW10 0RN
020 7351 1755
www.nordicstyle.com
Pages 98–99, 230cl, 230c

Roger Oates
Shop and showroom:
1 Munro Terrace, off Cheyne Walk
London SW10 0DL
Studio shop:
The Long Barn
Eastnor, Ledbury
Herefordshire HR8 1EL
Rugs and Runners mail-order
catalogue: 01531 631611
www.rogeroates.co.uk
Pages 50l, 227r

Ogawa/Depardon Architects
137 Varick Street, Suite 404
New York, NY 10013
USA
+1 212 627 7390
www.oda-ny.com
Page 20bl

OKA Direct
0870 160 6002
www.okadirect.com
Page 100r

Colin Orchard Consultants
C8 & C9 The Old Imperial Laundry
71 Warriner Gardens
London SW11 4XW
020 7720 7550
info@colinorchard.com
Pages 30, 31, 32a both, 78l,
124–125, 208ar, 209l

Orefelt Associates
4 Portobello Studios
5 Haydens Place
London W11 1LY
020 7243 3181
fax 020 7792 1126
orefelt@msn.com
Pages 156 both, 177al

Ory Gomez
Didier Gomez, interior designer
15 Rue Henri Heine
75016 Paris
France
+33 01 44 30 8823
orygomez@free.fr
Pages 33, 158al, 204ar

Carole Oulhen
Interior designer
+33 6 80 99 66 16
fax +33 4 90 02 01 91
With the help of contractors:
Icardi Soditra Entreprise
+33 4 90 89 31 52
icardi@wanadoo.fr
Pages 185al, 187

Parnassus
Chichi Meroni Fassio
Corso Porta Vittoria, 5
Milano
Italy
+39 02 78 11 07
Page 90c both

Caroline Paterson
Paterson Gornall Interiors
50 Lavender Gardens
London SW11 1DN
020 7738 2530
Pages 192–193

Alan Power Architects
5 Haydens Place
London W11 1LY
020 7229 9375
fax 020 7221 4172
Page 61r

Project Orange
1st Floor Morelands
7 Old Street
London EC1V 9HL
020 7689 3456
www.projectorange.com
Page 60l

Mark Pynn A.I.A
McMillen Pynn Architecture LLP
P.O. Box 1068
Sun Valley, Idaho 83353
USA
+1 208 622 4656
mpynn@sunvally.net
www.sunvalleyachitect.com
Pages 126cr, 127r, 216bl

Ratia Brand Co Oy
Kapteeninkatu 1 E
00140 Helsinki
Finland
+35 89 622 72820
Pages 86cr, 218r

Kristiina Ratia Designs
+1 203 852 0027
Pages 50r, 52bl, 97al, 185bc

Michèle Rédélé
Interior designer
90 Boulevard Malegerbes
Paris 75008
France
Pages 34, 127c

Jonathan Reed
Reed Creative Services Ltd
151a Sydney Street
London SW3 6NT
020 7565 0066
Pages 122 both, 205

**Retrouvius Reclamation &
Design**
2A Ravensworth Road
Kensal Green
London NW10 5NR
020 8960 6060
mail@retrouvius.com
www.retrouvius.com
Pages 15b, 74c, 120–121, 149

Johanne Riss
35 Place du Nouveau Marché aux
Graens
1000 Brussels
Belgium
+32 2 513 0900
fax +32 2 514 3284
www.johanneriss.com
Page 212c

R. K. Alliston
173 New King's Road
Parsons Green
London SW6 4SW
6 Quiet Street
Bath
Somerset BA1 2JS
www.rkalliston.com
Mail order: 0845 130 5577
International line:
+44 (0)20 7751 0077
Page 46a

Carla Saibene
Womenswear collection,
accessories and antiques
Shop: Carla Saibene
Via San Maurilio 20
Milano
Italy
+39 2 77 33 15 70
xaibsrl@yahoo.com
Pages 235c, 235r

Lucy Salem
Makes and sources soft furnishings
and decorative items for the home
020 8563 2625
lucyandmarcsalem@hotmail.com
Pages 62al, 106bl

Sanaksenaho Architects
Tehtaankatu 13C
00140 Helsinki
Finland
+35 89 177 341
arch@sanaks.pp.fi
Pages 41b, 132r

SCDA Architects
10 Teck Lim Road
Singapore, 088386
+65 324 5458
fax +65 324 5450
Pages 15 inset, 37ar, 173al

Schefer Design
David Schefer and Eve-Lynn
Schoenstein
41 Union Square West, No. 1427
New York, NY 10003
USA
+1 212 691 9097
scheferdesign@mindspring.com
www.scheferdesign.com
Page 217

Sheila Scholes
Designer
01480 498 241
Page 212ar

Lloyd Schwan/Design
195 Chrystie Street, # 908
New York, NY 10002
USA
+1 212 375 0858
fax +1 212 375 0887
Page 206al

Steven Sclaroff, Designer
801 Greenwich Street
New York, NY 10014
USA
+1 212 691 7814
fax +1 212 691 7793
sclaroff@aol.com
Pages 84–85

Shamir Shah
shahdesign@earthlink.net
Page 151br

Paul Simmons
Bespoke, hand-printed textiles
Timorous Beasties
0141 959 3331
Pages 15b, 74c, 120–121

Daisy Simon
Architecte d'interieur décoration
55 Cours Mirabeau, Passage Agard
13100 Aix-en-Provence
France
daisy.simonaix@wanadoo.fr
Page 154

Site Specific Ltd
Interior design and architecture
60a Peartree Street
London EC1V 3SB
020 7490 3176
office@sitespecificltd.co.uk
www.sitespecificltd.co.uk
Pages 22–23b, 83r

Stephen Slan AIA
Variations in Architecture
5537 Hollywood Boulevard
Los Angeles, CA 90028
USA
+1 323 962 9101
www.viarc.com
Page 27

Mark Smith at Smithcreative
15 St George's Road
London W4 1AU
020 8747 3909
mark@smithcreative.net
Ceramics by David Garland
01285 720307
Pages 51, 97ar, 97bl, 140r, 226bl

Angela Southwell
Interior designer
01732 763246
angsouthwell@hotmail.com
Page 184l

Enrica Stabile
Antiques dealer, interior decorator
and photographic stylist
L'Utile e il Dilettevole
Via della Spiga, 46
Milano
Italy
+39 02 76 00 84 20
e.stabile@enricastaile.com
www.enricastabile.com
Pages 181ac, 181ar, 181bc, 181br,
183 both, 222al, 222r, 223

Seth Stein Architects
15 Grand Union Centre
West Row
Ladbroke Grove
London W10 5AS
020 8968 8581
Page 159br

Stelton A/S
P.O. Box 59
Gl. Vartov Vej 1
DK 2900 Hellerup
Denmark
+45 3962 3055
stelton@stelton.dk
www.stelton.com
Page 131ar

John L. Stewart SIT, L.L.C.
113–115 Bank Street
New York, NY 10014-2176
USA
+1 212 620 0777
JLSCollection@aol.com
Pages 63a, 150br, 150–151a

Stickland Coombe Architecture
258 Lavender Hill
London SW11 1LJ
020 7924 1699
nick@scadesign.freeserve.co.uk
Pages 118ar, 204bl

William W. Stubbs, IIDA
William W. Stubbs and Associates
2100 Tanglewilde, Suite 17
Houston, Texas 77063
USA
stubbsww1@aol.com
Pages 25ar, 74ar, 74br

Studio Nurmesniemi
Antti Nurmesniemi
+35 89 6847055
fax +35 89 6848325
Page 86c

The Swedish Chair
020 8657 8560
www.theswedishchair.com
Pages 226ar, 227l

Marisa Tadiotto Cavalli
Via Solferino, 11
20121 Milano
Italy
+39 02 36 51 14 49
marisacavalli@hotmail.com
Page 106bc

Bruno Tanquerel
Artist
2 Passage St. Sébastien
75011 Paris
France
+33 1 43 57 03 93
Page 173bc

Tessuti
Interiors and fabrics
Doorniksewijk 76
8500 Kortrijk
Belgium
+32 56 25 29 27
www.tessuti.be
Pages 18, 21, 68al, 140l

Melanie Thornton
Stylist
01453 885952
Page 47br

Todhunter Earle
Chelsea Reach, 1st Floor
79–89 Lots Road
London SW10 0RN
020 7349 9999
enquiries@todhunterearle.com
www.todhunterearle.com
Pages 56, 79bl, 209r, 230ar

Totem Design
Ian Hume
2 Alexander Street
London W2 5NT
020 7243 0692
totem.uk@virgin.net
Pages 74bl, 117l, 117c

Touch Interior Design
020 7498 6409
Pages 57b, 165

Tsao & McKown
Architects
20 Vandam Street, 10th Floor
New York, NY 10013
USA
+1 212 337 3800
fax +1 212 337 0013
Pages 158ar, 158–159a, 159ar

Tyler London Ltd
22a Ives Street
London SW3 2ND
020 7581 3677
fax 020 7581 8115
www.tylerlondon.com
Pages 25ar, 74ar, 74br

Constanze von Unruh
Constanze Interior Projects,
interior design company
Richmond, Surrey
020 8948 5533
constanze@constanzeinterior
  projects.com
Pages 94r, 97cr

Urban Research Lab/ Jeff Kirby
Ground Floor, Lime Wharf
Vyner Street
London E2 9DJ
020 8709 9060
info@urbanresearchlab.com
www.urbanresearchlab.com
Page 163l

Urban Salon Ltd
Unit D, Flat Iron Yard
Ayres Street
London SE1 1ES
020 7357 8000
Page 177bc

USE Architects
Unit 12, 47–49 Tudor Road
London E9 7SN
020 8986 8111
fax 020 8986 8555
use.arch@virgin.net
www.usearchitects.com
Page 106c

David Vanderhook
020 7729 3645
Pages 157bc, 177br

**VX design & architecture/
Ian Chee**
ianchee@vxdesign.com
www.vxdesign.com
Pages 20al, 68ar, 112al, 157ar

Sasha Waddell
269 Wandsworth Bridge Road
London SW6 2TX
020 7736 0766
Pages 136b, 220bl

Daniela Micol Wajskol
Interior designer
Via Vincenzo Monti 42
20123 Milano
Italy
daniela.w@tiscalinet.it
Pages 32b, 79c, 96ar, 97br, 123bl,
168bl, 210–211

Wallensteen & Co ab
Architect and design consultants
Floragatan 11
114 31 Stockholm
Sweden
+46 8 210151
wallensteen@chello.se
Lighting: Konkret Architects/
Gerhard Rehm
Pages 132l, 133, 178r

Emma Wilson
London home available for
photographic shoots:
www.45crossleyst.com
Moroccan home available for
holiday lets:
www.castlesinthesand.com
Pages 15al, 37br, 105bc, 126al

Heidi Wish and Philip Wish
Interior design and build
020 7684 8789
Pages 173bl, 176

Voon Wong Architects
Unit 27, 1 Stannary Street
London SE11 4AD
020 7587 0116
voon@btconnect.com
Pages 22l, 22c, 110, 114–115, 200al,
204br

Woodnotes OY
Tallberginkatu 1B
00180 Helsinki
Finland
+35 89 694 2200
woodnotes@woodnotes.fi
www.woodnotes.fi
Pages 40r, 179

William Yeoward
270 King's Road
London SW3 5AW
020 7349 7828
store@williamyeoward.com
www.williamyeoward.com
Pages 30, 31, 32a both, 78l,
124–125, 208ar, 209l

Yves-Claude Design
199 Layfayette Street
New York, NY 10012
USA
info@kanso.com
www.kanso.com
Pages 70–71a, 71ar, 71bl

Caroline Zoob
Textile artist and interior design
For commissions please contact:
01273 479274
Caroline Zoob's work is available at:
Housepoints
48 Webbs Road
London SW11 6SF
020 7978 6445
Pages 17ar, 182r

index

Figures in *italics* indicate captions.